The WINNERS! Handbook

A Closer Look at Judy Freeman's Top-Rated Children's Books of 2007

Grades K-6

Judy Freeman

LIBRARIES
UNLIMITED
A Member of the Greenwood Publishing Group

Westport, Connecticut • London

Library of Congress Cataloging-in-Publication Data available at www.loc.gov

British Library Cataloguing in Publication Data is available.

ISBN: 978-1-59158-712-5

First published in 2008

Libraries Unlimited, 88 Post Road West, Westport, CT 06881
A Member of the Greenwood Publishing Group, Inc.
www.lu.com

Printed in the United States of America

The paper used in this book complies with the
Permanent Paper Standard issued by the National
Information Standards Organization (Z39.48–1984).

10   9   8   7   6   5   4   3   2   1

The WINNERS! Handbook
A CLOSER LOOK AT JUDY FREEMAN'S
100 TOP-RATED CHILDREN'S BOOKS OF 2007
GRADES K-6

Judy Freeman

CONTENTS

CONTENTS, cont.

WHAT IS THE PURPOSE OF THIS PROGRAM?

Every year, well over 5,000 new books are published for children. In order to review and evaluate those new books properly, a conscientious book selector would have to read more than 13 books every day of the year. Most already-overworked librarians therefore depend on the book reviews in professional journals and online for guidance, but even a good review can be misleading.

Each year, several prestigious professional organizations and periodicals present their nominations for the "best" books of the year. Libraries with limited budgets may decide that the "best of the year" list is what they should buy, but even those critical lists frequently disagree with each other! So how *do* you decide which books you really need to buy for your classroom or library, and why?

Having been burned too often by inaccurate reviews and incomprehensible lists, in 1985, I began, along with Alice Yucht, another children's books maven and New Jersey librarian, what became an annual project: to critically examine and compare all the books from four of those yearly lists: "Notable Children's Books" from the Association of Library Services to Children (ALSC), a division of the American Library Association; "Editors Choice" from *Booklist*; "Fanfare" from *Horn Book*; and Best of the Year" from *School Library Journal*.

Each year Alice and I found that many titles were on only one or two of the lists, that we were unimpressed (or even astonished) by some of the books chosen, and that some of the titles *we* considered outstanding had been ignored. That's why we began presenting *WINNERS!*, our own original all-day workshop for teachers, librarians, and other book-lovers, then sponsored by the Professional Development Studies Department of Rutgers University's School of Communication, Information, and Library Studies. After ten years, in 1994, Alice decided to bid a fond cheerio, and ever since, I've done the program on my own. After twenty years of Rutgers sponsorship, *WINNERS!* is now presented under the auspices of my publisher, Libraries Unlimited, which also publishes this spiffy handbook for the workshop.

As the former children's book reviewer for *Instructor* magazine and current reviewer for *School Library Media Activities Monthly*, **NoveList**, the online database, and *School Library Journal's Curriculum Coinnections*; writer of professional books about children's literature; and a presenter of many workshops, seminars, and speeches throughout the U.S. and abroad, I read a lot. I spend much of my professional time each year evaluating and considering which books teachers and librarians would love to use with their students. I search for memorable and exemplary read-alouds and teacher resources from every publisher, seeking a multicultural treatment of the world—an eclectic mixture of picture books, fiction, nonfiction, biography, poetry, folklore—with varied interest and reading levels, that you can use as welcome companions to your curriculum.

In order to share with you, my colleagues, what I've learned, I develop and present an all-new, all-day edition of *WINNERS!* each year, showing and telling my reactions to the past year's "best" books for pre-kindergarten through sixth grade. Reading thousands of children's books each year, I choose 100 or so titles, all published in the past year, pulling together my favorites on and off the major "Best of the Year" lists into my own personal list of significant, controversial, and/or award-winning books I feel teachers and librarians will want to know.

I'll give you my honest opinions and those of other professional book reviewers; then it's up to you to examine the books and decide what *you* think. After all, you are the one who makes the decision on what books you find to be the best to introduce to your students. I would never expect everyone to agree with all my choices, and relish discussing our differing opinions.

HOW IS "WINNERS!" PUT TOGETHER?

Although I read reviews and new books all year, the serious work for *WINNERS!* can't really begin until mid-December, when the first of the "year's best" lists come out. By then I have already started to predict much of what will be on the lists, and what will win major awards, but I am always surprised at some of the final choices. I read, and reread. As each list is published, I start to see the overlaps, disagreements, and gaps. I weed out titles that I don't consider especially noteworthy.

I compile my list of personal favorites and then consult the lists to fill in award-winners, significant, controversial, or provocative titles, and books I may have overlooked or not seen. I try to choose books I personally think no teacher or librarian should live without, most of which are glorious read-alouds, but also great read-alones, and if/when they come out in paperback, ideal for Book Club groups.

It's one thing for me to like a book, but until I've tried it out with the people for whom it is intended—actual children—I can't know for sure how it will go over. So I field-test as many books as possible with children, fellow librarians, and teachers, since each book should be judged both intrinsically, and in its targeted "user context." Since leaving my school library job in 2000, I have stayed current by visiting classes of children in grades kindergarten to six at five New Jersey schools. Several times a year, I visit these schools to work with the teachers, librarian, and children.

For each visit, I bring in a big box of my favorite new books to try out, and spend the day working with many classes of children and their wonderful teachers and librarians. I test out, read aloud, and booktalk a batch of books with each group. I give the teachers suggested lesson plans, detailing some ideas for making each book come alive through writing and discussion prompts, curricular and research projects, drama, music, art, movement, and games. The teachers use their knowledge of their kids, their innate creativity, and their sense of fun to do interesting, fulfilling, and often amazing follow-ups with their classes, and give me samples to bring with me to my workshops.

I am indebted to all the wonderful educators and students at these schools My heartfelt thanks for their time, generosity, coordinating skills, ideas, and friendship go to: Kathy Marceski, librarian, at Van Holten School in Bridgewater, NJ, where I was school librarian for 23 of my 26 librarian-ing years; Maren Vitali, librarian at Milltown School in Bridgewater; Matt Barbosa, principal, and Sharon Boyle, librarian, at Old York School in Branchburg, Cyndi Tufaro, reading specialist extraordinaire at James Monroe School in Edison, NJ; and Jennifer Fisher, librarian at Irving School in my hometown, Highland Park, NJ.

By March, my eyeballs are falling out, but I begin to see a pattern in the year's publishing, and that shapes the program I present to you. To the booktalks and show-and-tell descriptions, I add songs, chants, stories, related titles, curricular ideas I call "*GERMS*," and assorted fun but educationally relevant schtick that you can take back to try out on your own children.

In this handbook you will find my annotated booklists of my 100 favorite or noteworthy books of the past year, 2007. You'll find a list of the books I chose not to review during the workshop on page 54, and the list of young adult titles for grades seven and up that don't fit our grade K-6 audience on page 58.

Follett Library Resources, thanks to the wonderful David Rothrock, has been kind enough, for the past many years, to put together the annotated order list attendees will find in their packets and on the amazing Follett website. *(Open your free Titlewave account at Follett's indispensable website at <www.titlewave.com>. You can even find, for easy ordering, all my best books lists there from past and current BER and Winners conferences. After you log in, click on: Curriculum > Browse Other Book Lists > Popular Subject Lists > Judy Freeman.)*

ABOUT THE RATINGS

THE "BEST OF THE YEAR" LISTS

As you will see, the four following well-known and respected "Best of the Year" booklists often disagree with each other. In fact, each year very few titles make it onto all four lists! This year, out of a total of *182* books, only *5* were on all four lists. (Look for *A|B|H|S|.* to find them.) Only *8* were on three lists, *25* were on two lists, and *118* were on only one list. I also included *26* of my own additional choices to the list, for a grand total of *182* titles, out of which I chose *100* to cover in my program and in this handbook.

|A| *American Library Association's "ALSC's Notable Children's Books"*
Announced at the ALA Midwinter Conference, and published in ***Booklist's*** March 15th issue and ***School Library Journal's*** March issue. Compiled by the Notable Children's Books Committee (different members each year) of the Association for Library Service to Children, a division of ALA. Included are books for children up to age 14. *<www.ala.org/ala/alsc/awardsscholarships/childrensnotable>*

|B| *Booklist "Children's Editors' Choice"*
Published in the January issue. Selected by the Children's Books Editors as being examples of the year's most outstanding picture books, fiction, and nonfiction. These titles represent their best-of-the-year selections, based on literary and artistic quality, and on special appeal to older and middle readers and the young. *<www.booklistonline.com>*

|H| *The Horn Book "Fanfare"*
Published in the January/February issue. Honor list of titles chosen by the editors.
<www.hbook.com/booklists/fanfare_about.asp>

|S| *School Library Journal "Best Books of the Year"*
Published in the December issue. Selected by the SLJ book review editors as the best of the titles reviewed in the magazine that year. " . . . books . . . have been selected as the best among the year's output on the basis of their originality, quality of writing and art, presentation of material, and appeal to the intended audience." *<www.schoollibraryjournal.com/article/CA6395088.html>*

ABOUT JUDY FREEMAN'S PERSONAL RATINGS

[J]   Judy considers this book a winner. Included in this category are marvelous titles that you won't want to miss, including a handful of books all the other review journals and established lists overlooked, and which Judy felt deserved to be included.

[J *]   Judy starred those titles she considered to be the best of the best.

[j]   Judy didn't consider this book to be one of her "best of the year" choices, but she liked it well enough to consider it worth buying.

[_]   Judy felt that this book was not worth purchasing. Her opinion of this book ranges from mild indifference to strong dislike. (NOTE: There were only a few [_] books this year.)

[X]   Judy loathed this book, and/or vehemently disagreed with its inclusion on a "best books" list. (NOTE: There were no [X] books this year.)

WHAT HAPPENS AT THE WORKSHOP?

During the workshop, we'll examine each book's possible classroom and library connections, from story hour to school curriculum tie-ins, including writing and drawing prompts, lots of comprehension and critical thinking skills, songs, plenty of great across-the-curriculum poetry, creative drama and Reader's Theater, storytelling, and, of course, nonstop booktalking all day long.

All day I hope to model hundreds of useful strategies, ideas, activities, lessons, read-aloud techniques, writing prompts, and ways you can incorporate literature into every aspect of your day and your life. Many if my ideas are what I call "quick and dirty"—you hear it today, and take it back to inflict on your kids tomorrow. I'll show you what I've found really works with real kids.

Will every book or idea apply to your situation? Well, no, not every one. This is a K-6 workshop. It's always up to you to pick and choose those books and ideas *you* can use and develop, that *you* feel will work best with *your* kids, whether you're a teacher looking for classroom read-alouds, writing prompts, and curriculum ties ins; a school librarian looking for library lesson ideas and books to recommend to staff and students; or a public librarian, who needs to be a reader's advisory expert in every aspect of children's lit, pre-birth to post-teen.

My best advice: Read off your grade level. Enjoy fooling around with the books you might never get to see otherwise. Today is a day for reveling, for wading, and for wallowing in print. It's a day for readers, and also a day for writers. Over the course of the day, we'll model, appreciate, and emulate dozens of writing techniques, strategies, and styles to try out with your children. Keep an open mind as we look at this past year's treasures and trends.

This year, students have created fabulous projects including animal haiku, a Library Book Hunt, poems of apology and forgiveness, library rules, a story told backwards, research projects and guides, apple dolls, stick puppets, job descriptions, and biography comic books. Children made predictions and inferences, and made lots of text to text, text to life, and text to world connections. I love to bring in examples of their work to showcase at the Winners! Workshop.

This program, which I create from scratch every year, my five-hour vaudeville act and passion play for all book-lovers, grades K-6, is set up like a school day: language arts in the morning, when we're fresh and ready to read, and a tour of the curriculum after lunch, with an end-of-day cool down of folklore-based stories and fantasies. It is my aim to recommend stimulating, enticing, and practical ways to use these books with their intended audience—*children.*

And once I finish presenting this year's best books program, there are already shelves and boxes bursting with the Spring, 2008 books waiting for me in my garret, so I can get started on next year's seminars . . .

ACKNOWLEDGMENTS

I GIVE GRATEFUL THANKS TO:

FOLLETT LIBRARY RESOURCES and DAVID ROTHROCK for once again providing the Follett booklist and the online order list for this program.

Debby LaBoon, for making the Winners Conference tick every year.
Emma Bailey for editing and producing the Handbook each year in no time flat.

THE STUDENTS AND STAFF AT IRVING PRIMARY SCHOOL, HIGHLAND PARK, NJ; JAMES MONROE SCHOOL, EDISON, NJ; OLD YORK SCHOOL, BRANCHBURG, NJ; VAN HOLTEN SCHOOL, BRIDGEWATER, NJ; AND MILLTOWN ELEMENTARY SCHOOL, BRIDGEWATER, NJ; for helping me test out, evaluate, come up with wonderful ideas for, and fool around with so many new books.

A special thanks for their generosity, good humor, and numerous spectacular follow-up projects, to librarian JENNIFER FISHER at Irving Primary School, reading specialist CYNDI TUFARO at James Monroe School, librarian KATHY MARCESKI at Van Holten School, librarian SHARON BOYLE at Old York School, and librarian MAREN VITALI at Milltown School, all of whom also devoted inordinate amounts of time and energy to coordinate my visits.

The following teachers generously gave of their time and expertise; their students' wonderful responses to the books we shared made me laugh out loud, they were so innovative, clever, and inspirational:

Irving Primary School, Highland Park, NJ
KINDERGARTEN:	Barbara Holzhauser, Priscilla Pericas, Nancy Rosenthal
GRADE 1:	Jennifer Lugo, Beth Seifer

James Monroe Elementary School, Edison, NJ
GRADE 1:	Jennifer Altman , Jennifer Rommel, Maureen Speckin, Marjorie Weinfeld
GRADE 2:	Claudine Fanous, Lisa Romeo, Margaret Sprunger
GRADE 5:	Amy Fuentes, Rochelle Schwarz, Ashleigh Snow, Maria Weber

Old York School, Branchburg, NJ:
GRADE 3:	Doris Jennings, Ellen Moore, Lisa Rice
GRADE 4:	Erica Patente, Rene Sakos, Barbara Weintraub
ART:	Rokiah Barry

Van Holten Elementary School, Bridgewater, NJ:
KINDERGARTEN:	Lori Foley, Carolyn Richardson, Jill Von Bischoffshausen,
GRADE 1:	Samantha Hopf, Michele Incao, Megan Kranich
GRADE 2:	Lisa D'Ascensio, Becky Gara, Meghan Kipila, Helen Kyritsis, Alicia Piniat
GRADE 3:	Lyndsay Bezak, Kristion Johnson
GRADE 4:	Curt Weaver

My brother Richard Freeman who once again volunteered to proofread. I owe you.
And, as always, to my husband, IZZY FELDMAN, who reads my mind.

Welcome to Judy Freeman's 24th Annual
WINNERS! CONFERENCE
A Closer Look at the 100 Top-Rated
Children's Books of 2007
Presented April 29-May 2, 2008

HIGHLIGHTS OF TODAY'S SCHEDULE:

8:30 -10:00 LANGUAGE ARTS:
           School Stories / Fowl Language

10:00-10:15 BREAK (& BOOK LOOK)

10:15-12:00 MORE LANGUAGE ARTS:
           Graphic Novels / Words and Wordplay /
           Emergent Readers / Reader's Theater

12:00 - 1:00 LUNCH (& BOOK LOOK)

1:00 - 2:10 BOOKS ACROSS THE CURRICULUM
           The Arts, Math, Science

2:10 - 2:20 BREAK (& BOOK LOOK)

2:20 - 3:00 BOOKS ACROSS THE CURRICULUM
           Social Studies / Folklore & Storytelling

WINNERS!
A Closer Look at the
Top-Rated Children's Books of 2007:
THE ANNOTATED BOOKLIST
Compiled and written by Judy Freeman, Spring, 2008

The following "WINNERS!" booklist, arranged in alphabetical order by title order, contains 100 of the most memorable, interesting, distinguished, and award-winning titles published in 2007. The list is broken into four sections: Easy Fiction/Picture Books; Fiction Books; Nonfiction and Biography Books; and Poetry and Folklore Books. For easy access, refer to the Author and Title Index on page 61 and the Subject Index on page 68.

EACH BOOK ENTRY CONSISTS OF SIX PARTS:

1. **RATINGS:** You can compare each title to see if Judy Freeman, your seminar leader, adored it [J*]; loved it [J]; liked it OK [j]; disliked it [_]; or truly loathed it [X], and see which of the review journals (**A**=ALA Notables List, **B**=Booklist, **H**=Horn Book, and **S**=School Library Journal) included it on their "Best of the Year" lists. A book on all four lists will look like this: |A|B|H|S|. A book that was not on any of the four lists looks like this: | | | | |. (These are books Judy nevertheless thought were "bests.")

2. **BIBLIOGRAPHIC INFO:** Includes title, author, illustrator, publisher and date, ISBN number, number of pages ("unp." means unpaged, or no page numbers), call number (**E**=Easy Fiction/Picture Book; **FIC**=Fiction; **B**=Biography; **#**=Nonfiction), and suggested grade level range (though that is never set in stone; picture books so often can, should, must be used well beyond their intended grade levels—what I call Picture Books for All Ages).

3. **ANNOTATION:** To help you remember what the book is about, or to lure you into reading it.

4. **GERM:** A good, practical, do-able, useful, pithy idea; a way to use the book for reading, writing, and illustrating prompts and other activities across the curriculum, and for story hour programs, including creative drama, Reader's Theater, storytelling, group discussion, booktalks, games, crafts, research, and problem-solving. Your mission is to take that *Germ* of an idea, nurture it, grow it, expand upon it, and incorporate it into your own lessons, programs, and story hours to make them shine.

5. **RELATED TITLES LIST:** A carefully compiled list of exemplary books that share the same theme, subject, style, genre, or type of characters; are by the same author; or extend the reader's knowledge. The more than 600 related titles listed will give you a tour through the best children's books of the past many years. Use these for read-alouds, thematic units, story hour tie-ins, and booktalks; for Guided Reading, Literature Circles, or Book Clubs; and to recommend to kids as wonderful follow-up reads.

6. **SUBJECTS:** Subject designations for each title so you can ascertain where the book might fit thematically into your curricular plan, literary program, or your life. You'll find all of these listed in the Subject Index on page 68.

The 100 Top-Rated Children's Books of 2007

EASY FICTION / PICTURE BOOKS

[j] |A| | | |

The All-I'll-Ever-Want Christmas Doll. **McKissack, Patricia A. Illus. by Jerry Pinkney. Schwartz & Wade, 2007. {ISBN 978-0-375-83759-3; unp.} E (Gr. PreK-3)**

The week before Christmas Nella announces to her sisters that the Baby Betty doll is all she wants ever. Her big sister Eddy Bernice and little sister Dessa remind her about the Depression, but she writes to Santy Claus anyway. On Christmas morning, Mamma and Daddy give them each a sack of walnuts, a peppermint candy stick, an orange, and a box of raisins, which, as Nella tells it, is "the most Christmas we'd ever had." But, wait. Daddy has one more gift, for all three girls to share—a brand-new Baby Betty doll, which the girls fight over until their parents tell them to work it out and fix it. When Nella gets sole custody of the doll, she thinks she doesn't need anything else, but soon realizes the doll's no fun without her sisters to share in the playing. Pinkney's large full-bleed watercolors portray a warm and loving African American family with little in wealth or possessions, but an abundance of love.

GERM: Though it's a bit on the didactic side, this earnest story will have children comparing their overabundant holiday celebrations and gifts with Nella and her sisters. In her personal narrative, Nella alludes to the story of "Br'er Rabbit and the Tar Baby." Introduce that story with Virginia Hamilton's picture book ***Bruh Rabbit and the Tar Baby Girl***. Patricia Polacco's ***An Orange for Frankie*** is another thought-provoking picture book about Christmas during the Depression.

RELATED TITLES: Dewan, Ted. *Crispin, the Pig Who Had It All.* Doubleday, 2000. / Hamilton, Virginia. *Bruh Rabbit and the Tar Baby Girl.* Blue Sky/Scholastic, 2003. / Houston, Gloria. *The Year of the Perfect Christmas Tree.* Dial, 1988. / Leighton, Maxine Rhea. *An Ellis Island Christmas.* Viking, 1992. / Paterson, Katherine. *Marvin's Best Christmas Present Ever.* HarperCollins, 1997. / Polacco, Patricia. *An Orange for Frankie.* Philomel, 2004. / Rylant, Cynthia. *Silver Packages: An Appalachian Christmas Story.* Orchard, 1997. / Tews, Susan. *The Gingerbread Doll.* Clarion, 1993.

SUBJECTS: AFRICAN AMERICANS. CHRISTMAS. DEPRESSIONS, 1929. DOLLS. GIFTS. HISTORICAL FICTION. MULTICULTURAL BOOKS. SHARING. SISTERS.

EASY FICTION / PICTURE BOOKS, cont.

[J] | | | | |

The Apple Doll. **Kleven, Elisa. Illus. by the author. Farrar, 2007. {ISBN 978-0-374-30380-8; unp. E (Gr. PreK-2)**

Lizzy loves playing and pretending in her apple tree. On the morning she is to start school, she picks a red apple and tells it a secret: she's scared. Making it a twig body, she takes her new doll, Susanna, to school, but the children make fun of it. Lizzy's mother peels the apple, carves a face, soaks it in a lemon juice bath, and lets it dry for a week. They make clothes and a pipe cleaner body for the new wrinkle-faced doll, and now everyone at school wants one. In a wistful story about making friends and making dolls, Kleven's sweet soft collage illustrations are charming

GERM: When you read the instructions at the back of the book for making these dolls, you will look longingly at the refrigerator. It doesn't look too difficult. Collaborate with your art teacher on the project. Each child can make and dress a doll, and then write stories about it. Think how much fun the class would have, playing with their dolls together and acting out little scenes.

RELATED TITLES: Gibbons, Gail. *Apples.* Holiday House, 2000. / Hall, Zoe. *The Apple Pie Tree.* Scholastic, 1996. / Hopkinson, Deborah. *Apples to Oregon.* Atheneum, 2004. / Lerner, Harriet, and Susan Goldhor. *What's So Terrible about Swallowing an Apple Seed?* HarperCollins, 1996. / Maestro, Betsy. *How Do Apples Grow?* HarperCollins, 1992. / McGhee, Alison. *Countdown to Kindergarten.* Harcourt, 2002. / Noble, Trinka Hakes. *Apple Tree Christmas.* Dial, 1984. / Polette, Nancy. *The Hole by the Apple Tree: An A-Z Discovery Tale.* Greenwillow, 1992. / Powell, Consie. *Amazing Apples.* Albert Whitman, 2003. / Priceman, Marjorie. *How to Make an Apple Pie and See the World.* Knopf, 1994. / Robbins, Ken. *Apples.* Atheneum, 2002. / Schertle, Alice. *Down the Road.* Harcourt, 1995.

SUBJECTS: APPLES. DOLLS. FIRST DAY OF SCHOOL. SCHOOLS.

[j] | | | |S|

Captain Raptor and the Space Pirates. **O'Malley, Kevin, and Patrick O'Brien. Illus. by Patrick O'Brien. Walker, 2007. {ISBN 978-0-8027-9572-4; unp.} E (Gr. K-3)**

The dinosaur citizens of Jurassica are in a panic when the pirate ship Blackrot lands and a mob of space pirates raids the Imperial Palace, making off with the famous Jewels of Jurassica. The President calls in Captain Raptor to pursue the evildoers. Raptor and his fearless crew crash-land their starship Megatooth on a deserted moon and catch a spying scoundrel named Bloody Bart Scalawag, who sports a hook for a left hand and claims he was left behind by the pirates. Can Raptor trust him? Methinks not. This comic book-style picture book with glossy watercolor and gouache illustrations of dinosaur adventurers, spaceships, and scurvy pirates oozes testosterone and danger.

GERM: You could write this up pretty much verbatim as a Reader's Theater. Children will have a blast figuring out what the voices should sound like. Students can write new one-page adventures of Raptor, using paneled illustrations and a combination of narration and dialogue boxes. Pull out the first book, ***Captain Raptor and the Moon Mystery*** for readers to pore over.

RELATED TITLES: Dodson, Peter. *An Alphabet of Dinosaurs.* Scholastic, 1995. / French, Vivian. *T. Rex.* Candlewick, 2004. / O'Malley, Kevin. *Captain Raptor and the Moon Mystery.* Walker, 2005. / Schwartz, Henry. *How I Captured a Dinosaur.* Orchard, 1989. / Talbott, Hudson. *We're Back!* Crown, 1987. / Wallace, Karen. *I Am a Tyrannosaurus.* Atheneum, 2004. / Yolen, Jane. *Commander Toad and the Space Pirates.* Putnam, 1987. / Yolen, Jane. *How Do Dinosaurs Say Good Night?* Blue Sky/Scholastic, 2000. (And others in the "How Do Dinosaurs" series.)

SUBJECTS: ADVENTURE AND ADVENTURERS. ASTRONAUTS. CARTOONS AND COMICS. DINOSAURS. EXTRATERRESTRIAL BEINGS. PICTURE BOOKS FOR ALL AGES. PIRATES. READER'S THEATER. SCIENCE FICTION. SPACE FLIGHT.

[J*] | | | | |

Casey Back at Bat. Gutman, Dan. Illus. by Steve Johnson and Lou Fancher. HarperCollins, 2007. {ISBN 978-0-06-056026-3; unp.} E (Gr. K-8)

He's back for another swing at the old ball game. Who? Casey, of course, in Dan Gutman's droll narrative poem book, a new encounter with baseball's legendary blunderhead. It's the last game of the season, and with Mudville tied for first, it's once again up to Casey to hit in the clutch. Will he blow it this time, too? Not only is this picture book an homage to Ernest Lawrence Thayer's classic poem, "Casey at the Bat: A Ballad of the Republic Sung in the Year 1888," it's an around-the-world travelogue, and packs in a tall tale pourquoi element, too. Casey gives that ball such a mighty whack, it flies out of the stadium and across the Atlantic Ocean. The towering drive hits a certain building in Pisa, sending it sideways, knocks the nose off the Sphinx, races back through time to scare off the dinosaurs, and careens into outer space. No routine pop-up, this.

GERM: With your listeners, trace the ball's trajectory on a globe. Have them speculate about and then write and illustrate new verses describing other landmarks that the ball might have affected. Artists can emulate the style of Steve Johnson and Lou Fancher's striking and comical old-timey collage illustrations; take notice that the players' uniforms are created from strips of vintage newspapers. Pull out the sports section of your local newspaper to investigate how sporting events are described. Children can rewrite the story as game coverage, do a feature article about Mudville's season, or write a profile on supercilious athlete Casey. What about the other Casey, Katie Casey, the girl from Jack Norworth's 1908 baseball anthem, "Take Me Out to the Ball Game"? You can find the complete song on the endpapers of Shana Corey's *Players in Pigtails*, a fictional picture book about Katie Casey and the All-American Girls Professional Baseball League of the 1940s at :

<sniff.numachi.com/pages/tiTAKEBALL;ttTAKEBALL.html>. Then segue into a profusion of fascinating baseball facts with Sally Cook and James Charlton's *Hey Batta Batta Swing!: The Wild Old Days of Baseball.*

RELATED TITLES: Cook, Sally, and James Charlton. *Hey Batta Batta Swing!: The Wild Old Days of Baseball.* McElderry, 2007. / Cline-Ransome, Lesa. *Satchel Paige.* Simon & Schuster, 2000. / Corey, Shana. *Players in Pigtails.* Scholastic, 2003. / Gutman, Dan. *Honus and Me: A Baseball Card Adventure.* Avon, 1997. / Hopkins. Lee Bennett, comp. *Extra Innings: Baseball Poems.* Harcourt, 1993. / Janeczko, Paul B. *That Sweet Diamond: Baseball Poems.* Atheneum, 1998. / Norworth, Jack. *Take Me Out to the Ball Game.* Four Winds, 1993. / Thayer, Ernest Lawrence. *Casey at the Bat.* Illus. by C. F. Payne. Simon & Schuster, 2003. / Thayer, Ernest Lawrence. *Casey at the Bat.* Illus. by Christopher Bing. Handprint, 2000.

SUBJECTS: BASEBALL. HUMOROUS POETRY. NARRATIVE POETRY. PARODIES. PICTURE BOOKS FOR ALL AGES. SPORTS. STORIES IN RHYME.

[J] | | | | |

The Cheese. Palatini, Margie. Illus. by Steve Johnson, and Lou Fancher. HarperCollins, 2007. {ISBN 978-0-
06-052630-6; unp.} E (Gr. PreK-2)

"What a waste of a chunk of cheddar," the rat grumbles,looking down in the dell. It looks so yellow and tasty. In spite of the posted rules and regulations which state "The cheese stands alone," the rat grabs a napkin and heads for dinner. On the way and one-by-one, he is joined by the cat, the dog, a little girl, her Mother, and the Farmer in the Dell, too. Is this rule meant to be broken? The mixed media collage illustrations are so comic and expressive, with related words (like cheese, meow, nosh, and rules) integrated into the backgrounds. For maximum effect, stop before turning to the last page and ask your listeners what they think the rat, now alone with the cheddar, is going to do. Or hold a mini-debate. Should they eat that cheese? Why or why not? What could happen? Once again, parody master Palatini makes hay with her sprightly reworking of a classic nursery rhyme.

GERM: You can act out this whole story with your group, either with invented dialogue or using Judy Freeman's Reader's Theater script which you'll find on page 161 of this handbook. Also go to <**www.harpercollinschildrens.com**> and type "cheese" in the search bar. You'll find not just reproducible pages for children to do, but a wonderful free recording of author Margie Palatini reading the entire story. It's quite possible that your children are not familiar with the song or game upon which Palatini's book is based. So sing it together and then form a big circle with one child as the "farmer" in the middle. As everyone sings, the circle can rotate to the right. The farmer chooses a wife, who joins him in the center, and so on, until you get to the final verse. Once a child is picked to be the cheese, the others rejoin the outer circle, and circle him, singing that final verse. Pull out your Mother Goose books to share, along with two new visual knockouts full of easy child-friendly poems to recite with toddlers and on up to first grade: ***Here's a Little Poem: A Very First Book of Poetry*** by Jane Yolen and Andrew Fusek Peters, illustrated by Polly Dunbar and ***In Aunt Giraffe's Green Garden*** by the U.S. Children's Poet Laureate Jack Prelutsky and illustrated by Petra Mathers.

RELATED TITLES: Child, Lauren. *That Pesky Rat.* Candlewick, 2002. / DePaola, Tomie, comp. *Tomie dePaola's Mother Goose.* Putnam, 1985. / Edwards, Pamela Duncan. *The Neat Line: Scribbling Through Mother Goose.* HarperCollins, 2005. / Grey, Mini. *The Adventures of the Dish and the Spoon.* Knopf, 2006. / Krosoczka, Jarrett J. *Punk Farm.* Knopf, 2005. / Lobel, Arnold. *The Random House Book of Mother Goose.* Random House, 1986. / McClements, George. *Jake Gander, Storyville Detective.* Hyperion, 2002. / Palatini, Margie. *Moo Who?* HarperCollins, 2004. / Palatini, Margie. *Piggie Pie.* Clarion, 1995. / Palatini, Margie. *The Web Files.* Hyperion, 2001. / Prelutsky, Jack. *In Aunt Giraffe's Green Garden.* Greenwillow, 2007. / Scieszka, Jon. *The Stinky Cheese Man and Other Fairly Stupid Tales.* Viking, 1992. / Stevens, Janet, and Susan Stevens Crummel. *And the Dish Ran Away with the Spoon.* Harcourt, 2001. / Wallner, Alexandra. *The Farmer in the Dell.* Holiday House, 1998. / Yolen, Jane, and Andrew Fusek Peters. *Here's a Little Poem: A Very First Book of Poetry.* Candlewick, 2007

SUBJECTS: CHEESE. CUMULATIVE STORIES. HUMOROUS FICTION. NURSERY RHYMES. PARODIES. RATS. READER'S THEATER.

EASY FICTION / PICTURE BOOKS, cont.

[J*] |A|B|H| |

The Chicken-Chasing Queen of Lamar County. **Harrington, Janice N. Illus. by Shelley Jackson. Farrar, 2007.**
      {ISBN 978-0-374-31251-0; unp.} E (Gr. PreK-3)

Big Mama chides her granddaughter, the pigtailed African American narrator and a self-proclaimed chicken-chaser, "Don't you chase those chickens. If you make those girls crazy, they won't lay eggs. You like eggs, don't you?" Does that child listen? She can't help herself. She loves chasing those chickens, especially her favorite, Miss Hen, plump as a Sunday purse, with her "Pruck! Pruck! Pruck!" that " . . . sounds like pennies falling on a dinner plate." True, she's never caught her, but perhaps today is the day. What is Miss Hen up to and where could she be hiding? Miss Hen has a secret, hidden in the tall, tall grass. Discovering the wily chicken with her new brood of baby chicks, the girl swears off chasing chickens—until they grow up, of course. The full bleed collage illustrations of cut paper, fabric, and photographs, bursting with farmyard excitement and pecking chickens, will get kids squawking. There's one that's just priceless: the girl is peering out of one eye at the hen, who is peering back with the same hard stare. Listeners will want to try out that pose.

GERM: Before reading the last part, ask your children to speculate where Miss Hen is and what she's doing. Take everyone on a chicken strut around the room. Note that this exuberant story is filled with surprising similes and vivid, figurative language: The narrator brushes her teeth "whiter than a biscuit," and describes Miss Hen as "fast as a mosquito buzzing and quick as a fleabite." Compare and contrast her experiences with those of Saba, a girl from Pakistan who is terrified of chickens in Rukhsana Khan's ***Ruler of the Courtyard*** and with Amina, a girl who visits Mali with her family and gets two chickens for her loose tooth in ***I Lost My Tooth in Africa*** by Penda Diakité.

RELATED TITLES: Diakité, Penda. *I Lost My Tooth in Africa.* Scholastic, 2006. / Feldman, Thelma. *Who You Callin' Chicken?* Abrams, 2003. / Himmelman, John. *Chickens to the Rescue.* Henry Holt, 2006. / Khan, Rukhsana. *Ruler of the Courtyard.* Viking, 2003. / O'Malley, Kevin. *Gimme Cracked Corn and I Will Share.* Walker, 2007. / Pearson, Tracey Campbell. *Bob.* Farrar, 2002. / Piven, Hanoch. *My Dog Is as Smelly as Dirty Socks: And Other Funny Family Portraits.* Schwartz & Wade, 2007. / Rostoker-Gruber, Karen. *Rooster Can't Cock-a-Doodle-Doo.* Dial, 2004. / Wattenberg, Jane. *Henny-Penny.* Scholastic, 2000. / *Why Did the Chicken Cross the Road?* Dial, 2006.

SUBJECTS: AFRICAN AMERICANS. CHICKENS. ENGLISH LANGUAGE—SIMILES AND METAPHORS. FARM LIFE. HUMOROUS FICTION. MULTICULTURAL BOOKS. PERSONAL NARRATIVES.

[J] | | | | |

Cowboy & Octopus. **Scieszka, Jon. Illus. by Lane Smith. Viking, 2007. {ISBN 978-0-670-91058-8; unp.} E (Gr. PreK-2)**

Nine wacky short stories, told mostly in dialogue, display two unlikely friends, a well-dressed cowboy and a giant blue octopus, as they fix the see-saw, shake hands (and shake hands, and shake hands . . .), chow down on beans, and get ready for Halloween. The illustration, in mixed media, of Octopus in his pink crown and white lace Tooth Fairy costume is very scary, just like Cowboy says.

GERM: Their brief but punchy dialogues are just great for acting out in pairs with Reader's Theater scripts. They'll ratchet up the humor level in your room for sure. If you look on the title page, you'll see the genesis of the two pals. Cowboy is a paper doll cut from "Western Heroes Vol II," and Octopus was cut out of what looks like a comic book. What other unlikely friends can be cut out of the comics or magazines? Have your kids each cut out a pair, mount them on cardboard, and make up new buddy stories together. Older children can write down their dialogues.

RELATED TITLES: Denim, Sue. *Make Way for Dumb Bunnies.* Scholastic, 1996. (And others in the Dumb Bunnies series.) / Lobel, Arnold. *Frog and Toad Are Friends.* HarperCollins, 1970. (And others in the Frog and Toad series.) / Marshall, James. *George and Martha: The Complete Stories of Two Best Friends.* Houghton Mifflin, 1997. / Scieszka, Jon. *Squids Will Be Squids: Fresh Morals, Beastly Fables.* Viking, 1998. / Scieszka, Jon. *The Stinky Cheese Man and Other Fairly Stupid Tales.* Viking, 1992. / Scieszka, Jon. *The True Story of the 3 Little Pigs.* Viking, 1989. / Seeger, Laura Vaccaro. *Dog and Bear: Two Friends, Three Stories.* Roaring Brook, 2007. / Sherry, Kevin. *I'm the Biggest Thing in the Ocean.* Dial, 2007. / Smith, Lane. *The Happy Hocky Family!* Viking, 1993. / Smith, Lane. *The Happy Hocky Family Moves to the Country.* Viking, 2003. / Willems, Mo. *Today I Will Fly!* Hyperion, 2007. (And others in the Elephant & Piggie series.)

SUBJECTS: COWBOYS. FRIENDSHIP. HUMOROUS FICTION. OCTOPUSES. READER'S THEATER.

EASY FICTION / PICTURE BOOKS, cont.

[J] |A| | | |

Dimity Dumpty: The Story of Humpty's Little Sister. **Graham, Bob. Illus. by the author. Candlewick, 2007.** {ISBN 978-0-7636-3078-2; unp.} E (Gr. PreK-2)

You know the old nursery rhyme about the fall of that unfortunate egg, Humpty Dumpty? Now the truth can be told about the role his little sister, Dimity, played in his recovery. The Tumbling Dumpties are part of a traveling circus. Though Dimity loves to play her tiny silver flute her father crafted for her out of the tube inside an old pen, she is shy and has no interest in joining her parents and brother in their daring trapeze act. When naughty Humpty a high brick wall to spray paint the tag "Humpty Rules," he slips and falls. Lucky for that bad egg, Dimity saves him. What's so tantalizing about the oversized pen and ink and watercolor illustrations is the perspective of regular-sized humans interacting with those wee wee little personified eggs, complete with hair and hats and solemn expressions.

GERM: Review the original nursery rhyme so listeners have context to compare it with this story. Introduce the 398.8 section of the library where nursery rhymes reside. Bring in hard-boiled eggs for children to turn into eggfolk, and use the egg cartons to construct egg-friendly furniture. Read this book with older children who can then choose other well-known nursery rhymes and write and illustrate their back stories. (Why was Jack-Be-Nimble jumping over that candlestick? What's with those Three Blind Mice?) Other delightful nursery rhyme parodies include Pamela Duncan Edwards's ***The Neat Line: Scribbling Through Mother Goose***, Mini Grey's ***The Adventures of the Dish and the Spoon***, Margie Palatini's ***The Cheese*** and ***The Web Files***, and Janet Stevens and Susan Stevens Crummel's ***And the Dish Ran Away with the Spoon***.

RELATED TITLES: DePaola, Tomie, comp. *Tomie dePaola's Mother Goose.* Putnam, 1985. / Edwards, Pamela Duncan. *The Neat Line: Scribbling Through Mother Goose.* HarperCollins, 2005. / Grey, Mini. *The Adventures of the Dish and the Spoon.* Knopf, 2006. / Krosoczka, Jarrett J. *Punk Farm.* Knopf, 2005. / Lobel, Arnold. *The Random House Book of Mother Goose.* Random House, 1986. / McClements, George. *Jake Gander, Storyville Detective.* Hyperion, 2002. / Palatini, Margie. *The Cheese.* HarperCollins, 2007. / Palatini, Margie. *The Web Files.* Hyperion, 2001. / Scieszka, Jon. *The Stinky Cheese Man and Other Fairly Stupid Tales.* Viking, 1992. / Stevens, Janet, and Susan Stevens Crummel. *And the Dish Ran Away with the Spoon.* Harcourt, 2001. / Vail, Rachel. *Over the Moon.* Orchard, 1998.

SUBJECTS: BROTHERS AND SISTERS. CHARACTERS IN LITERATURE. CIRCUS. EGGS.

[J*] |A| | | |

Dog and Bear: Two Friends, Three Stories. **Seeger, Laura Vaccaro. Illus. by the author. Roaring Brook, 2007.** {ISBN 978-1-59643-053-2; unp.} E (Gr. PreK-1) Boston Globe-Horn Book Award (Picture Book)

Dog, an energetic little brown dachshund, and his sensible best friend Bear, a multicolored stuffed teddy, have three mini adventures together. Dog helps Bear get down from a tall table; Dog wants Bear to play, but Bear is reading a book; and Dog decides to change his boring name. ("From now on, call me SPOT." "But you don't have any spots.") The focus is on the two endearing characters, their bodies, one long and lean, the other plump and round, outlined in thick black scratchy lines and set against all-white pages. The spare words and pictures come together in a package that is so elemental but so satisfying.

GERM: An easy-to-read emergent reader, the three brief tales that make up this adorable book are just right to act out or write up as Reader's Theater scripts for pairs of children to read and dramatize. Note the book is written mostly in simple dialogue, which is ideal to use as a model when teaching or reinforcing punctuation and dialogue-writing skills. The first story, "Bear in the Chair," is a short story in microcosm, with rising action, a climax, falling action, and a perfect punchline at the conclusion. You could use it with older children to talk about the parts of a good story. Have children write new Dog and Bear stories and then pair up to read them aloud. Make the acquaintance of two other dachshunds in Caralyn Buehner's ***Superdog: The Heart of a Hero*** and Dav Pilkey's ***The Hallo-Wiener***.

RELATED TITLES: Bloom, Suzanne. *A Splendid Friend Indeed.* Boyds Mills, 2005. / Buehner, Caralyn. *Superdog: The Heart of a Hero.* HarperCollins, 2004. / Lobel, Arnold. *Frog and Toad Are Friends.* HarperCollins, 1970. (And others in the Frog and Toad series.) / Marshall, James. *George and Martha: The Complete Stories of Two Best Friends.* Houghton Mifflin, 1997. / Pilkey, Dav. *The Hallo-Wiener.* Scholastic, 1995. / Rohmann, Eric. *My Friend Rabbit.* Roaring Brook, 2002. / Scieszka, Jon. *Cowboy & Octopus.* Viking, 2007. / Seeger, Laura Vaccaro. *Black? White! Day? Night!* Roaring Brook, 2006. / Seeger, Laura Vaccaro. *Dog and Bear: Two's Company.* Roaring Brook, 2008. / Seeger, Laura Vaccaro. *The Hidden Alphabet.* Roaring Brook, 2003. / Seeger, Laura Vaccaro. *Lemons Are Not Red.* Roaring Brook, 2004. / Seeger, Laura Vaccaro. *Walter Was Worried.* Roaring Brook, 2005. / Willems, Mo. *My Friend Is Sad.* Hyperion, 2007. (And others in the Elephant & Piggie series.)

SUBJECTS: BEARS. BEST FRIENDS. DOGS. FRIENDSHIP. HUMOROUS FICTION. TEDDY BEARS.

EASY FICTION / PICTURE BOOKS, cont.

[J*] | | | | |

The End. **LaRochelle, David. Illus. by Richard Egielski. Arthur A. Levine/Scholastic, 2007. {ISBN 978-0-439-44011-4; unp. E (Gr. PreK-3)**

Open up the cover and the first page shows an elf tacking a sign reading "The End" to an old door. Starting (or ending) with, "And they all lived happily ever after," this entire story is told backwards in a lively exploration of cause-and-effect. See how the knight fell in love with the clever princess after she poured lemonade on his head because his curly red beard was on fire because he tickled a great green dragon who couldn't stop crying because . . . Egielski's action-filled watercolors are packed with rabbits, an enormous rolling tomato, a winged blue pig, and lots of lemons.

GERM: Not only do you put the story together sequentially as you read, but when you finish, you can also reread and retell it back to front, which is really front to back, starting with "Once upon a time a clever princess decided to make a big bowl of lemonade." Have your listeners add sound effects for each character, as described on page 197. Take a story you all know, like "The Three Bears" or "Cinderella," and see if your group can tell it backwards. Never tried telling stories before and don't know how to get started but want to give it a try? For practical advice, easy-to-follow techniques, literature-based ideas, and lots of wacky stories and songs you can try out on your students, take a look at my spiffy new book, ***Once Upon a Time: Using Storytelling, Creative Drama,and Reader's Theater with Children in Grades PreK-6*** (by Judy Freeman; Libraries Unlimited, 2007).

RELATED TITLES: Charlip, Remy. *Fortunately.* Aladdin, 1993, c1964. / Child, Lauren. *Beware of the Storybook Wolves.* Scholastic, 2001. / Child, Lauren. *Who's Afraid of the Big Bad Book?* Hyperion, 2003. / Egielski, Richard. *The Gingerbread Boy.* HarperCollins, 1997. / Garland, Michael. *Miss Smith's Incredible Storybook.* Dutton, 2003. / LaRochelle, David. *The Best Pet of All.* Dutton, 2004. / Noble, Trinka Hakes. *The Day Jimmy's Boa Ate the Wash.* Dial, 1980. / Palatini, Margie. *Three French Hens.* Illus. by Richard Egielski. Hyperion, 2005. / Palatini, Margie. *The Web Files.* Illus. by Richard Egielski. Hyperion, 2001. / Patschke, Steve. *The Spooky Book.* Walker, 1999. / Yorinks, Arthur. *Hey, Al.* Illus. by Richard Egielski. Farrar, 1986. / Zemach, Kaethe. *The Character in the Book.* HarperCollins, 1998.

SUBJECTS: CAUSE AND EFFECT. HUMOROUS FICTION. FAIRY TALES. PRINCES AND PRINCESSES.

[J] |A| | |S|

Fred Stays with Me! **Coffelt, Nancy. Illus. by Tricia Tusa. Little, Brown, 2007. {ISBN 978-0-316-88269-9; unp.} E (Gr. K-3)**

A little brown haired girl explains that sometimes she lives with her mom and sometimes with her dad, but of her brown-eared, white, sausage-bodied dog she says, "My dog, Fred, stays with me." The divorced child will recognize her situation, adjusting to the two homes of her parents, and she seems to be awfully well-adjusted and grounded, thanks to Fred, her lifeline, her friend, and her confidant. It's the parents who take it out on the dog, with mom tired of all the barking and dad mad at Fred for eating all his socks. There's no way she's going to let them reject her dog, though. "Excuse me," she announces to her parents (who remain unseen in the brown-toned illustrations). ". . . Fred doesn't stay with either of you. Fred stays with ME!" And he does, thank goodness.

GERM: Do you want to go into the girl's sensitive situation, living in two places? Maybe, in your discussion of different families, you do. If so, this book's so centered and pragmatic, it'll get kids talking about how they cope through difficult times. It's also a good story to use when talking about problems versus solutions. The girl and her parents come up with sensible plans to deal with Fred. Ask your children to recount problems they've solved with pets or siblings or parents or friends.

RELATED TITLES: Brown, Laurene Krasny. *Dinosaurs Divorce: A Guide for Changing Families.* Little Brown, 1986. / Calmenson, Stephanie. *May I Pet Your Dog?: The How-to Guide for Kids Meeting Dogs (and Dogs Meeting Kids).* Clarion, 2007. / Coy, John. *Two Old Potatoes and Me.* Knopf, 2003. / George, Kristine O'Connell. *Little Dog Poems.* Clarion, 1999. / Gottfried, Maya. *Good Dog.* Knopf, 2005. / Graham, Bob. *"Let's Get a Pup!" Said Kate.* Candlewick, 2001. / Polacco, Patricia. *Some Birthday!* Simon & Schuster, 1991.

SUBJECTS: DIVORCE. DOGS. FAMILY PROBLEMS.

[J] |A|B|H|S|

A Good Day. Henkes, Kevin. Illus. by the author. Greenwillow, 2007. {ISBN 978-0-06-114019-8; unp.} E (Gr. PreK-1)

It's a bad day for a little yellow bird who loses his favorite tail feather, a little white dog whose leash gets tangled, a little orange fox who can't find his mother, and a little brown squirrel who drops her nut. But then, something good happens to each of them, turning a bad day into a good one. The most elemental of texts and handsome brown bordered watercolors make this lost-and-found story just right for toddler and preschool story hours.

GERM: Ask your listeners if they're having a good day. If they say they are, ask them what has made it good. If anyone is having a bad day, ask what made it bad. Talk over what they think it would take to turn a bad day into a good one or vice versa. Have you ever had a bad day that turned into a good day? What happened to perk up your day? For more ideas, see Judy Freeman's teacher's guide for this book on page 115. For still more ideas on using books by Kevin Henkes, see Judy Freeman's teacher's guide, "The World of Kevin Henkes", which you can download at <**www.HarperCollinschildrens.com**>. Click on "Teachers & Librarians" and type Henkes in the Search Bar.

RELATED TITLES: Charlip, Remy. *Fortunately*. Aladdin, 1993, c1964. / Cuyler, Margery. *That's Good! That's Bad!* Henry Holt, 1991. / Henkes, Kevin. *Chrysanthemum*. Greenwillow, 1991. / Henkes, Kevin. *Kitten's First Full Moon*. Greenwillow, 2004. / Rosenthal, Marc. *Phooey!* HarperCollins, 2007. / Stevens, April. *Waking Up Wendell*. Schwartz & Wade, 2007.

SUBJECTS: ANIMALS. CAUSE AND EFFECT. CIRCULAR STORIES.

[J*] |A|B| | |

Henry's Freedom Box: A True Story. Levine, Ellen. Illus. by Kadir Nelson. Scholastic, 2007. {ISBN 978-0-439-77733-9; unp.} E (Gr. 2-6) Caldecott Honor

On his deathbed, the master of slave Henry Brown does not give the boy his freedom. Instead, he gives Henry to his son who sets him to work in a tobacco factory. Years later, Henry marries a woman named Nancy and they have three children. After his wife and children are sold at the slave market, Henry makes a bold plan to escape. He asks his friend James and Dr. Smith, a white abolitionist, to help pack him into a large wooden crate, and mail him from Richmond, Virginia to the doctor's friend in Philadelphia, 350 miles away. This dramatic story is all the more startling because it is true. After 27 hours of travel, some of it upside down, Henry "Box" Brown arrived in Philadelphia safe and sound on March 30, 1849. Kadir Nelson's breathtaking full bleed cross hatched paintings are somber, eloquent, and ultimately, hopeful.

GERM: Read aloud the Author's note to provide more facts. If you have a box from a TV or other large piece of equipment, cut holes in the side for air, and ask for a brave volunteer to get inside while you read the second half of the book. Have the child describe what it felt like to be in the dark box alone. There's a chapter about Henry Brown in Virginia Hamilton's *Many Thousand Gone: African Americans from Slavery to Freedom*. Also share Emily Arnold McCully's eye-opening picture book, *The Escape of Oney Judge: Martha Washington's Slave Finds Freedom*. In the late 1700s, upon discovering that first lady Martha Washington would never set her free, Oney Judge, a young seamstress, ran away, sailing to Portsmouth, New Hampshire where she lived till the end of her life.

RELATED TITLES: Curtis, Christopher Paul. *Elijah of Buxton*. Scholastic, 2007. / Fradin, Dennis Brindell. *Bound for the North Star: True Stories of Fugitive Slaves*. Clarion, 2000. / Hamilton, Virginia. *Many Thousand Gone: African Americans from Slavery to Freedom*. Knopf, 1993. / Hamilton, Virginia. *The People Could Fly: The Picture Book*. Knopf, 2004. / Hopkinson, Deborah. *Sweet Clara and the Freedom Quilt*. Knopf, 1993. / Johnson, Dolores. *Now Let Me Fly: The Story of a Slave Family*. Macmillan, 1993. / McCully, Emily Arnold. *The Escape of Oney Judge: Martha Washington's Slave Finds Freedom*. Farrar, 2007. / Nelson, Vaunda Micheaux. *Almost to Freedom*. Carolrhoda, 2003. / Ringgold, Faith. *Aunt Harriet's Underground Railroad in the Sky*. Crown, 1992. / Tingle, Tim. *Crossing Bok Chitto: A Choctaw Tale of Friendship & Freedom*. Cinco Puntos, 2006. / Weatherford, Carole Boston. *Moses: When Harriet Tubman Led Her People to Freedom*. Illus. by Kadir Nelson. Hyperion/Jump at the Sun, 2006. / Winter, Jeannette. *Follow the Drinking Gourd*. Knopf, 1989.

SUBJECTS: AFRICAN AMERICANS—BIOGRAPHY.   BROWN, HENRY BOX.   HISTORICAL FICTION. MULTICULTURAL BOOKS. SLAVERY. PICTURE BOOKS FOR OLDER READERS. UNDERGROUND RAILROAD.

[j] | | | |S|

Hurry! Hurry! **Bunting, Eve. Illus. by Jeff Mack. Harcourt, 2007. {ISBN 978-0-15-205410-6; unp.} E (Gr. PreK-1)**

A chicken, racing across the barnyard, exhorts, "Hurry! Hurry!" "Coming! Coming!" bleats the goat leaping over a fence. Between the green grass and the blue sky, the ducks, cows, pigs, sheep, and a sheepdog cavort eagerly to the barn, where they converge expectantly around the hatching egg centered in a straw nest on the earthen floor. "I'm here! I'm here!" proclaims the new chick to the exultant crowd. Their celebration of the newest member of the barnyard community, depicted in joyous full-bleed acrylics, will make listeners think about the preciousness of each new life, including theirs.

GERM: With each word repeated twice on each page, the animal's exclamations will be perfect to act out with the toddler or preschool storyhour set. Ask them how people welcome their new babies.

RELATED TITLES: Aston, Dianna. *An Egg Is Quiet.* Chronicle, 2006. / Berends, Polly Berrien. *I Heard Said The Bird.* Dial, 1995. / Braun, Trudi. *My Goose Betsy.* Candlewick, 1999. / Dunrea, Olivier. *Ollie.* Houghton Mifflin, 2003. / Hills, Tad. *Duck & Goose.* Schwartz & Wade, 2006. / Harrington, Janice N. *The Chicken-Chasing Queen of Lamar County.* Farrar/Melanie Kroupa, 2007.

SUBJECTS: CHICKENS. DOMESTIC ANIMALS. EGGS.

[J*] | | | | |

I Am Invited to a Party! **Willems, Mo. Illus. by the author. Hyperion, 2007. {ISBN 978-1-42310-687-6; 56p.} E (Gr. PreK-1)**

When Piggie gets a cool invitation to go to her first party, she is thrilled and invites her best friend, Elephant (AKA Gerald), to go with her. Elephant says, "I know parties," and that, as it turns out, is very true. But what kind of party will it be: a fancy party, a pool party, or a costume party? The two friends are prepared for all three.

GERM: Make invitations for an Elephant & Piggie party where you play games based on the other stories in the series, such as Balance the Nest on Your Head, Make Someone Laugh, and Pretend to Fly. Party on with the elephants in Arthur Howard's *The Hubbub Above.* For more ideas for using the first four books in the resplendent Elephant & Piggie series, see Judy Freeman's Activity Guide on page 119. You can also print out the activity pages at <**www.hyperionbooksforchildren.com**>. Type "Mo Willems" in the search bar, click on the title, and you'll see the link to the guide on the book's home page.

RELATED TITLES: Elya, Susan Middleton. *Eight Animals on the Town.* Putnam, 2000. / Howard, Arthur. *The Hubbub Above.* Harcourt, 2005. / Scieszka, Jon. *Cowboy & Octopus.* Viking, 2007. / Seeger, Laura Vaccaro. *Dog and Bear: Two Friends, Three Stories.* Roaring Brook, 2007. / Soto, Gary. *Chato and the Party Animals.* Putnam, 2000. / Waber, Bernard. *Bearsie Bear and the Surprise Sleepover Party.* Houghton Mifflin, 1997. / Willems, Mo. *Don't Let the Pigeon Drive the Bus.* Hyperion, 2003. (And others in the Pigeon series.) / Willems, Mo. *Leonardo the Terrible Monster.* Hyperion, 2005. / Willems, Mo. *Today I Will Fly!* Hyperion, 2007. (And others in the Elephant & Piggie series.)

SUBJECTS: BEST FRIENDS. ELEPHANTS. FRIENDSHIP. HUMOROUS FICTION. PARTIES. PIGS.

[j] |A| | | |

Jazz Baby. Wheeler, Lisa. Illus. by R. Christie Gregory. Harcourt, 2007. {ISBN 978-0-15-202522-9; unp.} E
     (Gr. PreK-1) Geisel Honor

The rhythm and rhyme of this rat-a-scat picture book will have babies bopping and clapping along with Baby's singing and dancing as he bounces and boogies with his whole extended African American family to a record on the record player. "Go, man, go!" calls that baby as Mama and Daddy dance and smile and sing the blues and put that "drowsy-dozy" baby, that "snoozy-woozy" baby in his crib. Flat gouache paintings with loose-limbed dancers on a white background will remind you of art from the hip '50s and '60s and of Chris Raschka's jazz books, too.

GERM: Play a little jazz for kids as you read this aloud in call-and-response fashion. Then get up and do a little dancing to the music. Oh yeah!

 RELATED TITLES: Cox, Judy. *My Family Plays Music.* Holiday House, 2003. / Dodds, Dayle Ann. *Sing, Sophie.* Candlewick, 1997. / Frame, Jeron Ashford. *Yesterday I Had the Blues.* Tricycle, 2003. / Gray, Libba Moore. *Little Lil and the Swing-Singing Sax.* Simon & Schuster, 1996. / Ho, Minfong. *Hush! A Thai Lullaby.* Orchard, 1996. / Lowery, Linda. *Twist with a Burger, Jitter with a Bug.* Houghton Mifflin, 1995. / McMullan, Kate. *Rock-a-Baby Band.* Little, Brown, 2003. / Moss, Lloyd. *Music Is.* Putnam, 2003. / Raschka, Chris. *Charlie Parker Played Bebop.* Orchard, 1992. / Wheeler, Lisa. *Mammoths on the Move.* Harcourt, 2006.

SUBJECTS: BABIES. JAZZ. MUSIC. STORIES IN RHYME.

[J*] |A| | |S|

Knuffle Bunny Too: A Case of Mistaken Identity. Willems, Mo. Illus. by the author. Hyperion, 2007. {ISBN
     978-1-42310-299-1; unp.} E (Gr. PreK-2) Caldecott Honor

We all fell in love with bald little toddler Trixie, who said her very first words in the Caldecott Honor winner, ***Knuffle Bunny***. Trixie's a yellow-haired preschooler now, and she and her dad and her one-of-a-kind stuffed rabbit are their way to someplace special . . . school! She's going to show her beloved Knuffle Bunny to all her friends and her teacher Ms. Greengrove. But what's this? It's classmate Sonja. And what's Sonja holding? Her own identical rabbit. The girls' subsequent spat leads to the toys being placed on top of a cabinet until the end of the day. In the middle of the night, Trixie awakens to a devastating realization. "That is not my bunny," she informs her sleeping daddy at 2:30 a.m. Mo Willems's story and illustrations—hand drawn ink sketches over silvery photographs of his Brooklyn, New York neighborhood, set against a shiny gray background—are every bit as original and innovative and hilarious as the first book.

GERM: Stop reading on the page where Trixie wakes her parents, and ask a few quick questions: How does Trixie know she has the wrong rabbit. Why did it take her so long to figure it out? And what should she do about it? You can download Judy Freeman's teacher's guide for Knuffle Bunny at <**www.hyperionbooksforchildren.com**>. Type "knuffle" in the search bar, click on the title, and you'll see the link to the guide on the book's home page. Judy's new activity guide for ***Knuffle Bunny Too*** is there, too—type the title in the search bar—and the uncut version is in this handbook on page 137. In the meantime, ask your students to compare and contrast the two titles. What elements of the first book do they see in the second?

RELATED TITLES: Clark, Emma Chichester. *Where Are You, Blue Kangaroo?* Doubleday, 2000. / Cocca-Leffler, Maryann. *Missing: One Stuffed Rabbit.* Albert Whitman, 1998. / Feiffer, Jules. *I Lost My Bear.* Morrow, 1998. / Fitzpatrick, Marie-Louise. *Lizzy and Skunk.* DK Ink, 2000. / Freeman, Don. *Corduroy.* Viking, 1968. / Galbraith, Kathryn O. *Laura Charlotte.* Philomel, 1990. / Hughes, Shirley. *Dogger.* Lothrop, 1988. / Ichikawa, Satomi. *La La Rose.* Philomel, 2004. / Willems, Mo. *Don't Let the Pigeon Drive the Bus.* Hyperion, 2003. / Willems, Mo. *Knuffle Bunny: A Cautionary Tale.* Hyperion, 2005. / Willems, Mo. *Leonardo the Terrible Monster.* Hyperion, 2005.

SUBJECTS: FAMILY LIFE. FRIENDSHIP. HUMOROUS FICTION. LOST AND FOUND POSSESSIONS. NEW YORK CITY. PICTURE BOOKS FOR ALL AGES. RABBITS. SCHOOLS. STUFFED ANIMALS. TEACHERS.

[j] |A| | | |
Little Rat Makes Music. Bang-Campbell, Monika. Illus. by Molly Bang. Harcourt, 2007. {ISBN 978-0-15-
205305-5; 48p.} E (Gr. K-3)

Enchanted with the sound of other young rats playing tiny violins at the Community Hall, Little Rat can't wait to take lessons. Her new teacher, a short-tempered rabbit named Miss Wingbutton, yells at Little Rat for sawing her bow back and forth on the strings, but when she finally gets to play her first real note, it sounds like this: SQWAAAAAAKK! She likes her lessons, she likes her violin, but she does not like practicing for a half hour each day. "Getting herself to do it was like wrestling a goat." Tutoring sessions with Kitty, one of the advanced students, gets her back in the swing, especially when she's asked to play a duet with Kitty at the holiday concert. The detailed pencil, gouache, and watercolor illustrations of this charming easy chapter book are irresistible.

GERM: Talk about what kinds of practice we need to do to become skilled at our undertakings, from learning an instrument to reading books to playing soccer. See how Little Rat pursues some of her other passions in *Little Rat Rides* and *Little Rat Sets Sail*. Have children think of other skills, sports, and activities they think she'd like to learn next (or that they'd like to learn how to do). They can draw up a list of procedural instructions on what one needs to do to get good at baseball or swimming or drawing.

RELATED TITLES: Bang-Campbell, Monika. *Little Rat Rides.* Harcourt, 2004. / Bang-Campbell, Monika. *Little Rat Sets Sail.* Harcourt, 2002. / Cox, Judy. *My Family Plays Music.* Holiday House, 2003. / Falconer, Ian. *Olivia Forms a Band.* Atheneum, 2006. / Howe, James. *Horace and Morris Join the Chorus (But What About Dolores?).* Atheneum, 2002. / Krosoczka, Jarrett J. *Punk Farm.* Knopf, 2005. / Krull, Kathleen. *M Is for Music.* Harcourt, 2003.
SUBJECTS: CONCERTS. MUSIC. RATS. VIOLIN.

[J] |A| | | |
Los Gatos Black on Halloween. Montes, Marisa. Illus. by Yuyi Morales. Henry Holt, 2006. {ISBN 978-0-8050-
7429-1; unp.} E (Gr. 1-4) Belpré Illustrator Award and Belpré Author Honor (NOTE: The Belpré
Awards are given every other year; this book was included in last year's *The Winners! Handbook*,
too.)

In a spooky graveyard on Halloween night, los gatos (cats) slink, las calabazas (pumpkins) burn bright, las brujas (witches) glide on their escobas (broomsticks), and los esqueletos (skeletons) rattle bones. The shivery rhyming text and creepy full bleed moonlit paintings introduce a host of horrifying creatures of the night who congregate in a haunted house to party. While you may find these apparitions mighty fearsome, there's one thing that frightens them most—human niños trick or treating.

GERM: Spanish words are defined and translated within each stanza. Try this as a choral reading or Reader's Theater, or even set it to music. (It would work wonderfully to the chorus of "Isabella the Glamor Cat" from the musical "Cats." Otherwise, make up a dirgelike tune in a minor key.)

RELATED TITLES: Bunting, Eve. *In the Haunted House.* Clarion, 1990. / Bunting, Eve. *Scary, Scary Halloween.* Clarion, 1986. / Cuyler, Marjorie. *Skeleton Hiccups.* Simon & Schuster, 2002. / DeFelice, Cynthia C. *The Dancing Skeleton.* Macmillan, 1989. / Johnston, Tony. *The Ghost of Nicholas Greebe.* Dial, 1996. / Krosoczka, Jarrett J. *Annie Was Warned.* Knopf, 2003. / Leuck, Laura. *One Witch.* Walker, 2003. / Loredo, Elizabeth. *Boogie Bones.* Putnam, 1997. / Park, Barbara. *Psssst! It's Me . . . the Bogeyman.* Atheneum, 1998. / Patschke, Steve. *The Spooky Book.* Walker, 1999. / San Souci, Robert D. *Cinderella Skeleton.* Harcourt, 2000. / Sierra, Judy. *Monster Goose.* Harcourt, 2001. / Silverman, Erica. *Big Pumpkin.* Macmillan, 1992. / Sklansky, Amy E. *Skeleton Bones and Goblin Groans: Poems for Halloween.* Henry Holt, 2004. / Stutson, Caroline. *By the Light of the Halloween Moon.* Lothrop, 1993. / Williams, Linda. *The Little Old Lady Who Was Not Afraid of Anything.* Crowell, 1986.
**SUBJECTS: HALLOWEEN.   HAUNTED HOUSES.   MONSTERS.   MULTICULTURAL BOOKS.
SPANISH LANGUAGE. STORIES IN RHYME.**

[j] | |B| | |

Max Counts His Chickens. **Wells, Rosemary. Illus. by the author. Viking, 2007. {ISBN 978-0-670-06222-5; unp.} E (Gr. PreK-1)**

Searching the house from room to room on Easter morning for the hot-pink marshmallow chicks hidden by the Easter Bunny, Ruby finds one after another, while poor hapless Max can't locate any chicks at all in the toothpaste tube, the coffee can, or even in the orange juice. Fortunately, Grandma and her friend, the Easter Bunny, come to the rescue.

GERM: Children will see the numbers one to ten and count the ever-increasing chicks across the top of each page. Ask children to explain why Max keeps having trouble finding chicks and Ruby does not. Hide your own marshmallow chicks (wrapped in plastic) around the room for children to find, count, and eat. Introduce other Max and Ruby books where Max makes a mess, like ***Max Cleans Up*** and ***Max's Dragon Shirt***. Another book of Max at Easter time is ***Max's Chocolate Chicken***.

RELATED TITLES: Bruel, Nick. *Poor Puppy.* Roaring Brook, 2007. / Catalanotto, Peter. *Daisy 1 2 3.* Atheneum, 2003. / Cronin, Doreen. *Click, Clack, Splish, Splash: A Counting Adventure.* Atheneum, 2006. / Falwell, Cathryn. *Turtle Splash!: Countdown at the Pond.* Greenwillow, 2001. / Rathmann, Peggy. *10 Minutes Till Bedtime.* Putnam, 1998. / Walton, Rick. *One More Bunny: Adding from One to Ten.* Lothrop, 2000. / Walton, Rick. *So Many Bunnies: A Bedtime ABC and Counting Book.* Lothrop, 1998. / Wells, Rosemary. *Emily's First 100 Days of School.* Hyperion, 2000. / Wells, Rosemary. *Max Cleans Up.* Viking, 2000. / Wells, Rosemary. *Max's Chocolate Chicken.* Dial, 1989. (And others in the Max and Ruby series.)

SUBJECTS: BROTHERS AND SISTERS. COUNTING BOOKS. EASTER. HUMOROUS FICTION. GRANDMOTHERS. MATHEMATICS. RABBITS.

[J] | | |H| |

May I Pet Your Dog?: The How-to Guide for Kids Meeting Dogs (and Dogs Meeting Kids). **Calmenson, Stephanie. Illus. by Jan Ormerod. Clarion, 2007. {ISBN 978-0-618-51034-4; 32p.} E (Gr. PreK-2)**

Harry, a longhaired, chocolate-dappled dachshund, encounters a young boy and gives him a series of concrete and practical instructions on how to be friends with a dog. The most important question to ask when approaching a person with a dog on a leash is, "May I pet your dog?" From that, the dog shows the boy how a dog likes to be petted: first letting it sniff your hand, then gently scratching its back. Pen and ink and watercolor illustrations of the yellow-hatted boy and a series of friendly and not-so-friendly dogs are reassuring and genial, as is the wealth of information about dog behavior, ending with a recap of the information learned. A final page provides color photos of the real Harry, whom the author adopted as a puppy.

GERM: After sharing the book with children, talk over what they learned about dogs that they never knew before. They can act out the different scenarios in pairs, with one person being the dog. You can then have them work in groups to write and illustrate other personal narratives—what would a cat or guinea pig or horse or snake have to say about how they would like to be treated? Take a further look at dog behavior in need of changing in Steven Kellogg's ***Pinkerton, Behave***, Nina Laden's ***Bad Dog***, David Shannon's ***Good Boy, Fergus!***, Mark Teague's ***Dear Mrs. LaRue: Letters from Obedience School***, and Rosemary Wells's ***McDuff Goes to School***.

RELATED TITLES: Bartoletti, Susan. *Nobody's Diggier than a Dog.* Hyperion, 2004. / Bruel, Nick, *Poor Puppy.* Roaring Brook, 2007. / Coffelt, Nancy. *Fred Stays with Me!* Little, Brown, 2007. / Gottfried, Maya. *Good Dog.* Knopf, 2005. / Graham, Bob. *"Let's Get a Pup!" Said Kate.* Candlewick, 2001. / Harvey, Amanda. *Dog Eared.* Doubleday, 2002. / Jenkins, Steve. *Dogs and Cats.* Houghton Mifflin, 2007. / Kalman, Maira. *What Pete Ate from A-Z.* Putnam, 2001. / Kellogg, Steven. *Pinkerton, Behave.* Dial, 1979. / Kirk, Daniel. *Dogs Rule!* Hyperion, 2003. / Meddaugh, Susan. *Martha Walks the Dog.* Houghton Mifflin, 1998. / Meyers, Susan. *Puppies! Puppies! Puppies!* Abrams, 2005. / Moxley, Sheila. *ABCD: An Alphabet Book of Cats and Dogs.* Little, Brown, 2001. / Shannon, David. *Good Boy, Fergus!* Scholastic/Blue Sky, 2006. / Sklansky, Amy E. *From the Doghouse: Poems to Chew On.* Henry Holt, 2002. / Teague, Mark. *Dear Mrs. LaRue: Letters from Obedience School.* Scholastic, 2002. / Wells, Rosemary. *McDuff Goes to School.* Hyperion, 2001. (And others in the McDuff series.)

SUBJECTS: DOGS. PETS. PROCEDURAL WRITING. SAFETY

EASY FICTION / PICTURE BOOKS, cont.

[j]　　|A| | | |

My Colors, My World/Mis Colores, Mi Mundo. **Gonzalez, Maya Christina. Illus. by the author. Children's Book Press, 2007. {ISBN 978-0-892-39221-6; unp.} E (Gr. PreK-2) Pura Belpré Illustrator Honor Book**

A little girl describes the colors in the desert where she lives, from the hot pink of the sunset to the green of the sharp cactus and the black of her Papi's hair. Double page spreads feature her words in English underneath the picture on the left side, and in Spanish on the right, with the words for each color written in that color for easy identification.

GERM: A bilingual glossary of colors will help children learn new words in English or Spanish. Children can recount and draw the colors that light up their lives.

RELATED TITLES: Elya, Susan Middleton. *Bebé Goes Shopping.* Harcourt, 2006. / Elya, Susan Middleton. *F Is for Fiesta.* Putnam, 2006. / Frame, Jeron Ashford. *Yesterday I Had the Blues.* Tricycle, 2003. / Jonas, Ann. *Color Dance.* Greenwillow, 1989. / Mora, Pat. *Yum! Mmmm! Que Rico!: Americas' Sproutings.* Lee & Low, 2007. / Seeger, Laura Vaccaro. *Lemons Are Not Red.* Roaring Brook, 2004.

SUBJECTS: COLOR. DESERTS. HISPANIC AMERICANS. SPANISH LANGUAGE.

[J*]　　| | | | |

My Friend Is Sad. **Willems, Mo. Illus. by the author. Hyperion, 2007. {ISBN 978-1-4231-0297-7; 57p.} E (Gr. PreK-1)**

Along with Frog and Toad, George and Martha, Henry and Mudge, and the new Dog and Bear series by Laura Vaccaro Seeger (see review above), make room on your shelves and in your hearts for two captivating new characters: the indefatigable Piggie and her pragmatic bespectacled companion, Elephant, AKA Gerald. "Ohhh . . ." moans Gerald, lost in his own misery. "My friend is sad," Piggie explains to us, her audience. "I will make him happy." Yee-haw! Piggie throws herself into cheering up Gerald, dressing up as a cowboy, a clown, and even a robot. Nothing works. Not until he sees Piggie sans adornment does Gerald even recognize his friend and shed his melancholia. "I need my friends," he says contentedly. "You need new glasses," Piggie quips, rolling her eyes. In this cleverest, most innovative emergent reader since Dr. Seuss's Beginner Books, the entire text is displayed in dialogue balloons, gray for Elephant, and pink for Piggie. Here's something that will cheer you right up: there are three companion books in the series, all published in 2007 (and four more on the way for 2008). In ***Today I Will Fly!,*** Piggie is determined to take to the air, despite Gerald's naysaying. Next, Elephant is not one bit happy when Piggie tells him there are two love birds building a nest on his head in ***There Is a Bird on Your Head!*** (The birds then lay three eggs that hatch, which is even worse.) And finally, in ***I Am Invited to a Party,*** Piggie gets a cool invitation to go to her first party and invites Elephant, who says, "I know parties." He does, too.

GERM: Have your children draw one thing that makes them sad and then something that cheers them up and makes them happy again. They can finish these sentences either verbally or in writing: I am sad when ____. I am happy when ____. For a Reader's Theater script of this book, turn to page 158 of this handbook. For more ideas for using the first four books in the Elephant & Piggie series, see Judy Freeman's Activity Guide on page 119. You can also print out her activity pages at <www.hyperionbooksforchildren.com>. Type "Mo Willems" in the search bar, click on the title, and you'll see the link to the guide on the book's home page.

RELATED TITLES: Chaconas, Dori. *Cork & Fuzz: Short and Tall.* Viking, 2006. / Freymann, Saxton, and Joost Elffers. *How Are You Peeling?: Foods with Moods.* Scholastic, 1999. / Rohmann, Eric. *My Friend Rabbit.* Roaring Brook, 2002. / Scieszka, Jon. *Cowboy & Octopus.* Viking, 2007. / Seeger, Laura Vaccaro. *Dog and Bear: Two Friends, Three Stories.* Roaring Brook, 2007. / Shannon, David. *Duck on a Bike.* Blue Sky/Scholastic, 2002. / Steig, William. *Pete's a Pizza.* HarperCollins, 1998. / Willems, Mo. *Don't Let the Pigeon Drive the Bus.* Hyperion, 2003. / Willems, Mo. *There Is a Bird on Your Head!* Hyperion, 2007. (And others in the Elephant & Piggie series.)

SUBJECTS: BEST FRIENDS. ELEPHANTS. FRIENDSHIP. HUMOROUS FICTION. PIGS. READER'S THEATER.

[j] | |B| | |
Nini Here and There. Lobel, Anita. Illus. by the author. Greenwillow, 2007. {ISBN 978-0-06-078768-4; unp.} E (Gr. PreK-2)

Nini, the striped tabby cat you might recall from the book *One Lighthouse, One Moon*, is distressed that her people are packing to leave the city on vacation without her. Instead, she's scooped up and zipped into the "big black thing," the carrying case where she falls asleep. She flies and floats and sails and bounces and rocks in her dreams, until there is a bump, and she emerges from the case in a whole new place where there are flowers and fluttering birds and butterflies and good things to eat. It's different here, in the country, but Nini is content, thinking, "Yes, everything is different. But they did not go away without me." Lobel's luscious watercolor and white gouache paintings aptly capture the mysterious thoughts of a cat who finds contentment in the small things.

GERM: Meet a lost cat with a tougher road to follow in *The Cat Who Walked Across France* by Kate Banks. Then see how another cat deals with a new experience in the Caldecott winner, *Kitten's First Full Moon* by Kevin Henkes and take a look at another cat's reveries in *When Cats Dream* by Dav Pilkey.

RELATED TITLES: Banks, Kate. *The Cat Who Walked Across France.* Farrar, 2004. / Henkes, Kevin. *Kitten's First Full Moon.* Greenwillow, 2004. / Lobel, Anita. *Away from Home.* Greenwillow, 1994. / Lobel, Anita. *One Lighthouse, One Moon.* Greenwillow, 2000. / McDonald, Joyce. *Homebody.* Putnam, 1991. / Myers, Christopher. *Black Cat.* Scholastic, 1999. / Pilkey, Dav. *When Cats Dream.* Orchard, 1992. / Rosen, Michael. *Moving.* Viking, 1993. / Voake, Charlotte. *Ginger Finds a Home.* Candlewick, 2003.

SUBJECTS: CATS. DREAMS. MOVING, HOUSEHOLD. VACATIONS.

[j] |A| | |S|
Orange Pear Apple Bear. Gravett, Emily. Illus. by the author. Simon & Schuster, 2007. {ISBN 978-1-4169-3999-3; unp.} E (Gr. PreK-1)

The four words of the title appear in different combinations as a brown bear examines, juggles with, and finally eats an orange, pear, and apple. Toddlers will delight in the simple silliness of the rhyming text and the spare charcoal bordered watercolors of fruit and bear against the stark white pages. Here's a book emergent readers can handle themselves.

GERM: Bring in stuffed bears, oranges, pears, and apples so children can act out the sequence of the story. Then hold the bear, add a banana, and make fruit salad.

RELATED TITLES: Ahlberg, Janet, and Ahlberg, Allen. *Each Peach Pear Plum.* Viking, 1979. / Bloom, Suzanne. *A Splendid Friend Indeed.* Boyds Mills, 2005. / Brown, Margaret Wise. *Goodnight Moon.* HarperCollins, 1947. / Campbell, Rod. *Dear Zoo: A Lift-the-Flap Book.* Little Simon, 2007, c1982. / Ehlert, Lois. *Color Zoo.* Harcourt. / Ehlert, Lois. *Eating the Alphabet: Fruits and Vegetables from A to Z.* Harcourt, 1989. / MacDonald, Suse. *Alphabatics.* Simon & Schuster, 1986. / Martin, Bill, Jr. *Brown Bear, Brown Bear, What Do You See?* Henry Holt, 1983. / Rathmann, Peggy. *Good Night, Gorilla.* Putnam, 1994.

SUBJECTS: BEARS. FRUIT. STORIES IN RHYME.

EASY FICTION / PICTURE BOOKS, cont.

[J] |A| |H|S|
Pictures from Our Vacation. Perkins, Lynne Rae. Illus. by the author. Greenwillow, 2007. {ISBN 978-0-06-085098-2; unp.} E (Gr. K-3)
A young girl with light brown braids describes her family's long car trip to the old family farm to join their grandparents for the summer. Mom gives her and her younger brother little instant cameras and a notebook so they can record, as souvenirs of their vacation, the sights they see and their reactions to them. Sprawled on the back seat of the car, the girl thinks about the ideal motel she would like to run, with rooms like the Jungle Cottage, which would feature hammocks for sleeping and a waterfall for a shower. And while the old farmhouse seems to be dusty and musty with not much to do, especially after days of rain, the arrival of lots of relatives makes their stay special. The detailed illustrations, done in pen and ink and watercolor paint, observe the many small events and ordinary but memorable moments that make up a vacation.
GERM: There's that perennial and ubiquitous first-day-of-school "What Did You Do on Your Summer Vacation" essay tie in here, sure, but instead, you could have your children begin their own spiral notebook jottings for the year, drawing or painting their most compelling memories and observations paired with some small moment writing that puts their experiences in words.
RELATED TITLES: Best, Cari. *When Catherine the Great and I Were Eight!* Farrar, 2003. / LaMarche, Jim. *The Raft.* HarperCollins, 2000. / Manzano, Sonia. *No Dogs Allowed!* Atheneum, 2004. / Rylant, Cynthia. *When I Was Young in the Mountains.* Dutton, 1982. / Schnur, Steven. *Summer: An Alphabet Acrostic.* Clarion, 2001. / Stewig, John Warren. *Making Plum Jam.* Hyperion, 2002. / Williams, Vera B. *Three Days on a River in a Red Canoe.* Greenwillow Books, 1981.
SUBJECTS: BROTHERS AND SISTERS. FAMILY REUNIONS. PHOTOGRAPHY. SUMMER. VACATIONS.

[J] | | | | |
Poor Puppy. Bruel, Nick. Illus. by the author. Roaring Brook, 2007. {ISBN 978-1-59643-270-3; unp.} E (Gr. PreK-2)
In this equally uproarious sequel to **Bad Kitty**, Puppy is sad that his best friend, Kitty, doesn't want to play with him today. The only things he has to play with are an entire alphabet of 26 toys, including 2 balls, 8 hula hoops, and 15 "old cat toys he found under the sofa." Listeners will point out the black and white kitten lurking in each of the exuberant action-filled paneled illustrations. Then Puppy takes a nap and dreams about playing with Kitty. They play Apple bobbing in Antarctica, Kick the Can in Kenya, and Tag in Turkey. So what you get here are two full alphabets, a counting book, an alliterative list of games and sports paired with the names of countries and cities, and a lot of laughs.
GERM: After reading Puppy's alphabet of games, ask your listeners to stand up, find a spot with a bit of elbow room, and then act out each of his activities as you reread them aloud. Locate the places on the map for a bit of a world tour. Children can design new counting pages or game and country (or states or cities) pages, illustrated with the antics of their own pets.
RELATED TITLES: Bruel, Nick. *Bad Kitty.* Roaring Brook, 2005. / Bruel, Nick. *Boing!* Roaring Brook, 2004. / Catalanotto, Peter. *Daisy 1 2 3.* Atheneum, 2003. / Catalanotto, Peter. *Matthew A.B.C.* Atheneum, 2002. / Cronin, Doreen. *Click, Clack, Quackity-Quack: An Alphabet Adventure.* Atheneum, 2005. / Cronin, Doreen. *Click, Clack, Splish, Splash: A Counting Adventure.* Atheneum, 2006. / Fleming, Denise. *Alphabet Under Construction.* Henry Holt, 2002. / Florian, Douglas. *Bow Wow Meow Meow: It's Rhyming Cats and Dogs.* Harcourt, 2003. / Kalman, Maira. *What Pete Ate from A-Z.* Putnam, 2001. / Lobel, Anita. *Away from Home.* Greenwillow, 1994. / Mahurin, Tim. *Jeremy Kooloo.* Dutton, 1995. / McFarland, Lyn Rossiter. *Widget.* Farrar, 2001. / Miller, Sara Swan. *Three Stories You Can Read to Your Cat.* Houghton Mifflin, 1997. / Miller, Sara Swan. *Three Stories You Can Read to Your Dog.* Houghton Mifflin, 1995.
SUBJECTS: ALLITERATION. ALPHABET. CATS. COUNTING BOOKS. CREATIVE DRAMA. DOGS. GAMES. HUMOROUS FICTION. MATHEMATICS. MULTICULTURAL BOOKS.

[j] |A| | |

Rainstorm. **Lehman, Barbara. Illus. by Barbara Lehman. Houghton Mifflin, 2007. {ISBN 978-0-8050-7389-8; unp.} E (Gr. PreK-2)**

Bored inside the big empty house on a rainy day, a boy finds an old fashioned key which fits into an old trunk. When he opens the lid, there's a ladder inside, which he climbs down, and finds himself in an unfamiliar passage that leads to a spiral staircase. Climbing all the way up, he opens a hatch and he's at the top of a red and white lighthouse on a tiny island overlooking the sea. (Sharp-eyed children will deduce it's the same lighthouse seen from the house on the title page.) Best of all, there are three other children up there, and they spend an idyllic day on the island flying kites and building sandcastles. Back at home, he wakes up the next morning and fetches the children back to his house to play.

GERM: Speech teachers have fun with Barbara Lehman's wordless books, since children can read the pictures and describe the story orally. Her precise, orderly, bordered watercolor, gouache, and ink illustrations offer wish fulfillment to children who wish they could find a hidden door or passageway in their houses. Lehman's other more magical and surreal adventures include *Museum Trip* and *The Red Book*.

RELATED TITLES: Banyai, Istvan. *Zoom.* Viking, 1995. / Faller, Regis. *The Adventures of Polo.* Roaring Brook, 2006. / Lehman, Barbara. *Museum Trip.* Houghton Mifflin, 2006. / Lehman, Barbara. *The Red Book.* Houghton Mifflin, 2004. / Varon, Sara. *Robot Dreams.* Roaring Brook/First Second, 2007. / Wiesner, David. *Flotsam.* Clarion, 2006. / Wiesner, David. *Free Fall.* Lothrop, 1988. / Wiesner, David. *Sector 7.* Clarion, 1999. / Yoo, Taeeun. *The Little Red Fish.* Dial, 2007.

SUBJECTS: ADVENTURE AND ADVENTURERS. PLAY. RAIN AND RAINFALL. STORIES WITHOUT WORDS.

[j] | |B| | |

A Second Is a Hiccup: A Child's Book of Time. **Hutchins, Hazel. Illus. by Katy MacDonald Denton. Scholastic/Arthur A. Levine, 2007. {ISBN 978-0-439-83106-2; unp.} E (Gr. PreK-1)**

Children who have little concept of time will be intrigued by the concrete examples of how long a second, minute, hour, day, week, month, and year are. Soft, sweet watercolors that will put you in mind of Maurice Sendak's early work introduce seven children who interact through play as units of time pass by. A second is "The time it takes to kiss your mom or jump a rope or turn around." Each measurement of time is defined in terms of its smaller unit ("Sixty seconds to a minute, sixty hiccups, sixty hops.") and then expanded upon as the children climb trees, sleep, wake, learn new skills, and, inevitably, grow.

GERM: Your children can time themselves with a stopwatch to see how long it takes to do common tasks and actions. They can demonstrate different brief actions, saying, "In one second I can _____." To show the passage of years and how children get bigger, read Margaret Wise Brown's *Another Important Book*.

RELATED TITLES: Behrman, Carol H. *The Ding Dong Clock.* Henry Holt, 1999. / Brown, Margaret Wise. *Another Important Book.* HarperCollins, 1999. / Crummel, Susan Stevens. *All in One Hour.* Marshall Cavendish, 2003. / Fraser, Mary Ann. *I. Q., It's Time.* Walker, 2005. / Harper, Dan. *Telling Time with Big Mama Cat.* Harcourt, 1998. / Hutchins, Pat. *Clocks and More Clocks.* Macmillan, 1970. / Kandoian, Ellen. *Is Anybody Up?* Putnam, 1989. / Singer, Marilyn. *Nine O'Clock Lullaby.* HarperCollins, 1991. / Walton, Rick. *Bunny Day: Telling Time from Breakfast to Bedtime.* HarperCollins, 2002.

SUBJECTS: MULTICULTURAL BOOKS. STORIES IN RHYME. TIME.

[J*] | | | |S|

***That Rabbit Belongs to Emily Brown.* Cowell, Cressida. Illus. by Neal Layton. Hyperion, 2007. {ISBN 978-1-42310-645-6; unp.} E (Gr. PreK-2)**

Emily Brown and her old gray stuffed rabbit called Stanley are having a busy day of adventures together—exploring outer space, riding through the Sahara Desert on their motorbike, and deep-sea diving off the Great Barrier Reef—but they are interrupted time and again by the Queen's emissaries knocking at Emily's door. The Chief Footman, the army, the navy, and even the air force demand that Emily hand over her Bunnywunny straightaway because Her Excellence, the Most Mighty Queen Gloriana the Third, wants him. Even though the Queen offers her all the toys a child could ever desire, will Emily Brown give up Stanley? Not a chance! ("This rabbit belongs to ME. And his name isn't Bunnywunny. It's STANLEY." Emily insists, indignantly.) When the Queen's special commandos sneak into her bedroom in the middle of the night and steal him from her bed, Emily Brown is so cross, she marches up to the palace to fetch him back. The big, bright, frantic mixed-media illustrations bring out the deadpan humor of this girl-loves-her-rabbit tale, which your listeners will understand firsthand.

GERM: When you get to the part in the story where Emily says, "I shall take Stanley HOME," and the naughty blond-tressed little girl queen starts to cry, shut the book for a moment. Ask your listeners how they think Emily can solve the queen's problem. And when you finish the story, ask them what they have done to transform their stiff brand-new toys into real toys of their own. Naturally, you can pair this story with Mo Willems's now-classic missing rabbit books, ***Knuffle Bunny*** and ***Knuffle Bunny Too*** for a themed storytime. Children can draw themselves having worldwide adventures with their own best toys.

RELATED TITLES: Clark, Emma Chichester. *Where Are You, Blue Kangaroo?* Doubleday, 2000. / Cocca-Leffler, Maryann. *Missing: One Stuffed Rabbit.* Albert Whitman, 1998. / Feiffer, Jules. *I Lost My Bear.* Morrow, 1998. / Fitzpatrick, Marie-Louise. *Lizzy and Skunk.* DK Ink, 2000. / Freeman, Don. *Corduroy.* Viking, 1968. / Galbraith, Kathryn O. *Laura Charlotte.* Philomel, 1990. / Ichikawa, Satomi. *La La Rose.* Philomel, 2004. / Willems, Mo. *Knuffle Bunny: A Cautionary Tale.* Hyperion, 2005. / Willems, Mo. *Knuffle Bunny Too: A Case of Mistaken Identity.* Hyperion, 2007.

SUBJECTS: HUMOROUS FICTION. KINGS AND RULERS. PLAY. RABBITS. STUFFED ANIMALS. TOYS.

[J*] |A| | |S|

***There Is a Bird on Your Head!* Willems, Mo. Illus. by the author. Hyperion, 2007. {ISBN 978-1-4231-0686-9; 56p.} E (Gr. PreK-1) Geisel Medal**

Elephant is not one bit happy when Piggie tells him there are two love birds building a nest on his head. Then they lay three eggs which hatch, and that is even worse.

GERM: Stop in mid-read and ask listeners what Elephant can do about his predicament. Mock up a template for kids to finish and illustrate: **PROBLEM:** Elephant has a bird's nest on his head. **SOLUTION:** _____. What you learn from this amusing emergent reader is that if someone is doing something to you and you are not happy about it, it can help if you simply say something. Such a simple lesson, but it packs a bit of a wallop. For more ideas for using the first four books in the resplendent Elephant & Piggie series, see Judy Freeman's Activity Guide on page 119. You can also print out her activity pages at <**www.hyperionbooksforchildren.com**>. Type "Mo Willems" in the search bar, click on the title, and you'll see the link to the guide on the book's home page.

RELATED TITLES: Franco, Betsy. *Birdsongs.* McElderry, 2007. / Hills, Tad. *Duck & Goose.* Schwartz & Wade, 2006. / Scieszka, Jon. *Cowboy & Octopus.* Viking, 2007. / Seeger, Laura Vaccaro. *Dog and Bear: Two Friends, Three Stories.* Roaring Brook, 2007. / Seuss, Dr. *Horton Hatches the Egg.* Random House, 1968. / Willems, Mo. *Don't Let the Pigeon Drive the Bus.* Hyperion, 2003. / Willems, Mo. *I Am Invited to a Party!* Hyperion, 2007. (And others in the Elephant & Piggie series.)

SUBJECTS: BEST FRIENDS. BIRDS. ELEPHANTS. FRIENDSHIP. HUMOROUS FICTION. NESTS. PIGS.

EASY FICTION / PICTURE BOOKS, cont.

[J*] |A| | |S|

Today I Will Fly! **Willems, Mo. Illus. by the author. Hyperion, 2007. {ISBN 978-1-42310-295-3; 57p.} E (Gr. PreK-1)**

You know that old saying, "Pigs will fly"? Well, Piggie intends to do just that—fly. Elephant tells her, "YOU WILL NEVER FLY!" Does that stop Piggie? Not for a second. With the help of an obliging dog, a pelican, and a strategically-tied piece of string, Piggie takes to the air.

GERM: Elephant and Piggie are two endearing characters in easy-to-read books kids can handle independently, but you'll also enjoy reading their adventures aloud. Told entirely in balloon dialogue, these little vignettes are waiting to be acted out in pairs and small groups. Other emergent readers in the Elephant & Piggie series include ***I Am Invited to a Party!***, ***My Friend Is Sad,*** and ***There Is a Bird on Your Head!***. For more ideas for using the books, see Judy Freeman's Activity Guide on page 119. You can also print out her activity pages at <**www.hyperionbooksforchildren.com**>. Type "Mo Willems" in the search bar, click on the title, and you'll see the link to the guide on the book's home page.

RELATED TITLES: Rohmann, Eric. *My Friend Rabbit.* Roaring Brook, 2002. / Scieszka, Jon. *Cowboy & Octopus.* Viking, 2007. / Seeger, Laura Vaccaro. *Dog and Bear: Two Friends, Three Stories.* Roaring Brook, 2007. / Shannon, David. *Duck on a Bike.* Scholastic, 2002. / Willems, Mo. *Don't Let the Pigeon Drive the Bus.* Hyperion, 2003. (And others in the Pigeon series.) / Willems, Mo. *Leonardo the Terrible Monster.* Hyperion, 2005. / Willems, Mo. *My Friend Is Sad.* Hyperion, 2007. (And others in the Elephant & Piggie series.)

SUBJECTS: BEST FRIENDS. ELEPHANTS. FLIGHT. FRIENDSHIP. HUMOROUS FICTION. PERSEVERANCE. PIGS.

[J] |A| | |S|

The Top Job. **Kimmel, Elizabeth Cody. Illus. by Robert Neubecker. Dutton, 2007. {ISBN 978-0-525-47789-1; unp.} E (Gr. PreK-3)**

On Career Day, Mrs. Feeny asks each student in class to stand up and talk about their parents' jobs. Their jobs are very interesting—UFO hunter, jeweler, NASCAR driver—but then, the long-haired narrator of the story stands up and says her dad changes lightbulbs. "Booooooooring," laughs classmate Anthony Swister, but she continues to describe how she helped her dad change the lightbulb at a tall building last weekend. They had to take an elevator up to the 102nd floor and then her dad climbed 117 feet up a special ladder built onto a big antenna. Colorful ink-outlined illustrations may make you a little queasy if you're afraid of heights, because the main facts of story are true, essentially.

GERM: As you read further in the story, children will guess that the special building is the Empire State Building. (How did they build it? Pull out Deborah Hopkinson's picture book, ***Sky Boys: How They Built the Empire State Building***). And where will the girl's dad be working next weekend? He's going to wash some windows. Children can guess where that might be. The final picture shows him outside the crown of the Statue of Liberty.

RELATED TITLES: Curlee, Lynn. *Liberty.* Atheneum, 2000. / DiPucchio, Kelly. *Liberty's Journey.* Hyperion, 2004. / Dorros, Arthur. *Abuela.* Dutton, 1991. / Hopkinson, Deborah. *Sky Boys: How They Built the Empire State Building.* Schwartz & Wade, 2006. / Jakobsen, Kathy. *My New York.* Little, Brown, 2003. / Melmed, Laura Krauss. *New York, New York!: The Big Apple from A to Z.* HarperCollins, 2005. / Neubecker, Robert. *Wow! City!* Hyperion, 2004. / Palatini, Margie. *Ding Dong Ding Dong.* Hyperion, 1999. / Wiesner, David. *Sector 7.* Clarion, 1999.

SUBJECTS: BUILDINGS. EMPIRE STATE BUILDING (NEW YORK, N.Y.). FATHERS AND DAUGHTERS. NEW YORK CITY. OCCUPATIONS. STATUE OF LIBERTY.

EASY FICTION / PICTURE BOOKS, cont.

[j] |A| | | |
Tracks of a Panda. **Dowson, Nick. Illus. by Rong Yu. Candlewick, 2007. {ISBN 978-0-7636-3146-8; 29p.} E (Gr. PreK-2)**
Tender Chinese-style watercolors in blacks, greys, and bamboo greens depict a mother panda cradling her blind, furless newborn cub, "small as a pinecone, pink as a blob of wriggling sunset." We follow Panda over a year as she cares for her cub, protects him from wild dogs, and teaches him to climb and swim. With her patch of bamboo dying, the starving mother must lead her six-month-old cub through the snowy mountains to find a new home.
GERM: While this story is fictionalized, it is not at all anthropomorphized, and could just as easily be catalogued as narrative nonfiction. With your group, make a list of the facts they now know about pandas, including why they are endangered. Use the simple index at the back for a lesson on how to use an index to locate information.
RELATED TITLES: Allen, Judy. *Panda.* Candlewick, 1993. / Dowson, Nick. *Tigress.* Candlewick, 2004. / Muth, Jon. *Zen Shorts.* Scholastic, 2005. / Nagda, Ann Whitehead, and Cindy Bickel. *Panda Math: Learning About Subtraction from Hua Mei and Mei Sheng.* Henry Holt, 2005. / Ryder, Joanne. *Little Panda: The World Welcomes Hua Mei at the San Diego Zoo.* Simon & Schuster, 2001.
SUBJECTS: ANIMALS—INFANCY. ENDANGERED SPECIES. GIANT PANDA. PANDAS.

[J*] |A| | |S|
Waking Up Wendell. **Stevens, April. Illus. by Tad Hills. Schwartz & Wade, 2007. {ISBN 978-0-375-93893-1; unp.} E (Gr. PreK-1)**
"TWEET-TWEEET-TA-TA-TA-TWEEEEET," sings the little yellow bird outside the window at #1 Fish Street, waking up Mr. Krudwig, the pig at #2 Fish Street. He lets out his dog Leopold whose barking wakes up Mrs. Musky at #3, and her whistling teakettle arouses oversleeper Mrs. Depolo, the kindergarten teacher. Each noise summons sleepers on down the block until little Wendell Willamore, a sweet little piglet, awakes with a squeal of happiness. Full bleed oil paint and colored pencil illustrations are as endearing as you can get, and the cause-and-effect story will be a read-aloud hit for sure.
GERM: In your first reading, your listeners can join in on each sound effect; afterwards, they can act out the whole story in sequence. Have them talk about and draw pictures of unexpected ways they've woken up.
RELATED TITLES: Barton, Byron. *Buzz Buzz Buzz.* Macmillan, 1973. / Crummel, Susan Stevens. *All in One Hour.* Marshall Cavendish, 2003. / DiCamillo, Kate. *Mercy Watson to the Rescue.* Candlewick, 2005. / Falconer, Ian. *Olivia.* Atheneum, 2000. / Gackenbach, Dick. *Claude Has a Picnic.* Clarion, 1993. / Henkes, Kevin. *A Good Day.* Greenwillow, 2007. / Hills, Tad. *Duck & Goose.* Schwartz & Wade, 2006. / Lillegard, Dee. *Wake Up House!: Rooms Full of Poems.* Knopf, 2000. / McPhail, David. *Pigs Aplenty, Pigs Galore.* Dutton, 1993. / Numeroff, Laura. *If You Give a Mouse a Cookie.* HarperCollins, 1985. / Palatini, Margie. *Oink?* Simon & Schuster, 2006. / Pomerantz, Charlotte. *The Piggy in the Puddle.* Macmillan, 1974. / Rosenthal, Marc. *Phooey!* HarperCollins, 2007. / Rylant, Cynthia. *Poppleton.* Scholastic, 1997. (And others in the Poppleton series.) / Willems, Mo. *Today I Will Fly!* Hyperion, 2007. (And others in the Elephant & Piggie series series.)
SUBJECTS: ANIMALS. CAUSE AND EFFECT. CIRCULAR STORIES. CREATIVE DRAMA. MORNING. PIGS.

EASY FICTION / PICTURE BOOKS, cont.

[j] |A| | | |

When Dinosaurs Came with Everything. **Broach, Elise. Illus. by David Small. Simon & Schuster/Atheneum, 2007. {ISBN 978-0-689-86922-8; unp.} E (Gr. PreK-2)**

On an otherwise boring errand day with his mother, a boy notes the interesting sign at the bakery: "BUY A DOZEN, GET A DINOSAUR." Sure enough, as they walk out with their box of doughnuts, the lady behind the counter brings out a dinosaur—a prodigious green triceratops that follows the boy to the doctor's. Today, instead of getting a sticker after his checkup, the boy is elated to receive a stegosaurus. His mom does not look amused. By the time the boy gets home, he has acquired two more dinos, a pterosaur and a little hadrosaur. What could be better? David Small's reptile-infused watercolors are plenty fun, and the matter-of-fact narration will get listeners pining for their own take-home creatures.

GERM: Children can draw the dinosaurs they'd like to bring home and write a sentence about what they'd do together. See how the boy's mom makes use of the new pets, having them help with chores around the house. Ask children to speculate on how their parents would use a dinosaur around the house. Pull out a book on real dinosaurs like Peter Dodson's ***An Alphabet of Dinosaurs*** so they can compare them to the dinosaurs in the story.

RELATED TITLES: Carrick, Carol. *Patrick's Dinosaurs.* Clarion, 1983. / Dodson, Peter. *An Alphabet of Dinosaurs.* Scholastic, 1995. / Edwards, Pamela Duncan. *Dinorella: A Prehistoric Fairy Tale.* Hyperion, 1997. / Grambling, Lois G. *Can I Have a Stegosaurus, Mom? Can I? Please!?* BridgeWater, 1995. / Hoff, Syd. *Danny and the Dinosaur.* HarperCollins, 1986. / Kellogg, Steven. *The Mysterious Tadpole.* Dial, 1977. / LaRochelle, David. *The Best Pet of All.* Dutton, 2004. / Nolan, Dennis. *Dinosaur Dreams.* Macmillan, 1990. / Schwartz, Henry. *How I Captured a Dinosaur.* Orchard, 1989. / Talbott, Hudson. *We're Back!* Crown, 1987. / Whybrow, Ian. *Sammy and the Dinosaurs.* Orchard, 1999. / Willems, Mo. *Edwina, the Dinosaur Who Didn't Know She Was Extinct.* Hyperion, 2006. / Wolf, Jake. *Daddy, Could I Have an Elephant?* Greenwillow, 1996. / Yolen, Jane. *How Do Dinosaurs Say Good Night?* Blue Sky/Scholastic, 2000. (And others in the "How Do Dinosaurs" series.)

SUBJECTS: DINOSAURS. HUMOROUS FICTION. MOTHERS AND SONS.

[J] | | | |S|

Wolf's Coming! **Kulka, Joe. Illus. by the author. Carolrhoda, 2007. {ISBN 978-1-57505-930-3; unp.} E (Gr. PreK-1)**

All of the animals are in a rush to hide when they see Wolf approaching, looking dapper and dangerous in his blue suit and tie and with his yellow eyes gleaming and fangs drooling. They race inside a house built into a tree trunk and wait silently, concealed behind and beneath the furniture until Wolf opens the door. SURPRISE!!! It's a birthday party with cake, pizza, and presents for the delighted guest of honor—Wolf.

GERM: Children will of course predict outcomes here, in a rhyming story that will give them delicious shivers up till the unexpected ending. They'll assume Wolf is the bad guy, of course, as wolves so often are in stories. Read the story a second time, paying attention to the building of suspense in the darkening illustrations on each page as night falls, adding to the scary ambiance. Listeners will note Wolf's pet tarantula accompanying him. As you read each couplet, leave off the final word for listeners to fill in.

RELATED TITLES: Bloom, Becky. *Wolf!* Orchard, 1999. / Child, Lauren. *Beware of the Storybook Wolves.* Scholastic, 2001. / Cowell, Cressida. *Little Bo Peep's Library Book.* Orchard, 1999. / Ernst, Lisa Campbell. *Little Red Riding Hood: A Newfangled Prairie Tale.* Simon & Schuster, 1995. / Hartman, Bob. *The Wolf Who Cried Boy.* Putnam, 2002. / Scieszka, Jon. *The True Story of the 3 Little Pigs.* Viking, 1989. / Trivizas, Eugene. *The Three Little Wolves and the Big Bad Pig.* McElderry, 1993.

SUBJECTS: ANIMALS. BIRTHDAYS. PARTIES. STORIES IN RHYME. WOLVES.

The 100 Top-Rated Children's Books of 2007

FICTION BOOKS

[J*] |A|B|H|S|

The Arrival. **Tan, Shaun. Illus. by the author. Scholastic/Arthur A. Levine, 2007. {ISBN 978-0-439-89529-3; unp.} FIC (Gr. 6-12)**

When you first pick up this very brown battered-looking wordless picture book with the sepia-toned photograph on the cover of a man in a suit and 1950s-style fedora, carrying an old suitcase, it looks like an old photo album you found up in your grandparents' attic. Then you look closer. What is that creature the man is contemplating? It's the size of a small white dog, but the head is part of the egg-shaped body and there are no real feet—each of its four legs comes to a point, and it has a big upswept pointy tail. It looks sort of like a walking fish. Open the book and leaf through the stained pages filled with little snapshots interspersed with sweeping double-page landscapes. We follow the bittersweet journey of a poor man who leaves his wife and daughter behind to travel by ship to a marvelous new land. His old country seems to be infested with long, spiky-tailed serpents, but this new place is filled with imponderable wonders, including that small white creature who becomes the man's pet. Slowly he is befriended by other immigrants who tell him their life stories, he looks for work, and in a hopeful ending, is reunited with his family. This saga of one immigrant family trying to work out all the rules, customs, and wonders of their new home is a stunning achievement, told entirely through pictures that look familiar and fantastical at the same time, just as this country must've looked to your ancestors when they got here.

GERM: There's more to pore over and puzzle out in the meticulous illustrations than you may have the concentration to do, but your children, who are probably far more visually literate than you will figure out lots of it. Have them put into words a description of the new land, describing the architecture, housing, food, pets, animals, work, money, alphabet, customs, music, transportation, and recreation. Since the illustrations are all in shade of brown, perhaps they can draw a picture of what the city looks like in color. Add this very important book to your immigration and emigration units.

RELATED TITLES: Avi. *Silent Movie.* Atheneum, 2003. / Freedman, Russell. *Immigrant Kids.* Dutton, 1980. / Sís, Peter. *The Wall: Growing Up Behind the Iron Curtain.* Farrar, 2007. / Tan, Shaun. *The Lost Thing.* Simply Read, 2004.

SUBJECTS: CARTOONS AND COMICS. FANTASY. GRAPHIC NOVELS. IMMIGRATION AND EMIGRATION. STORIES WITHOUT WORDS.

[j] | |B| | |

The Black Book of Secrets. **Higgins, F. E. Feiwel and Friends, 2007. {ISBN 978-0-312-36844-9; 273p.} FIC (Gr. 5-7)**

Ludlow Fitch manages to escape from the dank basement where, with the support of his larcenous parents, the notorious tooth surgeon of Old Goat's Alley, Barton Gumbroot, plans to extract the boy's teeth for money. There's no place he can hide in the City, so Ludlow hitches a ride on a carriage bearing the snoring Mr. Ratchet to his opulent house in the mountain village of Pagus Parvus, and then nicks the man's purse, scarf and gloves. Needing shelter from the cold and snow, Ludlow climbs a nearby hill, heading for a vacant building, when he first encounters Joe Zabbidou. Because the boy can read and write, Joe takes him in and offers him a job. Joe calls himself the Secret Pawnbroker, and makes it known in the village that he will pay people money to relieve them from the terrible secrets that haunt their dreams. Ludlow's job will be to write down their tearful and guilty confessions, from grave robbing to murder, in Joe's big black book. Who is this enigmatic man who pays good money for secrets and asks for nothing in return?

GERM: A little too grisly to use as a read-aloud, this chiller explores the line between good and evil. Readers who are riveted by the scariness of Joseph Delaney's The Revenge of the Witch and others in The Last Apprentice series, are going to find this one suitably creepy. When you booktalk it, introduce it by asking listeners if they've ever had a terrible secret they would love to see go away. The sequel's due out in 2008: *The Bone Magician.*

RELATED TITLES: Billingsley, Franny. *The Folk Keeper.* Simon & Schuster, 1999. / Delaney, Joseph. *The Revenge of the Witch.* (The Last Apprentice, Book One). Greenwillow, 2005. / Divakaruni, Chitra Banerjee. *The Conch Bearer.* Roaring Brook, 2003. / Higgins, F. E. *The Bone Magician.* Feiwel and Friends, 2008. / Hirsch, Odo. *Bartlett and the City of Flames.* Bloomsbury, 2003. / Langrish, Katherine. *Troll Fell.* HarperCollins, 2004.

SUBJECTS: APPRENTICES. FANTASY. PAWNBROKERS. SECRETS.

FICTION BOOKS, cont.

[j]   **|A| | |S|**

Chaucer's Canterbury Tales. **Williams, Marcia, retel. Illus. by the author. Candlewick, 2007. {ISBN 978-0-7636-3197-0; 45p.} 821 (Gr. 4-8)**

As an introduction to Chaucer and his storytelling, this oversized picture book with multitudes of characters, rendered in meticulous pen and ink and watercolors, provides a merry window into fourteenth-century medieval English life. On a pilgrimage from London to Canterbury to visit the shrine of martyr Saint Thomas à Becket at Canterbury Cathedral, a group of travelers pass the time by telling tales. Chaucer himself accompanies the nine pilgrims, each of whom relates a humorous and sometimes slightly off-color tale (though it's been toned down a fair bit with nothing too bawdy for children here, save a farting joke or two and a pair of naked bottoms).

GERM: While the comic strip illustrations complement these tales wonderfully, they are too tiny to be used with a group. Also, the use of old English dialogue in the illustrations can be frustrating since there's no pronunciation guide or more than a cursory glossary. If you're studying medieval times, however, it will be great fun to read each of those sentences aloud and puzzle out what the characters are saying. Compare "The Wife of Bath's Tale," which is a retelling of the King Arthur story, with the picture book ***Sir Gawain and the Loathly Lady*** by Selena Hastings. A far more sanitized version of "The Nun's Priest's Tale" can be found in the picture books ***Chanticleer and the Fox*** by Barbara Cooney and ***The Rooster and the Fox*** by Helen Ward. For another look at English life in the very old days, read Laura Amy Schlitz's Newbery Medal winner, ***Good Masters! Sweet Ladies!: Voices from a Medieval Village***.

RELATED TITLES: Chaucer, Geoffrey. *The Canterbury Tales.* Retold by Geraldine McCaughrean. Oxford University Press, 1996. / Cooney, Barbara. *Chanticleer and the Fox.* HarperCollins,1986. / Hastings, Selena. *Sir Gawain and the Loathly Lady.* Lothrop, 1985. / Schlitz, Laura Amy. *Good Masters! Sweet Ladies!: Voices from a Medieval Village.* Candlewick, 2007. / Ward, Helen. *The Rooster and the Fox.* Carolrhoda, 2004. / Williams, Marcia. *Charles Dickens and Friends.* Candlewick Press, 2006. / Williams, Marcia. *More Tales from Shakespeare.* Candlewick Press, 2005. / Williams, Marcia. *Tales from Shakespeare: Seven Plays.* Candlewick Press, 2004.

SUBJECTS: CHAUCER, GEOFFREY. ENGLAND. MIDDLE AGES. SHORT STORIES. STORYTELLING.

[J*]   **| | | | |**

City of Dogs. **Michael, Livi. Putnam, 2007. {ISBN 978-0-399-24356-1; 251p.} FIC (Gr. 4-7)**

On Sam's birthday, the one he thinks will be the worst ever, his Aunty Dot brings to the house a small white dog she has just hit with her car. The dog, which Sam names Jenny, has no obvious injuries, though in her mouth, she is holding a sprig of mistletoe carved like a dart. What Sam does not know is that Jenny has come from another one of the nine worlds, where she inadvertently altered the course of destiny when she saved her master, Baldur, the Golden Boy, from death. Jenny will need the assistance of all the dogs she meets in Sam's neighborhood, because the fate of this world is now at stake, too. There's Pico, a Chihuahua with a bark like a Great Dane; Gentleman Jim, a massive old fellow, on his last legs; Boris, a gentle, slightly-deaf Lab; excitable Checkers; and nervous Flo, a standard poodle dyed pink by her eccentric owner. Are they up to the task? You bet.

GERM: The modern world collides with the ancient worlds of Norse and Greek mythology in this adventuresome and winsome fantasy where dogs save the world. You'll want to dig into some Norse myths about Baldur, and Greek myths about Orion, Charon, Cerebus, and the Furies, each of whom plays an important role in the story. Children who love Rick Riordan's ***The Lightning Thief*** will be taken with this one, too.

RELATED TITLES: Climo, Shirley. *Stolen Thunder: A Norse Myth.* Clarion, 1994. / D'Aulaire, Ingri, and Edgar Parin. *Ingri and Edgar Parin D'Aulaire's Book of Greek Myths.* Doubleday, 1962. / Farmer, Nancy. *The Sea of Trolls.* Atheneum, 2004. / McCaughrean, Geraldine. *The Golden Hoard: Myths and Legends of the World.* Simon & Schuster, 1996. / Osborne, Mary Pope. *Favorite Greek Myths.* Scholastic, 1989. / Osborne, Mary Pope. *Favorite Norse Myths.* Scholastic, 1996. / Riordan, Rick. *The Lightning Thief.* (Percy Jackson & the Olympians, Book 1). Miramax/Hyperion, 2005. / Rupp, Rebecca. *Journey to the Blue Moon: In Which Time Is Lost and Then Found Again.* Candlewick, 2006.

SUBJECTS: ADVENTURE AND ADVENTURERS. DOGS. FANTASY. GODS AND GODDESSES. MYTHOLOGY.

FICTION BOOKS, cont.

[J*] | | | | |

***A Crooked Kind of Perfect.* Urban, Linda. Harcourt, 2007. {ISBN 978-0-15-206007-7; 213p.} FIC (Gr. 4-6)**
"I was supposed to play the piano," Zoe Elias begins. The piano is dignified, elegant, glamorous, and sophisticated. You could wear a tiara. You could play Carnegie Hall. Zoe, now 11, would like to be considered a child prodigy the way Vladimir Horowitz was. What does her dad get her instead? A "wood grained, vinyl-seated, wheeze-bag organ. The Perfectone D-60." Which she learns to play, taking lessons from Mabelline Person (pronounced Per-saaahn). And enters a competition. Mom, the comptroller for the state of Michigan, is the breadwinner in the family. Dad stays home cooking and cleaning and taking courses from Living Room University, like Golden Gloves: Make a Mint Coaching Boxing. He's agoraphobic, and never leaves the house. Her best friend, Emma, has just dumped her for a more popular girl in school, and Wheeler Diggs, a boy known for punching kids in the stomach, starts hanging out at her house and baking cookies with her dad. The short chapters are on-target funny and quirky and always not quite what you expect, making this one of the true charmers of the year, like last year's **Rules** by Cynthia Lord.
GERM: Just reading this book aloud will bring you great pleasure. (And my thanks to the lovely and effervescent Lisa Von Drasek for making me read it.) There's lots to talk about. Like how Zoe brings socks as a present to Emma's surprise birthday party. What's wrong with socks and why won't the "in" girls wear them, even in winter? And why does Zoe's dad stay in the house all the time? Zoe reveres Horowitz. Whom do you admire? What talent could make you famous, if you only practiced? You'll want to get a recording of Neil Diamond singing "Forever in Blue Jeans," since that's the song Zoe is planning to play at the Perform-O-Rama. And if you start salivating for Dad's Bada-Bing cookies, you'll find the recipe here: <**www.lindaurbanbooks.com/recipe.html**>.
RELATED TITLES: Bauer, Joan. *Rules of the Road.* Putnam, 1998. / Bauer, Joan. *Squashed.* Putnam, 1992. / Blume, Lesley M. M. *The Rising Star of Rusty Nail.* Knopf, 2007. / Creech, Sharon. *Love That Dog.* HarperCollins, 2001. / DiCamillo, Kate. *Because of Winn-Dixie.* Candlewick, 2000. / Hannigan, Katherine. *Ida B: And Her Plans to Maximize Fun, Avoid Disaster, and (Possibly) Save the World.* Greenwillow, 2004. / Lisle, Janet Taylor. *How I Became a Writer and Oggie Learned to Drive.* Philomel, 2002. / Lord, Cynthia. *Rules.* Scholastic, 2006. / Park, Barbara. *The Graduation of Jake Moon.* Atheneum, 2000. / Tarshis, Lauren. *Emma-Jean Lazarus Fell Out of a Tree.* Dial, 2007.
SUBJECTS: FAMILY LIFE. FAMILY PROBLEMS. HUMOROUS FICTION. INTERPERSONAL RELATIONS. MUSIC INSTRUCTION AND STUDY. ORGAN (MUSICAL INSTRUMENT). PERSONAL NARRATIVES. SCHOOLS.

[J*] | | | | |

***Diary of a Wimpy Kid: Greg Heffley's Journal.* Kinney, Jeff. Illus. by the author. Amulet, 2007. {ISBN 978-0-8109-9313-6; 217p.} FIC (Gr. 5-8)**
The surprise hit of the year, this easy-to-read first person expose of middle school life told by sixth grader Greg Heffley through cartoons and hand-written journal entries has sold more than a million copies. Its throw-yourself-on-the-floor-and-roll-around-howling hilarious, and boys, especially, are inhaling this book. All those 97-pound weaklings out there can really identify with a kid who figures he's somewhere around 52nd or 53rd most popular at school and whose slacker older brother, Rodrick, belongs to a heavy metal band called Löded Diaper. Reluctant readers? Not anymore.
GERM: Thankfully, for the kids who will demand another books just like this one, there's a sequel, **Rodrick Rules**, that readers may decide is even funnier. Let's hope Jeff Kinney can keep them coming. Guaranteed, there will be copycat titles in the next few years by other writers who latch on to the contemporary, clueless, and earnest style of this post-Captain Underpants phenomena. Go to <**www.wimpykid.com**> to find out more about the books and the author. If you want to read Kinney's original comics on which the books were based, go to <**www.funbrain.com**>. Kids will want to compare their print version to what's online. And then check out the author's blog at <**gregheffley.blogspot.com**>.
RELATED TITLES: Byars, Betsy. *The 18th Emergency.* Viking, 1973. / Gantos, Jack. *Joey Pigza Swallowed the Key.* Farrar, 1998. / Gauthier, Gail. *A Year with Butch and Spike.* Putnam, 1998. / Getz, David. *Almost Famous.* Henry Holt, 1992. / Gorman, Carol. *Dork on the Run.* HarperCollins, 2002. / Kinney, Jeff. *Diary of a Wimpy Kid: Rodrick Rules.* Amulet, 2008. / Korman, Gordon. *No More Dead Dogs.* Hyperion, 2000. / Korman, Gordon. *Schooled.* Hyperion, 2007. / Korman, Gordon. *This Can't Be Happening at Macdonald Hall.* Scholastic, 1978. / Naylor, Phyllis Reynolds. *The Boys Start the War.* Delacorte, 1993. / Park, Barbara. *The Graduation of Jake Moon.* Atheneum, 2000. / Spinelli, Jerry. *Loser.* HarperCollins, 2002. / Tarshis, Lauren. *Emma-Jean Lazarus Fell Out of a Tree.* Dial, 2007.
SUBJECTS: DIARIES. FRIENDSHIP. HUMOROUS FICTION. MIDDLE SCHOOLS. SCHOOLS.

FICTION BOOKS, cont.

[J*] |A|B|H|S|
Elijah of Buxton. **Curtis, Christopher Paul. Scholastic, 2007. {ISBN 978-0-439-02344-3; 341p.} FIC (Gr. 5-8)**
         Newbery Honor and Coretta Scott King Author Award
It's the singular voices of all the main characters in Christopher Paul Curtis's books that pull you into his novels. Joining my favorites narrators, Kenny from ***The Watsons Go to Birmingham, 1963*** and ***Bud from Bud, Not Buddy*** is 11-year-old Elijah Freeman. In this latest masterpiece, set in 1859 in Buxton, Ontario, Canada, a village founded by freed slaves, Elijah knows he is considered special. He was the first child to be born free in the Settlement and, as an infant, the one who threw up all over visiting dignitary, Frederick Douglass. He's all boy, Elijah, sneaking a toady-frog in his Ma's knitting basket with predictable results, but is "terrorfied" and cries himself silly when Ma retaliates by putting a snake in the cookie jar for him to discover. She wants him to be less fra-gile, as she puts it, but he is ever naive and often bamboozled by a fast-talking con man known as the Preacher. For all Elijah's gut-busting stories and observations about his best friend Cooter, school days, and attending a Carnival of Oddities, this extraordinary novel has a dead serious component when new-free slaves make it to Buxton, bad news comes from America, and Elijah finds out first hand the difference between slavery and freedom.
GERM: What an eye-opener as a read-aloud, whether read independently as a sterling example of personal narrative and voice, or tied in with the social studies curriculum looking at the realities of slavery.
RELATED TITLES: Adler, David A. *A Picture Book of Frederick Douglass.* Holiday House, 1993. / Curtis, Christopher Paul. *Bud, Not Buddy.* Delacorte, 1999. / Curtis, Christopher Paul. *The Watsons Go to Birmingham, 1963.* Delacorte, 1995. / Douglass, Frederick. *Escape from Slavery: The Boyhood of Frederick Douglass in His Own Words.* Knopf, 1994. / Hamilton, Virginia. *Many Thousand Gone: African Americans from Slavery to Freedom.* Knopf, 1996. / Hamilton, Virginia. *The People Could Fly: The Picture Book.* Knopf, 2004. / Hurmence, Belinda. *A Girl Called Boy.* Clarion,1982. / Johnson, Dolores. *Now Let Me Fly: The Story of a Slave Family.* Macmillan, 1993. / Landau, Elaine. *Fleeing to Freedom on the Underground Railroad: The Courageous Slaves, Agents, and Conductors.* Twenty-First Century, 2006. / Levine, Ellen. *Henry's Freedom Box: A True Story.* Scholastic, 2007. / Nelson, Vaunda Micheaux. *Almost to Freedom.* Carolrhoda, 2003.
SUBJECTS: AFRICAN AMERICANS. BLACKS—CANADA. CANADA. FREEDOM. HISTORICAL FICTION. MULTICULTURAL BOOKS. SLAVERY.

[J] | | | |S|
Emma-Jean Lazarus Fell Out of a Tree. **Tarshis, Lauren. Dial, 2007. {ISBN 978-0-8037-3164-6; 199p.} FIC**
         (Gr. 5-7)
When seventh grader Emma-Jean Lazarus encounters the popular Colleen Pomerantz crying in the girl's bathroom, she ignores her usual instincts to stay out of the messy lives of her classmates, and promises to help. Emma-Jean's adored father, a brilliant and eccentric mathematician, died in a car accident two years ago, and it doesn't bother her that people think she's strange, just like he was. She thinks of a "multistepped, highly logical plan of action" to thwart the powerful, bossy, and insidious Laura Gilroy from going on a ski trip with Colleen's best friend, Kaitlin. Told by an omniscient narrator in alternating chapters focusing on Emma-Jean and Colleen, it's an insightful and ultimately poignant look at the life of a popular student who tries to be nice to everyone and an unpopular one who accepts her own exclusion from the in crowd.
GERM: You'd probably place Emma-Jean, a girl who doesn't quite get it when others are mocking her and who misinterprets her classmates' requests for help, as someone on the Asperger's spectrum, and it's true, she is very different from other kids. But she sees a wrong and decides, for the first time ever, to get involved, and it changes her life. This will be a wonderful book to use for a book club discussion, since it delves into both girls' personalities with such compassion and clarity, and luckily, it's due out in paperback in Spring, 2008.
RELATED TITLES: Creech, Sharon. *Granny Torrelli Makes Soup.* HarperCollins, 2003. / Davies, Jacqueline. *The Lemonade War.* Houghton Mifflin, 2007. / Hannigan, Katherine. *Ida B: And Her Plans to Maximize Fun, Avoid Disaster, and (Possibly) Save the World.* Greenwillow, 2004. / Hest, Amy. *Remembering Mrs. Rossi.* Candlewick, 2007. / Kinney, Jeff. *Diary of a Wimpy Kid: Rodrick Rules.* Amulet, 2008. / Lord, Cynthia. *Rules.* Scholastic, 2006. / O'Connor, Barbara. *How to Steal a Dog.* Frances Foster/Farrar, 2007. / Spinelli, Jerry. *Loser.* HarperCollins, 2002. / Urban, Linda. *A Crooked Kind of Perfect.* Harcourt, 2007.
SUBJECTS: DEATH. FATHERS AND DAUGHTERS. FRIENDSHIP. INTERPERSONAL RELATIONS. MIDDLE SCHOOLS. MOTHERS AND DAUGHTERS. PROBLEM SOLVING. SCHOOLS.

FICTION BOOKS, cont.

[J*] | |B| |S|

Emmy and the Incredible Shrinking Rat. **Jonell, Lynne. Illus. by Jonathan Bean. Henry Holt, 2007. {ISBN 978-0-8050-8150-3; 346p.} FIC (Gr. 3-6)**

The more Emmy tries to be good, the more everyone seems to ignore her—her parents, classmates and even her teacher don't notice her at all. The Rat who lives in a cage in her classroom tells her, "The bad ones get all the attention . . . Try being bad for once. You might like it." Her wealthy parents are off on another vacation, and her strict and slightly sinister nanny, Miss Barmy, hovers over her, giving her tofu bars and tonics. The day Emmy sneaks the Rat outside and sets him free, she stumbles upon The Antique Rat store and begins to uncover the secrets she's not supposed to know. This engaging fantasy introduces talking (and soccer-playing) rodents, a rat who can make you small, jet-setting parents, and a nanny who isn't very nice.

GERM: For a Reader's Theater script of the first chaspter dialoigue between Emmy and the Rat, go to page 169. There's some delicious social commentary about the grown-up world woven into this book's narrative, presenting the drive for success, riches, and status as less-than-admirable qualities. Could it be that the reason some parents are too wrapped up in own lives to pay any mind to their children is that they have eaten potato rolls stamped with the footprint of a rare chinchilla? Students can speculate on the rodent curative powers they'd like to use in their own lives. Professor Capybara, the brilliant rodentologist, has an instrument called a charoscope that shows a person's character elements in one drop of blood. Have your students diagram the character elements they'd expect to find in their own blood. The most well-rounded character is the rat. Make a list of his traits. Read Albert Marrin's nonfiction book, *Oh, Rats!* to see what they're really like.

RELATED TITLES: Child, Lauren. *That Pesky Rat.* Candlewick, 2002. / Collins, Suzanne. *Gregor the Overlander.* Scholastic, 2003. / Cutler, Jane. *Rats.* Farrar, 1996. / DiCamillo, Kate. *The Tale of Despereaux.* Candlewick, 2003. / Marrin, Albert. *Oh, Rats!: The Story of Rats and People.* Dutton, 2006. / O'Brien, Robert C. *Mrs. Frisby and the Rats of NIMH.* Atheneum, 1971. / Pullman, Philip. *I Was a Rat!* Knopf, 2000. / Stewart, Trent Lee. *The Mysterious Benedict Society.* Little, Brown, 2007.

SUBJECTS: FANTASY. HUMOROUS FICTION. RATS. RODENTS. SIZE. TRANSFORMATIONS.

[J*] | | | | |

The Fabled Fourth Graders of Aesop Elementary School. **Fleming, Candace. Schwartz & Wade, 2007. {ISBN 978-0-375-83672-5; 186p.} FIC (Gr. 2-5)**

Hired to teach the robust, high-energy, and just plain naughty fourth graders at Aesop Elementary, Mr. Jupiter is more than prepared for his rambunctious group. "Raise your hand if you're not here," he says, and they have lots of creative excuses for being absent. Each fable-based chapter ends with a moral, like, "He laughs best who laughs last." You'll laugh at the antics of Mr. Jupiter's class, and appreciate the talents of a teacher who shepherds his charges through class pictures, a poetry contest, and the Lost and Found.

GERM: Have your listeners keep a running list of artifacts in Mr. Jupiter's classroom and try to figure out all the places he's visited around the world. Take Mr. Jupiter's lead to have your kids write excuses for being absent, memorize poems, and play a Dewey Decimal game. Read aloud corresponding Aesop's fables and compare and contrast them. Also take note of teacher's names in the book, including Miss Paige Turner, the librarian and Mrs. Bunz, the lunchroom lady. Your fabled students can write new tales about themselves, with morals at the end. See page 173 for a Reader's Theater script of the chapter, "The Boy Who Cried Lunchroom Monitor." It can also be found on Fleming's website, <**www.candicefleming.com**>.

RELATED TITLES: Birney, Betty G. *The World According to Humphrey.* Putnam, 2004. / Calmenson, Stephanie. *The Children's Aesop.* Doubleday, 1988. / Fletcher, Ralph. *Flying Solo.* Clarion, 1998. / Gutman, Dan. *Miss Daisy Is Crazy.* HarperCollins, 2004. (And others in series.) / Morpurgo, Michael. *The McElderry Book of Aesop's Fables.* McElderry, 2005. / Pinkney, Jerry. *Aesop's Fables.* SeaStar, 2000. / Sachar, Louis. *Sideways Stories from Wayside School.* Morrow, 1978. / Untermeyer, Louis. *Aesop's Fables.* Golden, 1965.

SUBJECTS: BEHAVIOR. FABLES. READER'S THEATER. SCHOOLS. TEACHERS.

[j] |A| | | |

Feathers. **Woodson, Jacqueline. Putnam, 2007. {ISBN 978-0-399-23989-2; 118p.} FIC (Gr. 4-7) Newbery Honor**

In winter of 1971, a new boy joins Mrs. Johnson's sixth grade class, a tall, skinny white boy with long, curly hair almost to his back, "his face pale and calm and quiet." Frannie observes him with interest, though the boys in class are not friendly to him. They call him the Jesus Boy, and the boy doesn't mind that. Franny's friend Samantha, who goes to One People Baptist church where her father is a fire-and-brimstone type of preacher, speculates that maybe the boy is Jesus. Franny's not a church-goer, and she's skeptical at first, but she can't help being intrigued by the Jesus Boy, who even knows sign language. Franny's older brother Sean is deaf and they sign at home. Mama is tired all the time, with a new baby coming, and Franny's worrying and wondering about a lot of things these days. Set at a time of peace signs, bell-bottoms, and Black Power, this is a quiet, introspective first-person exploration of hope and change.

GERM: This slim story pulls in many issues, including religion, racial prejudice, handicaps, friendship, and a bit of Emily Dickinson, whose poem, "Hope is the thing with feathers" inspires the title and the main character. Unlike *Belle Teal*, where an African American boy comes into an all-white classroom, Feathers looks at an all-black school where the children are suspicious of a white boy crossing the tracks to go to their school. You can booktalk this one with other historical fiction books about the Vietnam War era like Barbara Kerley's ***Greetings from Planet Earth*** and Gary D. Schmidt's ***The Wednesday Wars***.

RELATED TITLES: Curtis, Christopher Paul. *The Watsons Go to Birmingham, 1963.* Delacorte, 1995. / Kerley, Barbara. *Greetings from Planet Earth.* Scholastic, 2007. / Lynch, Chris. *Gold Dust.* HarperCollins, 2000. / Martin, Ann M. *Belle Teal.* Scholastic, 2001. / Schmidt, Gary D. *The Wednesday Wars.* Clarion, 2007. / Woodson, Jacqueline. *Show Way.* Putnam, 2005.

SUBJECTS: AFRICAN AMERICANS. DEAF. FAMILY LIFE. MULTICULTURAL BOOKS. RACE RELATIONS. RELIGION. SCHOOLS.

[J*] |A|B| | |

Harry Potter and the Deathly Hallows. **Rowling, J. K. Scholastic/Arthur A. Levine, 2007. {ISBN 978-0-545-01022-1; 759p.} FIC (Gr. 5-12)**

What can you say about the end of an era, the last book in a miraculous and groundbreaking series that changed everyone's perceptions of children's books and turned on so many readers worldwide? We bid a bittersweet and loving adieu to Harry and Hermione and Ron, and all the other characters we've grown to know and love (or loathe) like family. Some survive the final showdown with Voldemort; some don't. If you're not already a fan, it's not likely you'll have gotten to this final one; if you are, you read it the first month it came out. I am grateful to J. K. Rowling for the experience and am bowled over that she continued to surprise me with her humor, insights, and the sheer originality in her plot and fantasy elements. I have my seven books lined up on my bookshelf, and sometime, when I'm feeling disillusioned with life and politics, I'll start at book one again and relive the whole adventure.

GERM: For Life After Harry, you'll need to put together a booklist of good titles, some of which I've listed here.

RELATED TITLES: Alexander, Lloyd. *The Book of Three.* Henry Holt, 1964. / Billingsley, Franny. *The Folk Keeper.* Simon & Schuster, 1999. / Collins, Suzanne. *Gregor the Overlander.* Scholastic, 2003. / Divakaruni, Chitra Banerjee. *The Conch Bearer.* Roaring Brook, 2003. / Hirsch, Odo. *Bartlett and the City of Flames.* Bloomsbury, 2003. / Ibbotson, Eva. *The Secret of Platform 13.* Dutton, 1998. / LaFevers, R. L. *Theodosia and the Serpents of Chaos.* Houghton Mifflin, 2007. / Langrish, Katherine. *Troll Fell.* HarperCollins, 2004. / L'Engle, Madeleine. *A Wrinkle in Time.* Farrar, 1962. / Lowry, Lois. *The Giver.* Houghton Mifflin, 1993. / Pratchett, Terry. *The Wee Free Men.* HarperCollins, 2003. / Pullman, Philip. *The Golden Compass.* Knopf, 1996. (And others in the His Dark Materials series.) / Reeve, Philip. *Larklight.* Bloomsbury, 2006. / Riordan, Rick. *The Lightning Thief.* (Percy Jackson & the Olympians, Book 1) Miramax/Hyperion, 2005. / Rowling, J. K. *Harry Potter and the Sorcerer's Stone.* Scholastic, 1998. (And others in the Harry Potter series.) / Stroud, Jonathan. *The Amulet of Samarkand.* Hyperion, 2003.

SUBJECTS: ADVENTURE AND ADVENTURERS. ENGLAND. FANTASY. GOOD AND EVIL. MAGIC. SCHOOLS. WITCHES. WIZARDS.

FICTION BOOKS, cont.

[J*] | | | |S|

Home of the Brave. **Applegate, Katherine. Feiwel & Friends, 2007. {ISBN 978-0-312-36765-7; 249p.} FIC (Gr.**
Kek begins his heartfelt narrative of free verse poems on the day he gets off the "flying boat" to this place called
America where "this cold is like claws on my skin" and "dead grass pokes through the unkind blanket of white."
Back home in Somalia, before the soldiers came, Kek took care of the cows. After a long time living in a refugee
camp, he must now adjust to living in an apartment in Minnesota with his aunt and his cousin Ganwar, who lost his
left hand the night the men with guns killed Kek's father and brother. What keeps him going is the hope the people
at the Refugee Resettlement Center might find his mother, that she could still be alive, and that she could come for
him. Kek thrives in school, especially his lively ESL class, where he learns about that "strange and beautiful red
food," ketchup, and makes friends with Hannah, a foster child who lives in his building. What he wants most is to
get a job taking care of the sad cow he saw from the highway, and with Hannah's help, he does.
GERM: It's not easy to explain what it feels like to be lost in a new land, but listeners will feel a great outpouring of
love and empathy for Kek. Broken into four parts, each section is prefaced by an African proverb you can discuss
and see how it relates to the story. Talk over what are some of the other adjustments and new things a person coming
from a war-torn country would need to know to live here. (As when Kek puts his aunt's dishes in the washing
machine . . .) Shaun Tan's ***The Arrival***, a wordless graphic novel, deals with the bewilderment a newcomer feels
upon coming to a different place.
RELATED TITLES: Farmer, Nancy. *A Girl Named Disaster.* Orchard, 1996. / Jansen, Hanna. *Over a Thousand
Hills I Walk with You.* Carolrhoda, 2006. / Mazer, Norma Fox. *Good Night, Maman.* Harcourt, 1999. / Millman,
Isaac. *Hidden Child.* Farrar, 2005. / Naidoo, Beverly. *The Other Side of Truth.* HarperCollins, 2001./ Tan, Shaun.
The Arrival. Scholastic, 2007.
**SUBJECTS: AFRICAN AMERICANS. COUSINS. COWS. HOPE. IMMIGRATION AND EMIGRATION.
MINNEAPOLIS (MINN.). MULTICULTURAL BOOKS. SCHOOLS.**

[J*] | | | |S|

How to Steal a Dog. **O'Connor, Barbara. Frances Foster/Farrar, 2007. {ISBN 978-0-374-33497-0; 170p.} FIC**
    (Gr. 4-7)
"The day I decided to steal a dog was the same day my best friend, Luanne Godfrey, found out I lived in a car." That
first sentence will get your children talking. Live in a car? How can you live in a car? Daddy's deserted them,
Mama's working two jobs, and after school each day, Georgina and her little brother Toby wait outside the
Chevrolet for Mama to meet them. It's been a week now, and, as Luanne says, "No offense, Georgina. But you're
starting to look unkempt." When Georgina sees the missing dog sign with its offer of a $500 reward, tacked to a
telephone pole, she starts thinking, recording in her notebook lists of the rules and steps she needs to carry out her
plan.
GERM: Read aloud that first chapter, and look at the cute little black and white dog on the book's cover. Set up a
debate. Would it be justifiable for Georgina to abduct a little dog named Willy if the reward money will help her
family find a place to live? What should she do? Mind you, Georgina does steal that dog. What's compelling about
this fast-moving novel is the utter realism of it. Georgina is a sympathetic character, but as you read, you find
yourself talking to her in your head: Don't do it, Georgina! You wait in vain for someone else to come fix the
problem. Where are the DYFS workers in Darby, North Carolina? Does this really happen to people? And what on
earth would I do if it happened to me? Mookie, a homeless older man she encounters and the conscience of the
story, has a fitting motto, which you can discuss: "Sometimes the trail you leave behind you is more important than
the path ahead of you."
RELATED TITLES: Creech, Sharon. *Love That Dog.* HarperCollins, 2001. / DiCamillo, Kate. *Because of Winn-
Dixie.* Candlewick, 2000. / Hannigan, Katherine. *Ida B: And Her Plans to Maximize Fun, Avoid Disaster, and
(Possibly) Save the World.* Greenwillow, 2004. / Lindquist, Susan Hart. *Wander.* Delacorte, 1998. / Lisle, Janet
Taylor. *How I Became a Writer and Oggie Learned to Drive.* Philomel, 2002. / Lowry, Lois. *Stay!: Keeper's Story.*
Houghton Mifflin, 1997. / Myers, Anna. *Red-Dirt Jessie.* Walker, 1992. / Naylor, Phyllis Reynolds. *Shiloh.*
Atheneum, 1991.
**SUBJECTS: BROTHERS And SISTERS. CONDUCT OF LIFE. DOGS. FAMILY PROBLEMS.
HOMELESS PERSONS. NORTH CAROLINA. PROCEDURAL WRITING. SINGLE-PARENT
FAMILIES.**

FICTION BOOKS, cont.

[J*] |A| |H| |

The Invention of Hugo Cabret: A Novel in Words and Pictures. Selznick, Brian. Illus. by the author. Scholastic, 2007. {ISBN 978-0-439-81378-5; 533p.} FIC (Gr. 4-7) Caldecott Medal Winner

Brian Selznick does the cover art for all of Andrew Clements' middle grade novels, including ***No Talking***. But wait until you get a gander of his own new novel. Selznick, who won a Caldecott Honor for his spectacular illustrations in Barbara Kerley's extraordinary biography, ***The Dinosaurs of Waterhouse Hawkins***, has written and illustrated a wholly original, innovative and breathtaking masterpiece that bends all the rules of novel writing and illustrated stories. Part One is composed of crosshatched and shaded pencil drawings, double page spreads centered on a black background. First there's the moon and then the sun comes up over Paris. Page by page, we zoom in closer, like a movie, into a crowded train station where we watch a boy slip surreptitiously behind a grate in the wall. Next we observe a bearded older man sitting behind the counter of his toy booth, and the boy peering out at him from behind the face of a huge clock in the wall. Not until page 46 do the pictures give way to text, and we discover the boy's name: Hugo Cabret. When Hugo tries to steal a little blue toy mouse, the old man catches him and apprehends, in return, Hugo's priceless notebook, filled with sketches of an automaton, a mechanical man built out of clockworks. Who is this 12-year-old boy who secretly winds all 27 clocks in the train station each day, lives alone in the walls of the train station, and no longer attends school? And who is the old toymaker whose granddaughter befriends Hugo and says she'll help him get his notebook back?

GERM: Anyone finishing the book as a read-aloud will then want to play Selznick's interviews with NPR and with ExpandedBook.com, listen to him reading a chapter, and view a narrated version of George Méliès' famous silent movie from 1902, *A Trip to the Moon*, which figures in the story. Go to <**www.theinventionofhugocabret.com**>. Pass the book along to teachers doing take-apart units in science, where children use tools to dismantle old clocks, radios, and broken machinery to see how they work. Or show and read the first 80 pages, which you can easily do in one class period, tie in books on magic and magicians, movies, Paris, and pull out some simple wind-up toys for the finale and you've got yourself a fine booktalk.

RELATED TITLES: Fleming, Candace. *Ben Franklin's Almanac: Being a True Account of the Good Gentleman's Life*. Atheneum, 2003. / Kerley, Barbara. *The Dinosaurs of Waterhouse Hawkins*. Illus. by Brian Selznick. Scholastic, 2001. / Kerley, Barbara. *Walt Whitman: Words for America*. Illus. by Brian Selznick. Scholastic, 2004. / Selznick, Brian. *The Houdini Box*. Knopf, 1991. / St. George, Judith. *So You Want to Be an Inventor?* Philomel, 2002. / Yolen, Jane, and Robert J. Harris. *Odysseus in the Serpent Maze*. HarperCollins, 2001.

SUBJECTS: FRANCE. INVENTIONS. MOVIES. ORPHANS. PARIS (FRANCE). RAILROAD STATIONS. ROBOTS.

[J*] | | | | |

The Lemonade War. Davies, Jacqueline. Houghton Mifflin, 2007. {ISBN 978-0-618-75043-6; 175p.} FIC (Gr. 2-5)

Evan Treski has been feeling angry and humiliated ever since he found out that his little sister Jessie will be skipping third grade. "You ruin everything . . . I hate you," he tells her. Evan has always been her friend and protector, and Jessie can't understand why he's not happy she'll be joining his fourth grade class in September. Jessie is great at reading and math and academics, while Evan is not. On the other hand, Evan gets along so well with everybody, and Jessie often doesn't comprehend how other people tick. When Evan pairs up with a friend he doesn't even like to open a lemonade stand without her, Jessie enlists the help of fourth grader Megan, a girl Evan secretly likes, and the two girls go into the lemonade business, too. The increasingly cutthroat competition between Evan and Jessie leads to a bet: whoever makes the most money by Saturday wins the loser's earnings as well. The children's mother is a public relations consultant who has written a booklet called "Ten Bright Ideas to Light Up Your Sales," and her many useful pointers help them develop their selling skills. In alternating chapters told by a limited omniscient narrator, we follow each of the two siblings as they compete, undersell, go global, negotiate, and undertake malicious mischief against their competition.

GERM: What a fun tie-in to the math curriculum. Each fast-paced chapter starts off with the definition of a marketing term that figures into and foreshadows the plot. Learning about economics is a thirsty-producing enterprise, so mix up some frozen lemonade with your kids, calculate the costs together, and sample the goods. Pair this with ***Lunch Money*** by Andrew Clements, another enjoyable novel about business and competition. Find the teacher's guide at <**www.houghtonmifflinbooks.com/readers_guides/davies_lemonade.shtml**> and the terrific trailer for the book at <**www.lemonadewar.com/book_trailer.shtml**>. Have your entrepreneurs write and film trailers for books they've read and loved.

RELATED TITLES: Adams, Barbara Johnston. *The Go-Around Dollar.* Four Winds, 1992. / Brittain, Bill. *All the Money in the World.* HarperCollins, 1979. / Clements, Andrew. *Lunch Money.* Simon & Schuster, 2005. / Clements, Andrew. *No Talking.* Simon & Schuster, 2007. / Conford, Ellen. *A Job for Jenny Archer.* Little, Brown, 1988. / Gill, Shelley, and Deborah Tobola. *The Big Buck Adventure.* Charlesbridge, 2000. / Gutman, Dan. *The Get Rich Quick Club.* HarperCollins, 2004. / Herman, Charlotte. *Max Malone Makes a Million.* Henry Holt, 1991. / Kennedy, Frances. *The Pickle Patch Bathtub.* Tricycle, 2004. / Leedy, Loreen. *Follow the Money.* Holiday House, 2002. / Polacco, Patricia. *Rotten Richie and the Ultimate Dare.* Philomel, 2006. / Schwartz, David M. *If You Made a Million.* Lothrop, 1989. / Van Leeuwen, Jean. *Benjy in Business.* Dial, 1983.

SUBJECTS: BROTHERS AND SISTERS. BUSINESS. ECONOMICS. LEMONADE. MATHEMATICS. MONEYMAKING PROJECTS. SUMMER.

FICTION BOOKS, cont.

[J] | |B| | |
Miss Spitfire: Reaching Helen Keller. **Miller, Sarah Elizabeth. Atheneum, 2007. {ISBN 978-1-41692-542-2; 208p.} FIC (Gr. 5-8)**

Reading this biographical novel, narrated by Anne Sullivan and based on her many letters, I was reminded once again why I, like so many others, have always been captivated by the story of Anne and Helen Keller, the little girl whose life she transformed. It starts in 1887 with 20-year-old Anne on the train to Alabama to meet her new student. Anne's thoughts drift back to her own traumatic childhood as a blind orphan living at Tewksbury, the Massachusetts state almshouse, losing her beloved little brother, Jimmy, and finally finding acceptance and training at the Perkins Institution for the Blind. Upon meeting her new pupil, the blind and deaf six-year-old Helen, Annie muses, "She seems so utterly alone, her look so familiar, for a moment I imagine I'm seeing the shadow of my own child-soul." Love-starved Annie is every bit as emotionally needy as her charge. Soon, though, the two are locked in battle over Helen's appalling mealtime behavior as Annie struggles to teach the wild child some manners, how to finger spell, and how to obey. You've seen the movie, *The Miracle Worker.* This is a prose version of it, but from Annie's viewpoint. It's every bit as riveting, especially the final moving chapter when Helen finally makes the connection between the finger-spelled word for water, her remembered word for it—wah-wah, and the water gushing from the pump.

GERM: Don't assume your children know this story. Pair it with straightforward biographies including Marfe Ferguson Delano's ***Helen's Eyes: A Photobiography of Annie Sullivan, Helen Keller's Teacher***, Laurie Lawlor's ***Helen Keller: Rebellious Spirit***, and George Sullivan's ***Helen Keller: Her Life in Pictures***. If you can show the video of *The Miracle Worker*, note that it's what inspired Sarah Miller to write this book. Also read Russell Freedman's fascinating biography ***Out of Darkness: The Story of Louis Braille***. More than half a century earlier, Braille, who spent his formative years at the Royal Institute for Blind Youth in Paris, devised the Braille system of writing. And look in the 419 section of the library for books about American Sign Language.

RELATED TITLES: Davis, Patricia A. *Brian's Bird.* Albert Whitman, 2000. / Delano, Marfe Ferguson. *Helen's Eyes: A Photobiography of Annie Sullivan, Helen Keller's Teacher.* National Geographic, 2008. / Freedman, Russell. *Out of Darkness: The Story of Louis Braille.* Clarion, 1997. / Garfield, James. *Follow My Leader.* Viking, 1957. / Hermann, Spring. *Seeing Lessons: The Story of Abigail Carter and America's First School for Blind People.* Henry Holt, 1998. / Hunter, Edith Fisher. *Child of the Silent Night: The Story of Laura Bridgman.* Houghton Mifflin, 1963. / Lawlor, Laurie. *Helen Keller: Rebellious Spirit.* Holiday House, 2001. / Little, Jean. *Little by Little: A Writer's Education.* Viking, 1987. / MacLeod, Elizabeth. *Helen Keller: A Determined Life.* Kids Can, 2004. / Millman, Isaac. *Moses Goes to a Concert.* Farrar, 1998. / Sullivan, George. *Helen Keller: Her Life in Pictures.* Scholastic, 2007. / Whelan, Gloria. *Hannah.* Knopf, 1991.

SUBJECTS: ALABAMA. BIOGRAPHICAL FICTION. BLIND. DEAF. HISTORICAL FICTION. KELLER, HELEN, 1880-1968. PEOPLE WITH DISABILITIES. SULLIVAN, ANNIE, 1866-1936. TEACHERS. WOMEN—BIOGRAPHY.

[j] |A|B| |S|
The Mysterious Benedict Society. Stewart, Trenton Lee. illus. by Carson Ellis. Little, Brown/Megan Tingley,
   2007. {ISBN 978-0-316-05777-6; 485p.} FIC (Gr. 4-7)
"ARE YOU A GIFTED CHILD LOOKING FOR SPECIAL OPPORTUNITIES?" That newspaper ad brings
together four resourceful and multitalented children, all of whom are orphans or alone in the world, to become secret
agents for Mr. Benedict, a genius who has uncovered a nefarious international mind-control plot. There's Reynie
Muldoon, whose logical thinking helps him solve puzzles; Kate Wetherall, who can climb anywhere and fix
anything with her tool-filled bucket; tenacious Sticky Washington, who has total recall of everything he's ever read;
and the diminutive Constance Contraire, whose crabby and belligerent demeanor is her greatest gift. Their mission
will be to infiltrate the exclusive Learning Institute for the Very Enlightened and to discover how and why the
school's founder is transmitting subliminal doctrinaire messages into people's brains.
GERM: Readers who thrive on problem-solving novels like Blue Balliett's *Chasing Vermeer*, Eric Berlin's *The
Puzzling World of Winston Breen*, and Ellen Raskin's *The Westing Game* will enjoy the fast-paced intrigue and
kids-save-the-world theme. In describing the special gifts possessed by these four intrepid children, ask your
students to make a list of their own singular and perhaps unrecognized talents and describe how these attributes have
helped them solve problems and puzzles in their own lives.
RELATED TITLES: Anderson, M. T. *Whales on Stilts.* Harcourt, 2005. / Balliett, Blue. *Chasing Vermeer.*
Scholastic, 2004. / Berlin, Eric. *The Puzzling World of Winston Breen.* Putnam, 2007. / Jonell, Lynne. *Emmy and the
Incredible Shrinking Rat.* Henry Holt, 2007. / Raskin, Ellen. *The Westing Game.* Dutton, 1978. / Rex, Adam. *The
True Meaning of Smekday.* Hyperion, 2007. / Snicket, Lemony. *The Austere Academy.* HarperCollins, 2000.
**SUBJECTS: ADVENTURE AND ADVENTURERS. MYSTERY AND DETECTIVE STORIES. SCHOOLS.
SCIENCE FICTION.**

[J*] | | | |S|
No Talking. Clements, Andrew. Illus. by Mark Elliott. Simon & Schuster, 2007. {ISBN 978-1-41690-983-5;
   135p.} FIC (Gr. 3-6)
As a former teacher, Andrew Clements understands from the inside out what goes on in schools and writes down-to-
earth, entertaining, kid-friendly novels that introduce ethical break-the-mold children who question authority and
take a stand. Meet New Jersey fifth grader Dave Parker, a known loudmouth who has decided, in spite of being
called on to give his oral social studies report on India, to stick with his experiment of not speaking for an entire day.
Reading a book about Mahatma Gandhi, Dave was struck to discover that for many years, one day a week, Gandhi
did not speak, believing his silence brought order to his mind. Dave holds his tongue until lunchtime, when another
tongue-flapper, Lynsey Burgess, won't stop jawing. "If you had to shut up for five minutes, I bet the whole top of
your head would explode!" Dave tells her. And that comment sparks a huge fifth grade competition, boys against
girls, to see who can go for two entire days without speaking—this from a group whose nickname among the
teachers is the Unshushables. Dave is sure the next 48 hours will be interesting, exciting, and even dangerous, since
their teachers have no idea what's going on, though they catch on pretty fast.
GERM: Try out some of the techniques the students use in their quest to stay silent. There's sign language, note-
writing, and, since the rules allow each child to answer a teacher's question in three words or less, some very funny
question-and-answer dialogues. You'll love Mr. Burton's story starter—"A woman screamed."—to which each
student adds on a three-word sentence. And his writing lesson where kids must write all period long, not stopping
for any longer than 15 seconds, and communicate with at least four other people in the room. Your students can
imagine they're fifth graders at Laketon and write about how they handled two days without speaking at school or at
home. See if your own unshushables can stay silent for one whole period.
RELATED TITLES: Clements, Andrew. *Frindle.* Simon & Schuster, 1996. / Clements, Andrew. *Lunch Money.*
Simon & Schuster, 2005. / Clements, Andrew. *The School Story.* Simon & Schuster, 2001. / Davies, Jacqueline. *The
Lemonade War.* Houghton Mifflin, 2007. / Demi. *Gandhi.* McElderry, 2001. / Fletcher, Ralph. *Flying Solo.* Clarion,
1998. / Naylor, Phyllis Reynolds. *The Boys Start the War.* Delacorte, 1993. / Wilkinson, Philip. *Gandhi: The Young
Protester Who Founded a Nation.* National Geographic, 2005.
**SUBJECTS: BEHAVIOR. COMMUNICATION. CONTESTS. HUMOROUS FICTION. SCHOOLS.
TEACHERS.**

FICTION BOOKS, cont.

[J*] | | | | |
The Puzzling World of Winston Breen. Berlin, Eric. Putnam, 2007. {ISBN 978-0-399-24693-7; 215p.} FIC (Gr. 4-6)

For his younger sister Katie's tenth birthday, twelve-year-old Winston gives her what he thinks is a small empty wooden box he bought at an antique store. Winston is a puzzle fanatic. He looks for puzzles and patterns in everything, so when Katie finds a secret bottom to the box and pulls out four mysterious little wooden strips with words on them, he is intrigued. Turns out the box came from the estate of the late Livia Little, whose father, Walter Fredericks, was a wealthy inventor who helped build their town. Mr. Fredericks's other daughter is the town librarian, Violet Lewis, but when Winston and his friend Mal approach her she goes nuts, screaming and crying, and kicks them out of the library. Winston, his friends, and his sister must solve the puzzle of the wooden strips to find a valuable ring, hidden for 25 years, before two unsavory treasure hunters do.

GERM: Remember the pleasure you felt when you solved your first Encyclopedia Brown mystery without peeking at the solution at the back of the book? Here's a new one to help you hone your puzzle-solving skills. Winston likes to find and solve a puzzle every day. Lucky for us, he provides at least one per chapter for us to work out, including word puzzles and math problems. You can stop at each one and have your students work out the solution. If they (and you) get stumped, the answers to all 18 puzzles are at the back. Go to <**www.winstonbreen.com**> to download and print out all of the puzzles.

RELATED TITLES: Hirsch, Robin. *FEG: Ridiculous Poems for Intelligent Children.* Little, Brown, 2002. / Sobol, Donald J. *Encyclopedia Brown Cracks the Case.* Dutton, 2007. (And others in the Encyclopedia Brown series.) / Stewart, Trent Lee. *The Mysterious Benedict Society.* Little, Brown, 2007. / Torrey, Michele. *The Case of the Gasping Garbage.* Dutton, 2001. / Townsend, Charles Barry. *The Curious Book of Mind-Boggling Teasers, Tricks, Puzzles & Games.* Sterling, 2003.

SUBJECTS: BROTHERS AND SISTERS. MYSTERY AND DETECTIVE STORIES. PUZZLES.

[J] |A| | | |
Remembering Mrs. Rossi. Hest, Amy. Illus. by Heather Maione. Candlewick, 2007. {ISBN 978-0-7636-2163-6; 184p.} FIC (Gr. 3-5)

All children come to school with emotional baggage; good books can help them deal with difficult issues. The toughest one of all is the death of a parent. In Amy Hest's wistful chapter book, third grader Annie Rossi and her Columbia University professor dad are finding their way together after Mrs. Rossi, a school teacher, dies unexpectedly. They're not the only ones affected; Mrs. Rossi's sixth grade class invites Annie and her dad to their Winter Assembly to present them with a special book of students essays about their beloved teacher. What the two discover is that somehow, in spite of bouts of tears and sadness and anger and missing Mommy, there's joy, too. Somehow, life continues. There's a snow day where Annie sits in on Daddy's college English class and a summer at the beach where she and her friend Helen walk to town alone, without permission. Told in present tense, the omniscient narrator shepherds us tenderly but carefully through what could be risky terrain for children—What if my mom died?—and lets us see how a family copes with tragedy.

GERM: The book of heartfelt essays by Mrs. Rossi's students, appended at the back, is a huge help to Annie and will be a source of writing ideas to use with your kids. Go to <**www.candlewick.com**>, type the title in the search bar, and you can download a good teacher's guide.

RELATED TITLES: Creech, Sharon. *Love That Dog.* HarperCollins, 2001. / DiCamillo, Kate. *Because of Winn-Dixie.* Candlewick, 2000. / Fry, Virginia Lynn. *Part of Me Died, Too: Stories of Creative Survival Among Bereaved Children and Teenagers.* Dutton, 1995. / Lowry, Lois. *Anastasia Again.* Houghton Mifflin, 1981. (And others in the Anastasia series.) / Park, Barbara. *Mick Harte Was Here.* Knopf, 1995. / Recorvits, Helen. *Goodbye, Walter Malinski.* Farrar, 1999.

SUBJECTS: DEATH. FATHERS AND DAUGHTERS. GRIEF. MOTHERS. NEW YORK CITY. TEACHERS.

FICTION BOOKS, cont.

[J*] |A| | | |

Revolution Is Not a Dinner Party: A Novel. **Compestine, Ying Chang. Henry Holt, 2007. {ISBN 978-0-8050-8207-4; 248p.} FIC (Gr. 5-8)**

"The summer of 1972, the year I turned nine, danger began knocking on doors all over China." Ling is the narrator, but the events that follow mirror the life of the author, whose parents were also doctors in the city of Wuhan at the time of the Cultural Revolution. Ling's father, a respected surgeon, learned about Western medicine from an American, Dr. Smith, and treasures the picture of the Golden Gate Bridge the doctor gave him before returning home to San Francisco. Ling reveres her kind and affectionate father who teaches her American folk songs and gives her English lessons, but has a more formal relationship with her prickly and hard to please mother. Then Comrade Li, the sanctimonious new political officer for the hospital and enforcer of Mao's policies, moves in to the family's apartment, appropriating Father's study for himself. To "help build a new China," he has the heat and then the power cut off in the building, demands food, and begins arresting "undercover enemies," including Ling's father. Taunted and bullied at school for being "bourgeois," Ling is bewildered and terrified by the growing chaos as the city's social fabric unravels.

GERM: A grim and frightening look at power run amok and how it destroys lives and families, Ling's compelling narrative is an instructive reminder of the differences between democracy and dictatorships. "What's freedom?" Ling whispers to her father when he tells her that people go to America to find it. "Freedom is being able to read what you want and say what you think," he tells her. These rights, which we take for granted in America, are not guaranteed in many countries today. First, discuss what other freedoms Ling did not have, and have students compare and contrast her childhood with theirs. Ask them Why do people from other countries still want to come to America today? Go to the America's Historical Documents page of the National Archives website **<www.archives.gov/historical-docs/>** to find out more about our Bill of Rights and Articles 11 to 27. ***Ji Li Jiang's Red Scarf Girl: A Memoir of the Cultural Revolution*** is another startling true account, describing the author's experiences in Shanghai in 1966. ***The Wall: Growing Up Behind the Iron Curtain*** is an autobiographical picture book by Peter Sís about his childhood in Prague during the same era.

RELATED TITLES: Jiang, Ji Li. *Red Scarf Girl: A Memoir of the Cultural Revolution.* HarperCollins, 1997. / Lin, Grace. *The Year of the Dog.* Little, Brown, 2006. / Sís, Peter. *The Wall: Growing Up Behind the Iron Curtain.* Farrar, 2007. / Yep, Laurence. *The Star Fisher.* Morrow, 1991.

SUBJECTS: AUTOBIOGRAPHICAL FICTION. BULLYING. CHINA. COMMUNISM. FAMILY LIFE. HISTORICAL FICTION. MULTICULTURAL BOOKS. PHYSICIANS. PERSECUTION. TOTALITARIANISM.

[J*] | | | | |

The Rising Star of Rusty Nail. **Blume, Lesley M. M. Knopf, 2007. {ISBN 978-0-375-83524-7; 270p.} FIC (Gr. 4-7)**

The Cold War may be heating up between the U.S. and Russia, but in the sleepy little town of Rusty Nail, Minnesota in 1953, Franny, who loves playing piano more than anything, is determined to outdo that spoiled brat, the richest girl in town, Nancy Orilee in a piano playing competition at school. Franny and her best friend Sandy, infamous as the town's peskiest troublemakers, are already grounded for lobbing water balloons at Nancy. Meanwhile, Charlie Koenig, the town's young lawyer, comes back to town with his new wife, a Russian pianist, and the townsfolk are abuzz, convinced she must be a Communist spy. In spite of the townfolk's growing hysteria, Franny's dream is to play the piano, even if it means begging the imperious young woman, Madame Olga Malenkov, to give her lessons.

GERM: There are plenty of discussable issues here, aside from the cast of eccentric and comical characters. Ask students about their dreams and how they plan to reach them, even if their friends and family may not approve. Give some background on the McCarthy era. Ask if there are any modern day parallels to the close-minded behavior of the citizens of Rusty Nail. An author's note states that she structured the book on Rachmaninoff's Piano Concerto no. 2, op. 18. Be sure to play a CD of that for your listeners, and, in honor of Franny's dad, some Duke Ellington, too. Another fabulous fiction book about a young pianist is Linda Urban's ***A Crooked Kind of Perfect.***

RELATED TITLES: Cameron, Ann. T*he Secret Life of Amanda K. Woods.* Farrar, 1998. / Fitzgerald, John D. *The Great Brain.* Dial, 1967. / Levine, Ellen. *Catch a Tiger by the Toe.* Viking, 2005. / Peck, Richard. *A Long Way from Chicago: A Novel in Stories.* Dial, 1998. / Peck, Richard. *A Year Down Yonder.* Dial, 2000. / Pinkney, Andrea Davis. *Duke Ellington: The Piano Prince and His Orchestra.* Hyperion, 1998. / Urban, Linda. *A Crooked Kind of Perfect.* Harcourt, 2007.

SUBJECTS: COMMUNISM. FRIENDSHIP. HISTORICAL FICTION. HUMOROUS FICTION. MINNESOTA. MUSICIANS. PIANO. RUSSIAN AMERICANS.

FICTION BOOKS, cont.

[j] |A| | | |

Robot Dreams. **Varon, Sara. Illus. by Sara Varon. Roaring Brook/First Second, 2007. {ISBN 978-1-59643-108-9; 208p.} 741.5 (Gr. 2-6)**

In a wordless graphic novel, a gray dog puts together a new friend from a mail-order Tin Robot Kit. Together, the dog and robot check books out at the library, cook popcorn, watch TV, and take a Greyhound bus to the beach where they cavort in the water and fall asleep on beach towels in the sun. When it's time to go, though, the robot can't get up, and his friend, not knowing what to do, leaves him there. Lying on the beach, Robot dreams that he never went in the water, but he awakens alone and in the dark. That's the August chapter. In September, Dog, feeling guilty about what he's done, checks out a robot repair manual from the library and takes a cab back to the beach. It's closed for the season, with a barbed wire separating him from the robot. Over the next months, we see the dog make new friends while the robot dreams of finding his friend again. The story, told within thick black-lined cartoon panels and soft pastel Mo Willems–like colors, is populated with expressive comic book-like animal characters and a clunky looking robot you'd surely want to have live at your house.

GERM: There's a lot to ponder here. You want to like the genial dog, but how could he walk off and leave his friend like that? Why didn't he try to get some help? You puzzle over the ways he deals with his own actions. Can they be justified? You see the robot lying immobile in the sand, covered with snow, and your heart breaks for him. How does the robot feel about the dog over the course of the year? You'll find no reconciliation of dog and robot here. Some friendships are like that, though I felt angry at the dog for giving up on his friend and for having so little sense of responsibility. Readers can talk about the personalities of the two principal characters and how they are like or unlike people they know. Friendships can be complicated, and life doesn't always go the way you want it to.

RELATED TITLES: Faller, Regis. *The Adventures of Polo.* Roaring Brook, 2006. / Faller, Regis. *Polo: The Runaway Book.* Roaring Brook, 2006. / Lehman, Barbara. *The Red Book.* Houghton Mifflin, 2004. / Varon, Sara. *Chicken and Cat.* Scholastic, 2006. / Weitzman, Jacqueline Preiss. *You Can't Take a Balloon into the Metropolitan Museum.* Dial, 1998. / Wiesner, David. *Flotsam.* Roaring Brook, 2005. / Wiesner, David. *Free Fall.* Lothrop, 1988. / Wiesner, David. *Sector 7.* Clarion, 1999. / Wiesner, David. *The Three Pigs.* Clarion, 2001. / Wiesner, David. *Tuesday.* Clarion, 1991.

SUBJECTS: CARTOONS AND COMICS. DOGS. FRIENDSHIP. GRAPHIC NOVELS. ROBOTS. STORIES WITHOUT WORDS.

[J*] | | | |S|

The Talented Clementine. **Pennypacker, Sara. Illus. by Marla Frazee. Hyperion, 2007. {ISBN 978-0-7868-3870-7; 137p.} FIC (Gr. 1-4)**

It's gratifying to see our new favorite third grader back in a sequel that is just as funny as her first fabulous first book, ***Clementine***. She jumps right in: "I have noticed that teachers get exciting confused with boring a lot. But when my teacher said, 'Class, we have an exciting project to talk about,' I listened anyway." Poor kid. Unlike her fourth grade friend and neighbor Margaret, who has a whole alphabet of talents to draw on for the upcoming Talent-Palooza, Night of the Stars, Clementine can't think of even one thing she could do on stage. Sure, she's great at art and math, and her dad says she is the queen of noticing things and is very empathetic to boot. Her attempts at juggling and tap dancing don't quite pan out, and dad won't let her bring her little brother for her "Elvis and the Laughing Dog" act. Don't worry about Clementine. Her own talents help her big time on the night of the big show when she helps out her formidable but understanding principal Mrs. Rice.

GERM: Have your students make an alphabetical list of their talents and all the things they're good at. Hold an impromptu talent show to show them off a bit. Bring in clementines to eat and empathize with that unforgettable girl who "got stuck" with a fruit name. Judy Freeman is writing the teacher's guide for the Clementine series, so keep your eyes peeled for it at <**www.hyperionbooksforchildren.com**>; type in the title of the book in the search bar and you'll be able to download it from the book's home page.

RELATED TITLES: Cleary, Beverly. *Ramona Quimby, Age 8.* Morrow, 1981. / Duffey, Betsy. *Spotlight on Cody.* Viking, 1998. / Kline, Suzy. *What's the Matter with Herbie Jones?* Putnam, 1987. (And others in the Herbie Jones series.) / McDonald, Megan. *Judy Moody, M.D.: The Doctor Is In!* Candlewick, 2004. (And others in the Judy Moody series.) / McDonald, Megan. *Stink!: The Incredible Shrinking Kid.* Candlewick, 2005. (And others in the Stink series.) / Park, Barbara. *Junie B. Jones and the Stupid Smelly Bus.* Random House, 1993. (And others in the Junie B. Jones series.)

SUBJECTS: BROTHERS AND SISTERS. FRIENDSHIP. HUMOROUS FICTION. PRINCIPALS. SCHOOLS. SELF-ESTEEM. TALENT SHOWS.

FICTION BOOKS, cont.

[J] | | | |S|

The True Meaning of Smekday. **Rex, Adam. Illus. by the author. Hyperion, 2007. {ISBN 978-0-7868-4900-0; 423p.} FIC (Gr. 4-8)**

Writing an essay about how the Smekday holiday (formerly called Christmas) has changed in the year since the aliens left, eighth grader Gratuity Tucci, known as Tip, offers her story of her singular experiences since the Boov invasion in 2013. Though the aliens have just announced that all Americans must relocate to Florida, Tip's mom has already been abducted, called up to the spaceships by signals from a mole on her neck. Tip figures she'll drive there in her mom's little hatchback and her cat Pig, but after avoiding a barricade and being shot at by a Boov patrol, she blows a tire at mile forty-eight where the road has been destroyed. Stopping at an abandoned convenience store, Tip encounters the enemy—a broad-headed many-legged Boov named J-Lo, who fixes her car so it can hover instead of roll. Wildly inventive, outrageously funny, and thoroughly original, this Girl Saves Earth with Help from a Boov roadtrip adventure is one of the most beguiling sci fi stories ever.

GERM: This will make an ambitious read-aloud, punctuated by comic strips and artwork you may want to photocopy and pass around for listeners to examine in greater detail. They can make charts of Boovian language and the words that J-Lo misinterprets, and tell the story from the Boov point of view. Weirdly, then, you can use the book with Shaun Tan's wordless graphic novel, ***The Arrival***, about the immigrant experience in a strange land.

RELATED TITLES: Anderson, M. T. *Whales on Stilts.* Harcourt, 2005. / Bechard, Margaret. *Star Hatchling.* Viking, 1995. / Brittain, Bill. *Shape-Changer.* HarperCollins, 1994. / Collins, Suzanne. *Gregor the Overlander.* Scholastic, 2003. / Conly, Jane Leslie. *The Rudest Alien on Earth.* Henry Holt, 2002. / Gauthier, Gail. *My Life Among the Aliens.* Putnam, 1996. / L'Engle, Madeleine. *A Wrinkle in Time.* Farrar, 1962. / Pratchett, Terry. *The Wee Free Men.* HarperCollins, 2003. / Reeve, Philip. *Larklight.* Bloomsbury, 2006. / Rex, Adam. *Frankenstein Makes a Sandwich.* Harcourt, 2006. / Riordan, Rick. *The Lightning Thief.* Miramax/Hyperion, 2005. / Service, Pamela. *Stinker from Space.* Scribner, 1988. / Sleator, William. *Into the Dream.* Dutton, 1979. / Sleator, William. *The Night the Heads Came.* Dutton, 1996. / Tan, Shaun. *The Arrival.* Scholastic, 2007.

SUBJECTS: AFRICAN AMERICANS. EXTRATERRESTRIAL BEINGS. FANTASY. HUMAN-ALIEN ENCOUNTERS. HUMOROUS FICTION. MISSING PERSONS. MULTICULTURAL BOOKS. MOTHERS AND DAUGHTERS. SCIENCE FICTION.

[j] |A|B| | |

The Wednesday Wars. **Schmidt, Gary D. Clarion, 2007. {ISBN 978-0-618-72483-3; 264p.} FIC (Gr. 6-8) Newbery Honor**

"Of all the kids in the seventh grade at Camillo Junior High School, there was one kid that Mrs. Baker hated with heat whiter than the sun. Me." So starts the account of Holling Hoodhood of the Wednesday afternoons he is forced to spend with his stern and demanding English teacher. The Jewish and Catholic kids get of class early for Hebrew School or Catechism, but Holling, being inconveniently Presbyterian, stays behind, washing chalkboards and pounding erasers (this being 1967 when they used these things), and cleaning out the cage of the classroom's two fearsome pet rats, which he inadvertently allows to escape into the school's ceiling. Whoops. Mrs. Baker decides that she and Holling will start reading Shakespeare together, starting with "The Merchant of Venice." Though they begin as adversaries, Mrs. Baker, whose husband has just been deployed to Vietnam, becomes his touchstone, who helps him deal with his perfectionist and bullying father, the disappointment at meeting a less-than-genial Mickey Mantle, and playing Ariel the Fairy in The Tempest for the Long Island Shakespeare Company.

GERM: Bruce Coville picture book, ***William Shakespeare's The Tempest***, will help a lot in explaining the plot behind Holling's acting debut. Anita Ganeri's book, *The Young Person's Guide to Shakespeare* is a book and a CD, so students can hear Shakespeare the way it should sound. The novel rehashes so vividly the era of the 1970s when Vietnam was raging, teachers taught sentence diagramming (which you might want to take up with your students), students hid under their desks during government-approved atomic bomb drills, and older sisters ran off to California with a boyfriend to find themselves. Not so different from now, really.

RELATED TITLES: Avi. *Romeo and Juliet—Together and Alive at Last.* Orchard, 1987. / Caputo, Philip. *10,000 Days of Thunder: A History of the Vietnam War.* Atheneum, 2005. / Coville, Bruce. *William Shakespeare's The Tempest.* Delacorte, 1994. / Ganeri, Anita. *The Young Person's Guide to Shakespeare.* (book and CD) Harcourt, 1999. / Kerley, Barbara. *Greetings from Planet Earth.* Scholastic, 2007. / Schmidt, Gary D. *Lizzie Bright and the Buckminster Boy.* Clarion, 2004. / Williams, Marcia. *Tales from Shakespeare: Seven Plays.* Candlewick Press, 2004. / Woodson, Jacqueline. *Feathers.* Putnam, 2007.

SUBJECTS: FAMILY LIFE. FAMILY PROBLEMS. HUMOROUS FICTION. JUNIOR HIGH SCHOOLS. NEW YORK (STATE). PLAYS. SCHOOLS. SHAKESPEARE, WILLIAM, 1564-1616. TEACHERS.

The 100 Top-Rated Children's Books of 2007

NONFICTION AND BIOGRAPHY BOOKS

[J*] |A|B| |S|

At Gleason's Gym. **Lewin, Ted. Illus. by the author. Roaring Brook, 2007. {ISBN 978-1-59643-231-4; unp.}**
796.83 (Gr. K-5)

Follow nine-year-old boxing champ Sugar Boy Younan as he spends a Saturday in Brooklyn training with other athletes—kids and adults, male and female—in "the most famous boxing gym in the world." Combining a poetic descriptive text, gritty, realistic watercolors, and shaded pencil sketches, this evocative picture book envelops the reader in a you-are-there experience of the sweat, excitement, noise, intense concentration, and fun of sparring in the ring. Lewin was himself a professional wrestler as a teen; his admiration and respect for the "music of the gym" captures and humanizes an unfamiliar world.

GERM: Note the onomatopoeia used on many of the pages to give a sense of the sounds of boxing. Make a list of unfamiliar boxing terminology and showcase the glossary that defines them. Ask children to write and illustrate an informational description of how they train for a sport or prepare for a hobby.

RELATED TITLES: Brown, Don. *Bright Path: Young Jim Thorpe.* Roaring Brook, 2006. / Hamm, Mia. *Winners Never Quit!* HarperCollins, 2004. / Krull, Kathleen. *Lives of the Athletes: Thrills, Spills (and What the Neighbors Thought).* Harcourt, 1995. / Krull, Kathleen. *Wilma Unlimited: How Wilma Rudolph Became the World's Fastest Woman.* Harcourt, 1996. / Lewin, Ted. *I Was a Teenage Professional Wrestler.* Orchard, 1993. / Nevius, Carol. *Karate Hour.* Marshall Cavendish, 2004. / Piven, Hanoch. *What Athletes Are Made Of.* Atheneum, 2006. / Stauffacher, Sue. *Nothing But Trouble: The Story of Althea Gibson.* Knopf, 2007.

SUBJECTS: ATHLETES. BOXING. MULTICULTURAL BOOKS. SPORTS.

[j] |A| | | |

Ballerina Dreams. **Thompson, Lauren. Illus. by James Estrin. Feiwel & Friends, 2007. {ISBN 978-0-312-37029-9; unp.} 618.92 (Gr. K-4)**

When you first pick up this pink book with the three little girl ballerinas on the cover, you think this is a book your little girls will love, and that's true. But the very young dancers—Nicole, Shekinah, Veronica, Abbey, and Monica— are not your everyday dancers. While they've always wanted to dance just like other girls, all of them have cerebral palsy or other muscle disorders, and some use wheelchairs or walkers to get around. Nevertheless, they take weekly ballet classes with their ballet teacher, physical therapist Joann Ferrara, and are preparing for their upcoming recital. Dressed in pink tutus and ballet shoes, they perform onstage for cheering parents, friends, classmates, and teachers. This endearing and inspiring color photo essay, printed on pink paper, takes the girls, each assisted and physically supported by a helper, through three numbers. The final pages profile each girl, their teacher, their helpers, and provide information on cerebral palsy.

GERM: Play music from "The Nutcracker" and "Swan Lake" and have your children move to it in their own way. Then introduce the book for children to see firsthand how the girls transcended their physical limitations through dance. Discussion Points: Why did the girls want to dance? What obstacles did they overcome? How did their experiences affect you?

RELATED TITLES: Carlson, Nancy L. *Arnie and the New Kid.* Viking, 1990. / Cowen-Fletcher, Jane. *Mama Zooms.* Scholastic, 1993. / Damrell, Liz. *With the Wind.* Orchard, 1991. / Geras, Adele. *Time for Ballet.* Dial, 2004. / Isadora, Rachel. *Max.* Macmillan, 1976. / Krementz, Jill. *A Very Young Dancer.* Random House, 1976. / Millman, Isaac. *Moses Goes to a Concert.* Farrar, 1998. / Stadler, Alexander. *Lila Bloom.* Farrar, 2004.

SUBJECTS: BALLET DANCERS. CEREBRAL PALSY. DANCING. PEOPLE WITH DISABILITIES. PERSEVERANCE. PHYSICALLY HANDICAPPED.

[J*] | | | | |
Delicious: The Life & Art of Wayne Thiebaud. **Rubin, Susan Goldman. Illus. with photos. and reprods.**
   Chronicle, 2007. {ISBN 978-0-8118-5168-8; 108p.} B (Gr. 5-12)
This innovative and enticing biography explores 20th century painter Wayne Thiebaud, famed for painting ordinary objects like cakes, ice cream cones, shoes, and pinball machines. Color runs riot, with each smooth-textured page a different solid color you'd need a box of 96 Crayolas to name. Facing each page of mostly white text is a reproduction of one of Thiebaud's luscious paintings, pastels, and prints, most of which have not been previously published. What's so compelling about Rubin's text is not just the absorbing and skillfully told chronology of Thiebaud's life, but also her clear-eyed descriptions and analysis of his style, technique, and paintings, integrated with many quotes from Thiebaud about how and why he paints.
GERM: What a delicious art project it will be, to bring in sweets for children to draw or paint, inspired by Thiebaud's wonderful renditions of assorted desserts.
RELATED TITLES: Duggleby, John. *Story Painter: The Life of Jacob Lawrence.* Chronicle, 1998. / Gherman, Beverly. *Norman Rockwell: Storyteller with a Brush.* Atheneum, 2000. / Greenberg, Jan, and Sandra Jordan. *Action Jackson.* Roaring Brook, 2002. / Greenberg, Jan, and Sandra Jordan. *Andy Warhol: Prince of Pop.* Delacorte, 2004. / Greenberg, Jan, and Sandra Jordan. *Chuck Close, Up Close.* DK Ink, 1998. / Krull, Kathleen. *Lives of the Artists: Masterpieces, Messes (and What the Neighbors Thought).* Harcourt, 1995. / Raczka, Bob. *Here's Looking at Me: How Artists See Themselves.* Millbrook, 2006. / Rubin, Susan Goldman. *Andy Warhol: Pop Art Painter.* Abrams, 2006. / Rubin, Susan Goldman. *Edward Hopper: Painter of Light and Shadow.* Abrams, 2007.
SUBJECTS: ARTISTS. BIOGRAPHY. PAINTERS. THIEBAUD, WAYNE.

[j] | | | |S|
Dogs and Cats. **Jenkins, Steve. Illus. by the author. Houghton Mifflin, 2007. {ISBN 978-0-618-50767-2; unp.}**
   636.7 (Gr. 1-5)
With Jenkins's usual flair for finding interesting facts and his fetching textured earth-toned illustrations done in cut and torn homemade paper collage, we are introduced to the history and personality of man's best friend, the dog. Then flip the book over for equal time for our feline friends. He pulls both pets together with inset facts about dogs in the corners of each cat page and vice versa.
GERM: Poll your class to see how many are dog-lovers versus cat-lovers, and then share some of the many nuggets of information about both. This would pair up howlingly well with Susan Campbell Bartoletti's pair of picture books, *Nobody's Diggier than a Dog* and *Nobody's Nosier than a Cat,* followed by a choral reading of Donald Hall's *I Am the Dog, I Am the Cat.*
RELATED TITLES: Bartoletti, Susan. *Nobody's Diggier than a Dog.* Hyperion, 2004. / Bartoletti, Susan. *Nobody's Nosier than a Cat.* Hyperion, 2003. / Calmenson, Stephanie. *May I Pet Your Dog?: The How-to Guide for Kids Meeting Dogs (and Dogs Meeting Kids).* Clarion, 2007. / Florian, Doug. *Bow Wow Meow Meow: It's Rhyming Cats and Dogs.* Harcourt, 2003. / Gottfried, Maya. *Good Dog.* Knopf, 2005. / Hall, Donald. *I Am the Dog, I Am the Cat.* Dial, 1994. / Hausman, Gerald, and Loretta Hausman. *Dogs of Myth: Tales from Around the World.* Simon & Schuster, 1999. / Kirk, Daniel. *Cat Power!* Hyperion, 2007. / Kirk, Daniel. *Dogs Rule!* Hyperion, 2003. / Singer, Marilyn. *It's Hard to Read a Map with a Beagle on Your Lap.* Henry Holt, 1993.
SUBJECTS: CATS. DOGS.

NONFICTION BOOKS, cont.

[j] |A| | | |

Down the Colorado: John Wesley Powell, the One-Armed Explorer. **Ray, Deborah Kogan. Illus. by Deborah Kogan Ray. Farrar, 2007. {ISBN 978-0-374-31838-3; 48p.} 917.91 (Gr. 3-5)**

In 1841, after seven-year-old Wes Powell was taunted, beaten, and stoned by classmates angry at his father, Reverend Powell's, abolitionist sermons, Wes left school and was tutored by a neighbor, a self-taught naturalist who believed in learning through observation and firsthand experience. After a wave of anti-abolitionist violence, the Powells left their farm in southern Ohio and moved to the Wisconsin frontier. A captain in the Union army, Powell lost his right arm at the Battle of Shiloh, but went on to teach biology in college and lead groups of students on field trips to the Rocky Mountains. In 1869, he and a crew of nine men set out to explore the Colorado River through the Grand Canyon, the first recorded expedition to do so, taking 99 days, traversing 1,000 miles and 500 rapids. Big, full-bleed paintings, both pensive and robust, on each facing page add additional drama to this picture book biography of an extraordinary man.

GERM: Do some group research on the Grand Canyon and its marvels. There's also a map and a timeline recapping their journey and a chronology of Powell's life at the back.

RELATED TITLES: Armstrong, Jennifer. *Audubon: Painter of Birds in the Wild Frontier.* Abrams, 2003. / Brenner, Barbara. *On the Frontier with Mr. Audubon.* Boyds Mills, 1997. / Burleigh, Robert. *Into the Woods: John James Audubon Lives His Dream.* Atheneum, 2003. / Dunlap, Julie, and Marybeth Lorbiecki. *John Muir and Stickeen: An Icy Adventure with a No-Good Dog.* NorthWord, 2004. / Fraser, Mary Ann. *In Search of the Grand Canyon: Down the Colorado with John Wesley Powell.* Henry Holt, 1995. / Lasky, Kathryn. *John Muir: America's First Environmentalist.* Candlewick, 2006. / Maurer, Richard. *The Wild Colorado: The True Adventures of Fred Dellenbaugh, Age 17, on the Second Powell Expedition into the Grand Canyon.* Crown, 1999. / Ray, Deborah Kogan. *The Flower Hunter: William Bartram, America's First Naturalist.* Farrar, 2004. / Waldman, Stuart. *The Last River: John Wesley Powell & the Colorado River Exploration Expedition.* Mikaya Press, 2005. / Schanzer, Rosalyn. *How We Crossed the West: The Adventures of Lewis & Clark.* National Geographic, 1997. / St. George, Judith. *So You Want to Be an Explorer?* Philomel, 2005.

SUBJECTS: ADVENTURE AND ADVENTURERS. COLORADO RIVER—DISCOVERY AND EXPLORATION. EXPLORERS. GRAND CANYON. POWELL, JOHN WESLEY, 1834-1902. U.S.—HISTORY—1865-1898. WEST (U.S.)—DISCOVERY AND EXPLORATION.

[J*] | | | | |

Edward Hopper: Painter of Light and Shadow. **Rubin, Susan Goldman. Illus. with reprods. Abrams, 2007. {ISBN 978-0-8109-9347-1; 48p.} B (Gr. 4-10)**

From the glossy cover with embossed lettering that mirrors the colors in the iconic cover painting, Hopper's "Nighthawks," to the textured pastel backgrounds on each page, this is a book that pulls you in with its handsome design. Hopper's biography is told skillfully and sequentially, starting with his early childhood when Eddie, as he was called, loved to draw and knew he wanted to be an artist. Each page showcases one or two of his paintings or sketches of ships and shadows, seasides and portraits. The thoughtful narrative is filled with primary quotes from Hopper and his artist friends and offers an insightful analysis of his art. For Hopper fans who think his work was all about loneliness, it will amuse you to read his take on that. "The loneliness thing is overdone," he told the director of the Whitney Museum.

GERM: It's interesting to compare Hopper's self-portraits with photographs of him, especially on the first page where you can compare the portrait he did in his 40s with the photo of him as a boy. He said, "In every artist's development the germ of the later work is always found in the earlier." Art-lovers can pore over his work to see how that is true. A thorough appendix includes bios of Hopper's fellow artists, including his wife Jo; a bibliography; and a list of museums where his work is housed. Art teachers, for sure, will be impressed with this handsome overview.

RELATED TITLES: Greenberg, Jan, and Sandra Jordan. *Action Jackson.* Roaring Brook, 2002. / Greenberg, Jan, and Sandra Jordan. *Andy Warhol: Prince of Pop.* Delacorte, 2004. / Greenberg, Jan, and Sandra Jordan. *Chuck Close, Up Close.* DK Ink, 1998. / Krull, Kathleen. *Lives of the Artists: Masterpieces, Messes (and What the Neighbors Thought).* Harcourt, 1995. / Raczka, Bob. *Here's Looking at Me: How Artists See Themselves.* Millbrook, 2006. / Rubin, Susan Goldman. *Andy Warhol: Pop Art Painter.* Abrams, 2006. / Rubin, Susan Goldman. *Delicious: The Life & Art of Wayne Thiebaud.* Chronicle, 2007.

SUBJECTS: ARTISTS. BIOGRAPHY. HOPPER, EDWARD. PAINTERS.

[J*] |A| |H| |

***First the Egg.* Seeger, Laura Vaccaro. Illus. by the author. Roaring Brook, 2007. {ISBN 978-1-59643-272-7; unp.} 571.8 (Gr. PreK-1) Caldecott Honor and Geisel Honor**

"First the EGG," it says on a red overlay, a heavystock painted page with a die-cut oval that gives texture and depth to the white egg revealed underneath. Turn the page and it says, "then the CHICKEN," with the left hand page showing the hatched chick, and the right hand page a big white chicken. "First the TADPOLE / then / the FROG" is the next progression. For each transformation, there are three stages. Just when you think you're looking at a nature book, you come to, "First the WORD, then the STORY" and "First the PAINT, then the PICTURE." In that picture are the chicken, frog, butterfly, and flower. Turn to the final page and it takes you back to the egg again. Look under the dust jacket to complete the magic of this so simple yet captivating book you can read over and over to all ages, toddler to teen.

GERM: It's another bravura concept book for Seeger, about transformations and how things develop from one stage to another and are interrelated. And you can introduce the chicken versus egg conundrum. Which one came first? Children can paint new connections. (First the apple, then the pie; first the wool, then the sweater.) Want your own egg that turns into a chicken? Look online at <www.mimismotifs.com>. George Shannon's concept books *Tomorrow's Alphabet* and White *Is for Blueberry* are also pleasing puzzlers.

RELATED TITLES: Carle, Eric. *Hello, Red Fox.* Simon & Schuster, 1998. / Ehlert, Lois. *Color Zoo.* HarperCollins, 1989. / Ehlert, Lois. *In My World.* Harcourt, 2002. / Hoban, Tana. *Look Again.* Macmillan, 1971. / Hoban, Tana. *Look! Look! Look!* Greenwillow, 1988. / Hoban, Tana. *Take Another Look.* Greenwillow, 1981. / MacDonald, Suse. *Alphabatics.* Simon & Schuster, 1986. / McCarthy, Mary. *A Closer Look.* Greenwillow, 2007. / Schaefer, Lola M. *What's Up, What's Down.* Greenwillow, 2002. / Seeger, Laura Vaccaro. *Black? White! Day? Night!* Roaring Brook, 2006. / Seeger, Laura Vaccaro. *The Hidden Alphabet.* Roaring Brook, 2003. / Seeger, Laura Vaccaro. *Lemons Are Not Red.* Roaring Brook, 2004. / Shannon, George. *Tomorrow's Alphabet.* Greenwillow, 1996. / Shannon, George. *White Is for Blueberry.* Greenwillow, 2005.

SUBJECTS: ANIMALS. CAUSE AND EFFECT. TOY AND MOVEABLE BOOKS.

[j] |A| | | |

***Hello, Bumblebee Bat.* Lunde, Darrin. Illus. by Patricia J. Wynne. Charlesbridge, 2007. {ISBN 978-1-570-91374-7; unp.} 599.4 (Gr. PreK-2) Geisel Honor**

The rare and tiny Bumblebee Bat answers nine basic questions about itself, each posed and answered on an indigo-colored left-hand page, including its size (one inch long), how it sees at night, what it eats, what it fears, and where it sleeps. Soulful and endearing watercolor, ink, and colored pencil full-bleed illustrations of our little bat friend soaring through the nighttime sky will promote bat empathy instead of reticence from readers, even the grown-up ones. The information and word choice is as basic as it gets, especially for emergent readers and young children who love learning about a new animal.

GERM: Pull in other fiction and nonfiction bat books to beef up your children's knowledge and affection for bats, including Janell Canon's *Stellaluna*, of course.

RELATED TITLES: Bash, Barbara. *Shadows of Night: The Hidden World of the Little Brown Bat.* Sierra Club, 1993. / Bruchac, Joseph. *The Great Ball Game: A Muskogee Story.* Dial, 1994. / Cannon, Annie. *The Bat In the Boot.* Orchard, 1996. / Cannon, Janell. *Stellaluna.* Harcourt, 1993. / Dragonwagon, Crescent. *Bat in the Dining Room.* Marshall Cavendish, 1997. / Goble, Paul. *Iktomi and the Boulder: A Plains Indian Story.* Orchard, 1988. / Hall, Katy, and Lisa Eisenberg. *Batty Riddles.* Dial, 1993. / Maestro, Betsy. *Bats.* Scholastic, 1994. / Mollel, Tololwa M. *A Promise to the Sun.* Little, Brown, 1992. / Pringle, Laurence. *Bats!: Strange and Wonderful.* Boyds Mills, 2000.

SUBJECTS: BATS.

[J*] | | | | |

Hey Batta Batta Swing!: The Wild Old Days of Baseball. **Cook, Sally, and James Charlton. Illus. by Ross MacDonald. McElderry, 2007. {ISBN 978-1-4169-1207-1; 48p.} 796.357 (Gr. 1-8)**

In a profusion of fascinating baseball facts, learn how teams developed their names, put numbers on their uniforms, gave nicknames to their players, and dealt with cheating on the field. Do you know what a "dinger," an "Uncle Charlie," or "a can of corn" is? Instead of the definitions being hidden in a glossary at the back, you'll find each colorful baseball colloquialism defined in the page's margins. Think vocabulary lesson here. (Answer: a home run, a curveball, and an easy fly ball.) Ross MacDonald takes the lively text and knocks it out of the box with his lighthearted watercolor and pencil-crayon cartoon-style illustrations infused with sunny yellow highlights. By the time the World Series is upon us, your students will be scanning the shelves for more books on the sport.

GERM: For old-timey fun, read a version of Ernest Lawrence Thayer's classic poem, "Casey at the Bat" followed by Dan Gutman's continuation, ***Casey Back at Bat.*** Meet some memorable players in picture book biographies of Lou Gehrig, Satchel Paige, and Babe Ruth. And finally, blow off some steam. Go out and play some ball.

RELATED TITLES: Adler, David A. *Lou Gehrig: The Luckiest Man.* Harcourt, 1997. / Burleigh, Robert. *Home Run: The Story of Babe Ruth.* Harcourt, 1998. / Cline-Ransome, Lesa. *Satchel Paige.* Simon & Schuster, 2000. / Gutman, Dan. *Casey Back at Bat.* HarperCollins, 2007. / Gutman, Dan. *Honus and Me: A Baseball Card Adventure.* Avon, 1997. / Hopkins. Lee Bennett, comp. *Extra Innings: Baseball Poems.* Harcourt, 1993. / Janeczko, Paul B. *That Sweet Diamond: Baseball Poems.* Atheneum, 1998. / Norworth, Jack. *Take Me Out to the Ball Game.* Four Winds, 1993. / Thayer, Ernest Lawrence. *Casey at the Bat.* Illus. by C. F. Payne. Simon & Schuster, 2003. / Thayer, Ernest Lawrence. *Casey at the Bat.* Illus. by Christopher Bing. Handprint, 2000. / Thayer, Ernest Lawrence. *Casey at the Bat.* Illus. by Gerald Fitzgerald. Atheneum, 1995.

SUBJECTS: BASEBALL. SPORTS.

[J] |A|B| | |

Lightship. **Floca, Brian. Illus. by the author. Atheneum, 2007. {ISBN 978-1-41692-436-4; unp.} 387.2 (Gr. PreK-2) Sibert Honor**

A simple, descriptive, lighthearted and poetic text explains the role of a lightship, a ship that stayed anchored close to shore and acted as floating lighthouses to other passing vessels. Cheerful and appealing watercolors show the daily life of the working crew (and cat) of the (fictional) lightship Ambrose, based on Light Vessel 87, which is now docked at the South Street Seaport Museum in New York City.

GERM: Even the youngest children will gain a working knowledge of lightships, the last of which was decommissioned in 1983, and how they worked back in the day in this appealing informational book. Don't miss the detailed endpapers which reveal a cross-section of the Ambrose.

RELATED TITLES: Crews, Donald. *Sail Away.* Greenwillow, 1995. / Floca, Brian. *The Racecar Alphabet.* Atheneum, 2003. / Gramatky, Hardie. *Little Toot.* Putnam, 1967. / McMullan, Kate, and Jim McMullan. *I'm Mighty!* HarperCollins, 2003. / Robbins, Ken. *Bridges.* Dial, 1991. / Sobel, June. *B Is for Bulldozer: A Construction ABC.* Harcourt, 2003. / Sturges, Philemon. *Bridges Are to Cross.* Putnam, 1998. / Swift, Hildegarde Hoyt. *The Little Red Lighthouse and the Great Gray Bridge.* Harcourt, 2002.

SUBJECTS: LIGHTSHIPS. SHIPS.

[J*] | |B| | |
Living Color. Jenkins, Steve. Illus. by the author. Houghton Mifflin, 2007. {ISBN 978-0-618-70897-0; unp.}
     591.47 (Gr. PreK-4)
In another innovative and intriguing Steve Jenkins book, illustrated with his dazzling cut paper collages, he explores the animal kingdom, sorted by color. There are four pages of red animals, with two or three profiles on each page, and an explanation of how the color red helps that animal stay alive. Take a gander at the poisonous Malaysian cherry-red centipede, whose color lets predators know it won't be tasty; the most poisonous fish in the world, the stonefish, who looks like a piece of red coral, hiding on the ocean floor; and the baby crow, whose open red mouth signals the parents that it is hungry. Other colors profiled are blue, yellow, green, orange, purple, and pink. What a visual feast for animal fans.
GERM: At the back of the book is an index, arranged by color, with a mini-sized picture of each creature, its length, habitat, diet, and a few extra facts. Children can categorize each animal into its family—insects, fish, birds, reptiles and amphibians, mammals—and list additional animals they know that use their colors for camouflage, courting, or communicating. This might spur a good simple research project where students pick an animal, find some facts in books, encyclopedias, or online, and design posters formatted like the index entries.
RELATED TITLES: Collard, Sneed B., III. *Animal Dads.* Houghton Mifflin, 1997. / Heller, Ruth. *Color.* Putnam, 1995. / Jenkins, Steve. *Actual Size.* Houghton Mifflin, 2005. / Jenkins, Steve. *Big and Little.* Houghton Mifflin, 1996. / Jenkins, Steve. *Biggest, Strongest, Fastest.* Ticknor & Fields, 1995. / Jenkins, Steve. *Hottest Coldest Highest Deepest.* Houghton Mifflin, 1998. / Jenkins, Steve. *Life on Earth: The Story of Evolution.* Houghton Mifflin, 2002. / Jenkins, Steve. *Prehistoric Actual Size.* Houghton Mifflin, 2005. / Jenkins, Steve. *What Do You Do When Something Wants to Eat You?* Houghton Mifflin, 1997. / Jenkins, Steve, and Robin Page. *What Do You Do With a Tail Like This?* Houghton Mifflin, 2003.
SUBJECTS: ANIMALS. COLOR.

[J*] | | | | |
The Long Gone Lonesome History of Country Music. Bertholf, Bret. Illus. by the author. Little, Brown, 2007.
     {ISBN 978-0-316-52393-6; 58p.} 781.642 (Gr. 3-6)
From back in the days of the early 1900s when, if people wanted music, they had to make it themselves, folks invented country music. Even if you think you don't care about country music, this rip-roaring, rib-tickling, never-been-done overview for kids will send you out looking for Hank Williams records for sure. Painter, writer, musician Bret Bertholf has put together a collection of ruminations on the history, styles, and stars of country music, with unforgettable old-timey illustrations done with colored pencil and Caran d'Ache crayon on Canson pastel paper. Why do you need to know this? Because the pictures are so personable and full of stuff to look at, you'll be smitten. Read first-person profiles of stars Minnie Pearl, Bob Wills, Hank Williams, Patsy Cline, and Bill Monroe. See how the times, from the Depression to WWII to the Vietnam War changed the music. And see if you don't change your radio dial to hear some of that music firsthand.
GERM: You'll find a page on how to yodel. Play a CD of Jimmie Rogers and give it a try. Learn about clothing, country pets (including the squeezal), country vee-hickles, and a vocabulary list of country words. Read that list to your kids and see how many of them they know. There's even a big alphabetical list of country nicknames so you can put together your own moniker. (Mine is Skeeter Gatorface!) Most of all, play some music by the stars profiled for everyone to hear.
RELATED TITLES: Aliki. *Ah, Music!* HarperCollins, 2003. / Igus, Toyomi, comp. *I See the Rhythm.* Children's Book Press, 1998. / Krull, Kathleen. *I Hear America Singing!: Folk Songs for American Families.* Knopf, 2003. / Krull, Kathleen. *Lives of the Musicians.* Harcourt, 1993. / Krull, Kathleen. *M Is for Music.* Harcourt, 2003. / Marsalis, Wynton. *Jazz A.B.Z.: An A to Z Collection of Jazz Portraits.* Candlewick, 2005. / Wargin, Kathy-jo. *M Is for Melody: A Music Alphabet.* Sleeping Bear, 2004.
SUBJECTS: COUNTRY MUSIC. MUSIC. MUSICIANS. U.S.—HISTORY—20TH CENTURY.

NONFICTION BOOKS, cont.

[J] |A| | | |
The Many Rides of Paul Revere. **Giblin, James Cross. Illus. with reprods. Scholastic, 2007. {ISBN 978-0-439-57290-3; 85p.} B (Gr. 4-7)**

Get to know the man behind the legend and the famous ride in a clearly written and handsomely laid out biography illustrated with stately brown-toned paintings, reproductions, maps, and photographs. As an apprentice to his French-born father, a master silversmith, Paul learned the family trade but also served in the Massachusetts militia alongside the British during the French and Indian War, and then became enmeshed in politics with the leading thinkers of Boston. The most compelling chapters deal with Paul's involvement as "The Messenger for the Revolution."

GERM: Appended is the famed poem by Henry Wadsworth Longfellow, "Paul Revere's Ride," and a comparison between the events as Revere lived them and the liberties taken in the poem. Next is a detailed timeline of his life; a map of Boston with an annotated list of sites to visit in Boston, Charlestown, Lexington, and Concord; an annotated bibliography; and a thorough index. Grand for reports, this will also be a fine book to pair with Robert Lawson's classic fiction book, ***Mr. Revere and I***, as told by his faithful horse, Scheherazade.

RELATED TITLES: Forbes, Esther. *America's Paul Revere.* Houghton Mifflin, 1974. / Fradin, Dennis Brindell. *Let It Begin Here!: Lexington and Concord: First Battles of the American Revolution.* Walker, 2005. / Fritz, Jean. *And Then What Happened, Paul Revere?* Coward, 1998. / Krensky, Stephen. *Paul Revere's Midnight Ride.* HarperCollins, 2002. / Lawson, Robert. *Mr. Revere and I.* Little, Brown, 1988, c1953. / Longfellow, Henry Wadsworth. *The Midnight Ride of Paul Revere.* Illus. by Christopher Bing. Handprint, 2001. / Longfellow, Henry Wadsworth. *Paul Revere's Ride.* Illus. by Ted Rand. Dutton, 1990. / Longfellow, Henry Wadsworth. *Paul Revere's Ride: The Landlord's Tale.* Illus. by Charles Santore. HarperCollins, 2003. / Minor, Wendall. *Yankee Doodle America: The Spirit of 1776 from A to Z.* Putnam, 2006. / Murphy, Jim. *A Young Patriot: The American Revolution as Experienced by One Boy.* Clarion, 1996. / Smith, Lane. *John, Paul, George & Ben.* Hyperion, 2006.
SUBJECTS: BIOGRAPHY. REVERE, PAUL. U.S.—HISTORY—REVOLUTION, 1775-1783.

[J*] |A| | |S|
Nic Bishop Spiders. **Bishop, Nic. Photos. by the author. Scholastic, 2007. {ISBN 978-0-439-87756-5; 48p.} 595.4 (Gr. K-6) Sibert Honor**

Even the squeamish and the spider-phobic will be awed by the oversized color photographs of spiders in their habitats, including the largest (the Goliath birdeater tarantula from South America), all taken by master photographer Nic Bishop. Find out, through his clear descriptive prose and dramatic close-up photos and captions, how spiders catch and poison their prey, shed their skins, spin webs, defend themselves from enemies, mate, lay eggs, and look after their young. In the afterword, Bishop explains how he took his remarkable photos of more than a dozen types of spiders, some of which he shot on location, and some of which he raised at home. Look at his photo on the back flap to see how he immersed himself in this project.

GERM: This type of descriptive nonfiction makes a fascinating read-aloud or read alone, and will lead spider fans to other spider books in the 595.4 shelves. For instance, those intrigued by the tarantulas will also be wowed by Sy Montgomery's more detailed book, ***The Tarantula Scientist***, from the topnotch "Scientists in the Field" series, with photos by—Nic Bishop! See the worksheet, "How Much Do You Know About Spiders," on page 187, to try with your students as a pre- and post-reading activity. For numerous spider activities to try with primary grade children, take a look at <**www.mrspohlmeyerskinderpage.com/spiders.htm**> and
<**www.zoomdinosaurs.com/themes/spiders.shtml**>.
RELATED TITLES: Berger, Melvin. *Spinning Spiders.* HarperCollins, 2003. / Cronin, Doreen. *Diary of a Spider.* HarperCollins, 2005. / Hoberman, Mary Ann. *The Eensy-Weensy Spider.* Little, Brown, 2000. / Jenkins, Steve. *Actual Size.* Houghton Mifflin, 2005. / Markle, Sandra. *Spiders: Biggest! Littlest!* Boyds Mills, 2004. / Montgomery, Sy. *The Tarantula Scientist.* Houghton Mifflin, 2004. / Murawski, Darlyne A. *Spiders and Their Webs.* National Geographic, 2004. / Raffi. *Spider on the Floor.* Crown, 1993. / Simon, Seymour. *Spiders.* Smithsonian/Collins, 2007. / Trapani, Iza. *The Itsy Bitsy Spider.* Whispering Coyote, 1993. / Tyson, Leigh Ann. *An Interview with Harry the Tarantula.* National Geographic, 2003.
SUBJECTS: ANIMALS. SPIDERS.

[J*] | |B| | |

Pocket Babies and Other Marsupials. **Collard, Sneed B., III. Illus. with photos. Darby Creek, 2007. {ISBN 978-1-58196-046-4; 72p.} 599.2 (Gr. 3-7)**

"Marveling at Marsupials," is the first of many lively chapter headings, and that's what you will do when you pore over the amiable narrative, fascinating descriptions, astonishing facts, and plethora of color photos of that third group of mammals, the metatherians. It's all here: contents page; charts; maps; a clean, attractive layout; quotes from experts in the field; phonetic pronunciations of difficult words; a "For Further Reading" annotated list of books and Web sites for children; extensive bibliography ; glossary, and index. Collard raised a baby opossum as a boy, and his delight in the subject reverberates on every page.

GERM: Excellent for reports and for pleasure reading for kangaroo-lovers, it'll make a welcome companion to Sy Montgomery's ***Quest for the Tree Kangaroo: An Expedition to the Cloud Forest of New Guinea.***

RELATED TITLES: Collard, Sneed B. *Birds of Prey: A Look at Daytime Raptors.* Franklin Watts, 1999. / Collard, Sneed B. *The Prairie Builders: Reconstructing America's Lost Grasslands.* Houghton Mifflin, 2005. / Montgomery, Sy. *Quest for the Tree Kangaroo: An Expedition to the Cloud Forest of New Guinea.* Houghton Mifflin, 2006.

SUBJECTS: ANIMALS—INFANCY. MARSUPIALS.

[J*] | | | | |

A Seed Is Sleepy. **Aston, Dianna. Illus. by Sylvia Long. Chronicle, 2007. {ISBN 978-0-8118-5520-4; unp.} 581.4 (Gr. PreK-4)**

"A seed is sleepy. It lies there, tucked inside its flower, on its cone, or beneath the soil. Snug. Still." That's a lovely, sleepy way to start. The beautiful accompanying watercolor shows the head of a spent sunflower, its black and white seeds nestled in the papery head, a few spilled into the dirt below. Find out about all sorts of seeds, their attributes, and bits of facts about them, along with pages of graceful, delectable labeled watercolors depicting more than three dozen fruits, vegetables, flowers, and trees. Did you know the seed of a redwood, the world's tallest tree, is as small as a freckle? Or that the coco de mer palm seed is the largest seed, sometimes weighing more than 60 pounds? The orchid is the smallest, with maybe a million seeds in one pod.

GERM: You'll finish this stately nonfiction picture book, the companion to ***An Egg Is Quiet***, with a starting background of seeds (and, maybe, a hunger for sunflower seeds). If you don't have a seed lesson in your curriculum, it'll make you want to plan one anyway. Need an extra excuse to read this aloud? Look at all the lovely adjectives, one per page, for a grammar lesson.

RELATED TITLES: Aston, Dianna. *An Egg Is Quiet.* Chronicle, 2006. / Cherry, Lynne. *How Groundhog's Garden Grew.* Scholastic, 2003. / Coy, John. *Two Old Potatoes and Me.* Knopf, 2003. / Ehlert, Lois. *Eating the Alphabet: Fruits and Vegetables from A to Z.* Harcourt, 1989. / Ehlert, Lois. *Growing Vegetable Soup.* Harcourt, 1987. / Gibbons, Gail. *From Seed to Plant.* Holiday House, 1991. / Gibbons, Gail. *The Vegetables We Eat.* Holiday House, 2007. / Hall, Zoe. *It's Pumpkin Time!* Scholastic, 1994. / Krauss, Ruth. *The Carrot Seed.* HarperCollins, 1945. / Morgan, Pierr. *The Turnip.* Philomel, 1990. / Oppenheim, Joanne. *Have You Seen Trees?* Scholastic, 1995. / Peck, Jan. *The Giant Carrot.* Dial, 1998. / Pfeffer, Wendy. *From Seed to Pumpkin.* HarperCollins, 2004. / Schaefer, Lola M. *Pick, Pull, Snap!: Where Once a Flower Bloomed.* HarperCollins, 2003. / Sloat, Teri. *Patty's Pumpkin Patch.* Putnam, 1999. / Stevens, Janet. *Tops & Bottoms.* Harcourt, 1995.

SUBJECTS: ENGLISH LANGUAGE—ADJECTIVES. FLOWERS. PLANTS. SCIENCE. SEEDS. TREES.

[J] | |B| | |

Strong Man: The Story of Charles Atlas. **McCarthy, Meghan. Illus. by the author. Knopf, 2007. {ISBN 978-0-375-92940-3; unp.} B (Gr. 1-5)**

While this is indeed a picture book biography of the famed bodybuilder, Charles Atlas, the Author's Note states that in researching his life, finding out facts about his personal and not just public persona was nigh impossible. Over the years, Atlas has become something of a legend or a folk hero. Born Angelo Siciliano, he came to Ellis Island with his parents from Italy, settled in Brooklyn, and got beat up a lot. On a date at the beach, he says he was humiliated when a man actually kicked sand in his face. He tried to bulk up by lifting weights; it didn't help. Observing a lion stretch at the zoo, Angelo recalled, "The muscles ran around like rabbits under a rug." He then devised a new fitness routine, pitting one muscle against another. Pretty soon he was strong as an ox, and his friends nicknamed him Charles Atlas, after the Greek god. As a strongman at Coney Island, he tore phone books in half, bent iron bars with his bare hands, and was ultimately crowned "The World's Most Perfectly Developed Man." An inspiration for all us flab-filled folks, this amiable account with winsome bug-eyed folks rendered in acrylics is by the same author who gave us last year's terrific ***Aliens Are Coming!: The True Account Of The 1938 War Of The Worlds Radio Broadcast***.

GERM: At the back of the book are four illustrated "Try It Yourself!" exercises for a split jump, mini squat, push-up on knees, and downward dog. It's never too late to build that body. Read aloud the Author's Note to see more about Atlas, including a very hunky black and white photo of him in a bathing suit. Wow. Time to work on those abs . . . Go to his website, <**www.charlesatlas.com**> and you can still order his fitness program. And at <**www.sandowplus.co.uk/Competition/Atlas/atlasindex.htm**> you'll find wonderful articles by and photos of the man himself. See how boxers and wrestlers get in shape in Brooklyn, New York at the most famous boxing gym in the world in Ted Lewin's gritty picture book profile ***At Gleason's Gym***.

RELATED TITLES: Buehner, Caralyn. *Superdog: The Heart of a Hero.* HarperCollins, 2004. / Lewin, Ted. *At Gleason's Gym.* Roaring Brook, 2007. / McCarthy, Meghan. *Aliens Are Coming!: The True Account Of The 1938 War Of The Worlds Radio Broadcast.* Knopf, 2006.

SUBJECTS: ATLAS, CHARLES, 1893-1972. BIOGRAPHY. BODYBUILDERS. EXERCISE. ITALIAN AMERICANS—BIOGRAPHY. PHYSICAL FITNESS. SPORTS. STRONG MEN.

[J] |A| | | |

Vulture View. **Sayre, April Pulley. Illus. by Steve Jenkins. Henry Holt, 2007. {ISBN 978-0-8050-7557-1; unp.} 598.9 (Gr. PreK-2) Geisel Honor**

Open this sweeping, soaring overview of turkey vultures and you'll sigh, it's so gorgeous. You never thought you'd care about those scavengers, but the combination of the poetic text and Steve Jenkins's magnificent cut paper collages against a deep blue sky will make you gasp. Watch the turkey vultures as they "sniff, search, seek / for foods that . . . reek. . . Vultures like a mess. They land and dine. Rotten is fine."

GERM: At the end you'll find a detailed "Get to Know Vultures" section, including the Turkey Vulture Society's website at <**www.vulturesociety.homestead.com**>.

RELATED TITLES: Bash, Barbara. *Urban Roosts: Where Birds Nest in the City.* Little, Brown, 1990. / Blake, Robert J. *Fledgling.* Philomel, 2000. / Cowcher, Helen. *Whistling Thorn.* Scholastic, 1993. / Davies, Nicola. *White Owl, Barn Owl.* Candlewick, 2007. / Demuth, Patricia Brennan. *Cradles in the Trees: The Story of Bird Nests.* Macmillan, 1994. / Florian, Douglas. *On the Wing: Bird Poems and Paintings.* Harcourt, 1996. / Franco, Betsy. *Birdsongs.* McElderry, 2007. / Sayre, April Pulley. *If You Should Hear a Honey Guide.* Houghton Mifflin, 1995. / Schaefer, Lola M. *Arrowhawk.* Henry Holt, 2004. / Yolen, Jane. *Bird Watch: A Book of Poetry.* Philomel, 1990. / Yolen, Jane. *Wild Wings: Poems for Young People.* Wordsong/Boyds Mills, 2002.

SUBJECTS: BIRDS. TURKEY VULTURES. VULTURES.

NONFICTION BOOKS, cont.

[J*] |A|B|H|S|

The Wall: Growing Up Behind the Iron Curtain. Sís, Peter. Illus. by the author. Frances Foster, 2007. {ISBN 978-0-374-34701-7; unp.} 943.7 (Gr. 4-12) **Caldecott Honor and Sibert Medal**

Award-winning children's book author and illustrator Peter Sís grew up in Prague, Czechoslovakia after World War II, and came to the U.S. in the 1970s. This remarkable autobiographical picture book, told in the third person, is about the making of an artist in a place where creativity was discouraged, free thought was considered dangerous and subversive, and the Soviet Union controlled the government and its citizens. There are two stories intertwined here; the text at the bottom of the page is a simply told description of an unnamed boy's passion for art as he grows up. On the margins of the paneled illustrations are captions that list the many restrictions, ordered by the Czech government, that governed his life. Sís's tiny crosshatched pen and inks start out mostly monochromatic, with touches of red flags and neckerchiefs to show the uniformity imposed on people. From drawing what he was told in school and not questioning the status quo, his life was transformed. The catalyst? The Beatles. Suddenly everyone wanted to be a rock star and grow long hair. Prague Spring of 1968 promised freedom, but then came the tanks. Interspersed in the narrative are double-pages of chronological excerpts from Sís's own journals, from 1954-1968; the Introduction and Afterword fill in still more details.

GERM: For explaining the difference between a democratic society and a dictatorship, Sís's book is extraordinary. Google the following words—YouTube Peter Sis The Wall—and watch the remarkable little movie Sís made about the book. Compare and contrast the differences of growing up in Prague back then and America now. **_Revolution Is Not a Dinner Party_** by Ying Chang Compestine and **_Red Scarf Girl_** by Ji Li Jiang are about growing up at in the same era in another totalitarian society, China, during its repressive Cultural Revolution.

RELATED TITLES: Compestine, Ying Chang. _Revolution Is Not a Dinner Party: A Novel._ Henry Holt, 2007. / Jiang, Ji Li. _Red Scarf Girl: A Memoir of the Cultural Revolution._ HarperCollins, 1997. / Sís, Peter. _Madlenka's Dog._ Farrar, 2002. / Sís, Peter. _Starry Messenger: Galileo Galilei._ Farrar, 1996. / Sís, Peter. _Tibet: Through the Red Box._ Farrar, 1998. / Sís, Peter. _The Tree of Life: A Book Depicting the Life of Charles Darwin, Naturalist, Geologist & Thinker._ Farrar, 2003.

SUBJECTS: AUTHORS. AUTOBIOGRAPHY. BIOGRAPHY. COMMUNISM. CZECH AMERICANS. CZECHOSLOVAKIA. ILLUSTRATORS. PICTURE BOOKS FOR OLDER READERS. SÍS, PETER. TOTALITARIANISM.

[j] |A|B|H|S|

Who Was First?: Discovering the Americas. Freedman, Russell. Illus. with photos and reprods. Clarion, 2007. {ISBN 978-0-618-66391-0; 88p.} 970.01 (Gr. 5-9)

Freedman's latest history book is filled with surprising facts and is beautifully designed with glossy pages, color reproductions, paintings, maps, and photographs. In looking at Columbus and other explorers who sailed the seas and perhaps visited the Americas before Columbus, it's thrilling to consider that Asians may have crossed the Pacific as long as 3,000 years ago. One of my favorite facts in the text is that Zheng He, the Chinese admiral who was said to be over seven feet tall and was also known as Sin-Bao, inspired the legend of Sinbad the Sailor, based on the seven epic voyages he led with his fleet from 1405 to 1433. Other chapters deal with Leif the Lucky, the various civilizations living in the Americas before Columbus and Cortés showed up, and new speculations about the earliest migrants to the Americas between 20,000 and 30,000 years ago.

GERM: Insightful readers will find the level of inquiry in this text to be challenging, as Freedman states and then disputes many popular views about the people who may have reached or settled in the Americas. Another fascinating book that covers some of the same material is Don Wulffson's **_Before Columbus: Early Voyages to the Americas_**.

RELATED TITLES: Freedman, Russell. _Buffalo Hunt._ Holiday House, 1988. / Freedman, Russell. _Children of the Wild West._ Clarion, 1983. / Freedman, Russell. _Immigrant Kids._ Dutton, 1980. / Freedman, Russell. _Lincoln: A Photobiography._ Clarion, 1987. / Freedman, Russell. _The Wright Brothers: How They Invented the Airplane._ Holiday House, 1991. / Higgins, Nadia. _Columbus and the Age of Explorers._ Rourke, 2007. / Kimmel, Elizabeth Cody. _The Look-It-Up Book of Explorers._ Random House, 2004. / Weintraub, Aileen. _Vikings: Raiders and Explorers._ Children's Press, 2005. / Wilkinson, Philip. _Explorers._ Kingfisher, 2002. / Wulffson, Don. _Before Columbus: Early Voyages to the Americas._ Twenty-First Century, 2008.

SUBJECTS: AMERICA—DISCOVERY AND EXPLORATION. EXPLORERS.

POETRY AND FOLKLORE

[j] |A| |H| |

***The Bearskinner: A Tale of the Brothers Grimm.* Schlitz, Laura Amy. Illus. by Max Grafe. Candlewick, 2007. {ISBN 978-0-7636-2730-0; unp.} 398.2 (Gr. 3-6)**

In an elegant retelling, with dark earth-toned mixed-media illustrations, a hungry soldier makes a deal with the devil in exchange for gold. For seven years, the man must wear the skin of a bear and neither wash nor pray or the devil will gain his soul. In a twist on the "Beauty and the Beast" theme, the filthy and odiferous soldier is promised in marriage to a gambler's daughter who believes he has a good heart.

GERM: Discussion Points: Look at the quote at the start of the story: "They say that when a man gives up hope, the devil walks at his side." What does this mean? What does the soldier accept the devil's bargain? Why do people reject the soldier? How does he redeem himself? Why does the gambler's daughter wait for him? Compare and contrast this pensive tale with Beauty and the Beast. In Howard Pyle's literary fairy tale, ***Bearskin***, a young man raised by a bear slays a dragon to win the hand of a princess. Natalie Babbit's ***Ouch***, based on another Grimm story "The Devil and His Grandmother," is far more lighthearted.

RELATED TITLES: Babbitt, Natalie. *Ouch: A Tale from Grimm.* HarperCollins, 1998. / Grimm, Jacob. *The Bearskinner.* Illus. by Felix Hoffman. Atheneum, 1978. / Hooks, William H. *Snowbear Whittington: An Appalachian Beauty and the Beast.* Macmillan, 1994. / Huck, Charlotte. *The Black Bull of Norroway: A Scottish Tale.* Greenwillow, 2001. / Mayer, Marianna. *Beauty and the Beast.* Four Winds, 1978. / Pyle, Howard. *Bearskin.* Morrow, 1997. / Ray, Jane. *Twelve Dancing Princesses.* Dutton, 1996. / Schlitz, Laura Amy. *A Drowned Maiden's Hair: A Melodrama.* Candlewick, 2006. / Schlitz, Laura Amy. *Good Masters! Sweet Ladies!: Voices from a Medieval Village.* Candlewick, 2007.

SUBJECTS: BEARS—FOLKLORE. DEVIL—FOLKLORE. FAIRY TALES. FOLKLORE—GERMANY. SOLDIERS—FOLKLORE.

[J] | | |H|S|

***Beowulf: A Hero's Tale Retold.* Rumford, James. Illus. by the author. Houghton Mifflin, 2007. {ISBN 978-0-618-75637-7; unp.} 398.2 (Gr. 3-8)**

Rumford's skillful retelling and distillation of the ninth century hero poem, Beowulf, is elemental enough for even third graders to comprehend. And what a saga it is. With his bare hands, the stalwart young knight Beowulf rips off the arm of the ogre Grendel, kills Grendel's evil mother, and, many years later, as King of the Geats, meets his end fighting and defeating a flying fire-snake. Rumford's pen and ink and watercolor illustrations, inspired by the works of Arthur Rackham and Edmond Dulac, are a visual feast, infused as they are with two pretty creepy green monsters who rise up from the marshes and an orange dragon that lurks outside of the page borders.

GERM: In his Author's Note, the author explains how, with the exception of three Old Norse words—they, their, and them—he used only worlds that can be traced back to the Old English, a language also called Anglo-Saxon. Online, you'll find many bits of side-by-side translations you can print out and audio clips of readings in Anglo-Saxon, including Ben Slade's site, <www.beowulftranslations.net/benslade.shtml>. Children will be amazed to find they can't understand a word of it.

RELATED TITLES: Farmer, Nancy. *The Sea of Trolls.* Atheneum, 2004. / Hastings, Selena. *Gawain and the Green Knight.* Lothrop, 1981. / Hastings, Selena. *Sir Gawain and the Loathly Lady.* Lothrop, 1985. / Hayes, Sarah. *Robin Hood.* Henry Holt, 1989. / Henderson, Kathy. *Lugalbanda: The Boy Who Got Caught Up in a War.* Candlewick, 2006. / Hinds, Gareth. *Beowulf.* Candlewick, 2007. / Hodges, Margaret. *Saint George and the Dragon.* Little, Brown, 1984. / Kimmel, Eric A. *The Hero Beowulf.* Farrar, 2005. / McCaughrean, Geraldine. *Gilgamesh the Hero: The Epic of Gilgamesh.* Eerdmans, 2003. / Morpurgo, Michael. *Beowulf.* Candlewick, 2006. / Morpurgo, Michael. *Sir Gawain & the Green Knight.* Candlewick, 2004. / Osborne, Mary Pope. *Favorite Medieval Tales.* Scholastic, 1998. / Sabuda, Robert. *Arthur and the Sword.* Atheneum, 1995. / San Souci, Robert D. *Young Arthur.* Doubleday, 1997. / Shannon, Mark. *Gawain and the Green Knight.* Putnam, 1994. / Talbott, Hudson. *King Arthur and the Round Table.* Morrow, 1995.

SUBJECTS: ADVENTURE AND ADVENTURERS—FOLKLORE. BEOWULF. FOLKLORE—ENGLAND. MONSTERS—FOLKLORE.

[J] |A| | |S|

Blue Lipstick: Concrete Poems. **Grandits, John. Illus. by the author. Clarion, 2007. {ISBN 978-0-618-56860-4; unp.} 811 (Gr. 5-9)**

You might have read the uproarious book, ***Technically It's Not My Fault: Concrete Poems***, narrated by Robert, who complains a lot about his annoying big sister, Jessie. Now it's Jessie's turn to snipe. She's in ninth grade, so she has lots more to agonize over: bad hair days, pep rallies, liking Elton Simpson, and, of course, her jerky little brother. Emotions erupt in 33 shape poems that meander and cascade across each page in a swirl of blue and black fonts. There's "A Chart of My Emotional Day," which she does for a math assignment, "Volleyball Practice" with sentences that bounce back and forth on the page, and "My Absolutely Bad Cranky Day," a simply glorious alphabet and timeline combined. How Grandits, a man, has gotten under the skin of a ninth grader with such resonance, honesty, and humor, I can't fathom, but if you were ever a ninth grade girl, you'll marvel. And if you weren't, you'll learn a lot.

GERM: To get the full effect of Grandits's books with your kids, you'll need to photocopy some pages and make transparencies of others. Collaborate with the art teacher and the computer teacher to integrate the art with the poetry, because your students are going to be full of ideas for composing concrete poems about their own experiences, both hideous and hilarious.

RELATED TITLES: Grandits, John. *Technically, It's Not My Fault: Concrete Poems.* Clarion, 2004. / Janeczko, Paul B. *A Kick in the Head: An Everyday Guide to Poetic Forms.* Candlewick, 2005. / Janeczko, Paul B. *A Poke in the I: A Collection of Concrete Poems.* Candlewick, 2001. / Lewis, J. Patrick. *Doodle Dandies: Poems that Take Shape.* Atheneum, 1998. / Stevenson, James. *Popcorn.* Greenwillow, 1998. (And others in the Corn series.)

SUBJECTS: BROTHERS AND SISTERS. HUMOROUS POETRY. PERSONAL NARRATIVES. POETRY—SINGLE AUTHOR. POINT OF VIEW—POETRY. SCHOOLS.

[J] | | |H| |

Comets, Stars, the Moon, and Mars: Space Poems and Paintings. **Florian, Douglas. Illus. by the author. Harcourt, 2007. {ISBN 978-0-15-205372-7; unp.} 811 (Gr. K-6)**

Studying astronomy? Even dusty old planets are poem-worthy, as the esteemed punmaster Douglas Florian proves with his tribute to the orbs in our solar system and beyond. His artwork is extraordinary here, incorporating die cut holes in each double page spread of swirling colors, actually done with gouache, collage, and rubber stamps on primed brown paper bags. His 20 poems will be understood by your youngest students, but witty enough to impress older ones, too. ("Mars is red, / And Mars is rusty, / Sandy, rocky, / Very dusty. / Mars has ice caps. / Once had streams. / Mars has Martians . . . / In your dreams!")

GERM: Read each poem aloud several times. Ask listeners to look for facts and wordplay, if you're planning on having them write new science-based poems. You could hand out a copy of one poem per pair and stage a scintillating reading, scientifically speaking.

RELATED TITLES: Florian, Douglas. *Bow Wow Meow Meow: It's Rhyming Cats and Dogs.* Harcourt, 2003. / Florian, Douglas. *Omnibeasts: Animal Poems and Paintings.* Harcourt, 2004. / Florian, Douglas. *Summersaults: Poems & Paintings.* Greenwillow, 2002. / McNulty, Faith. *If You Decide to Go to the Moon.* Scholastic, 2005. / Reeve, Philip. *Larklight.* Bloomsbury, 2006. / Todd, Traci N. *A Is for Astronaut: Exploring Space from A to Z.* Chronicle, 2006.

SUBJECTS: ASTRONOMY—POETRY. OUTER SPACE—POETRY. POETRY—SINGLE AUTHOR.

POETRY AND FOLKLORE, cont.

[J] | | | | |

Dogku. **Clements, Andrew. Illus. by Tim Bowers. Simon & Schuster, 2007. {ISBN 978-0-689-85823-9; unp.} 811 (Gr. PreK-4)**

A synopsis: Stray dog on the porch. / Mom and three kids fall for him, / Though he makes a mess. Will dad let the sweet little scraggly white mutt they name Mooch stay after he chews the laundry and trashes the kitchen? Seventeen haiku (one for each syllable in a haiku?) take us from the pup's appearance on the back porch to his settling in for the long haul. Sweet and soulful full bleed oil paintings will make listeners go home and demand a dog.

GERM: Check out Clements's Author's Note where he talks about haiku and why he used them in this book: "Adorable dog + haiku = Dogku. Simple." As will be the haiku your kids write and illustrate about their own pets or pets-to-be.

RELATED TITLES: Coffelt, Nancy. *Fred Stays with Me!* Little, Brown, 2007. / Crowley, Dave. *Cat Poems.* Wordsong/Boyds Mills, 2005. / Crowley, Dave. *Dog Poems.* Wordsong/Boyds Mills, 2007. / George, Kristine O'Connell. *Hummingbird Nest: A Journal of Poems.* Harcourt, 2004. / George, Kristine O'Connell. *Little Dog Poems.* Clarion, 1999. / Graham, Bob. *"Let's Get a Pup!" Said Kate.* Candlewick, 2001. / Grimes, Nikki. *When Gorilla Goes Walking.* Orchard, 2007. / Katz, Susan. *Oh, Theodore: Guinea Pig Poems.* Clarion, 2007. / Kirk, Daniel. *Cat Power!* Hyperion, 2007. / Kirk, Daniel. *Dogs Rule!* Hyperion, 2007. / McFarland, Lyn Rossiter. *Widget.* Farrar, 2001. / Prelutsky, Jack. *If Not for the Cat.* Greenwillow, 2004. / Simont, Marc. *The Stray Dog.* HarperCollins, 2001.

SUBJECTS: DOGS—POETRY. FAMILY LIFE—POETRY. HAIKU. POETRY—SINGLE AUTHOR.

[J*] | | | | |

Glass Slipper, Gold Sandal: A Worldwide Cinderella. **Fleischman, Paul. Illus. by Julie Paschkis. Henry Holt, 2007. {ISBN 978-0-8050-7953-1; unp.} 398.2 (Gr. K-6)**

Taking bits and pieces, motifs, and descriptions from 17 Cinderella variants worldwide, Fleischman offers up a composite story, a melting pot of Cinderellas. The busy paneled gouache paintings look like folk art stencils, and each one reflects its country of origin. Cinderella dresses in a sarong of gold (Indonesia), with a cloak of kingfisher feathers (China), and sandals of gold (Iraq). The man of her dreams is, alternately, a prince, a king, and even a magistrate (Korea), all searching for the girl who fits the shoe.

GERM: Have your globe handy to pinpoint each of the countries identified in the illustrations. Pair it with a French version of the story, such as Barbara McClintock's ***Cinderella***, which is how we know it best. Compare and contrast variations in the story, including the major characters (the girl, the boy, the fairy godmother), the setting, the plot, the motifs (the clothes, the transformations, the lost shoe, the party), the climax, and the resolution. You'll find detailed abstracts of 345 Cinderella variants, dozens of reproductions of classic illustrations, and cover art of scores of children's books of the story at the Web site Surlalune Fairy Tales: <**www.surlalunefairytales.com/cinderella/index.html**>. ***If the Shoe Fits: Voices from Cinderella*** by Laura Whipple, told in free verse, examines the story from each character's vantage point. Go to the "Looking at Cinderella" page in this handbook on page 191 to make a list of the elements children can compare and contrast after reading versions of the Cinderella story from other lands. For the craziest retelling of all, read aloud "Prinderella and the Cince" on page 195.

RELATED TITLES: Climo, Shirley. *The Egyptian Cinderella.* Crowell, 1989. / Climo, Shirley. *The Irish Cinderlad.* HarperCollins, 1996. / Climo, Shirley. *The Persian Cinderella.* HarperCollins, 1999. / Craft, K. Y. *Cinderella.* SeaStar Books, 2000. / Han, Oki S., and Stephanie Plunkett. *Kongi and Potgi: A Cinderella Story from Korea.* Dial, 1996. / Hickox, Rebecca. *The Golden Sandal: A Middle Eastern Cinderella Story.* Holiday House, 1998. / Hooks, William H. *Moss Gown.* Clarion, 1987. / Louie, Ai-Ling. *Yeh-Shen: A Cinderella Story from China.* Philomel, 1982. / McClintock, Barbara. *Cinderella.* Scholastic, 2005. / Pollock, Penny. *The Turkey Girl: A Zuni Cinderella Story.* Little, Brown, 1996. / San Souci, Robert D. *Cendrillon: A Caribbean Cinderella.* Simon & Schuster, 1998. / Sierra, Judy. *Cinderella.* Oryx, 1992. / Sierra, Judy. *The Gift of the Crocodile: A Cinderella Story.* Simon & Schuster, 2000. / Wilson, Barbara Ker. *Wishbones: A Folk Tale from China.* Bradbury, 1993.

SUBJECTS: CINDERELLA STORIES. FAIRY TALES. MULTICULTURAL BOOKS—FOLKLORE. STEPMOTHERS—FOLKLORE.

POETRY AND FOLKLORE, cont.

[J*] |A|B| |S|

***Good Masters! Sweet Ladies!: Voices from a Medieval Village.* Schlitz, Laura Amy. Illus. by Robert Byrd. Candlewick, 2007. {ISBN 978-0-7636-1578-9; 85p.} 812.6 (Gr. 5-9) Newbery Medal Winner**

Baltimore school librarian, storyteller, and playwright Laura Amy Schlitz, author of last year's novel, *A Drowned Maiden's Hair* and the biography *The Hero Schliemann: The Dreamer Who Dug For Troy* is proving quite the the Renaissance woman. What's the connection between these books with her new one? A passion for history. When her students were studying the Middle Ages, she set to writing 17 short monologues so each child could have a decent part. It evolved into this collection of 22 narratives, some rhyming, some free verse, told by the children living by an English manor in 1255. There's Taggot the blacksmith's daughter, shoeing a horse for Hugo, Sir Steven's dazzling nephew; Alice the shepherdess who sings to her favorite sheep Jilly to keep her from dying after birthing a stillborn lamb; and Thomas the doctor's son, who is learning his father's trade. ("A healthy man is careless with a bill— / You have to make them pay when they are ill.") A running glossary in the margins defines difficult words and concepts. Interspersed throughout are double page spreads—"A Little Background"—on more complex matters including medieval pilgrimage, the Crusades, and Jews in Medieval Society. Delicate ink and watercolor illustrations give the book the priceless feel of an illuminated manuscript.

GERM: Of course you can photocopy and hand out a monologue to each student to practice and read aloud. Booktalk other outstanding titles that give a realistic feel for medieval life in England, such as Avi's *Crispin: The Cross of Lead* and three treasures by Karen Cushman: *Catherine, Called Birdy*, *The Midwife's Apprentice*, and *Matilda Bone*.

RELATED TITLES: Avi. *Crispin: The Cross of Lead.* Hyperion, 2004. / Barrett, Tracy. *Anna of Byzantium.* Delacorte, 1999. / Cushman, Karen. *Catherine, Called Birdy.* Clarion,1994. / Cushman, Karen. *Matilda Bone.* Clarion, 2000. / Cushman, Karen. *The Midwife's Apprentice.* Clarion, 1995. / Osborne, Mary Pope. *Favorite Medieval Tales.* Hyperion, 2002. / Schlitz, Laura Amy. *The Bearskinner: A Tale of the Brothers Grimm.* Candlewick, 2006. / Schlitz, Laura Amy. *A Drowned Maiden's Hair: A Melodrama.* Candlewick, 2006. / Schlitz, Laura Amy. *The Hero Schliemann: The Dreamer Who Dug For Troy.* Candlewick, 2006. / Williams, Marcia, retel. *Chaucer's Canterbury Tales.* Candlewick, 2007.

SUBJECTS: MIDDLE AGES. MONOLOGUES. NEWBERY MEDAL. PLAYS. POETRY—SINGLE AUTHOR. POINT OF VIEW.

[J] |A|B| | |

***Here's a Little Poem: A Very First Book of Poetry.* Yolen, Jane, and Andrew Fusek Peters, eds. Illus. by Polly Dunbar. Candlewick, 2007. {ISBN 978-0-7636-3141-3; 108p.} 811.008 (Gr. PreK-1)**

This gathering of more than 60 poems from the U.S., Great Britain, the Caribbean, and Australia into one big luscious book is just the ticket for little ones. The poems are as simple and chantable as nursery rhymes, like Aileen Fisher's interactive verse which starts, "After my bath / I try, try, try / to wipe myself / till I'm dry, dry, dry." The oversized mixed media illustrations of red-cheeked little ones will put you in mind of early Sendak. There are poems about growing, bananas and cream, getting dressed, rain, and mud, mud, glorious mud. You'll know some poems and recognize some favorite poets like A. A. Milne, Jack Prelutsky, Charlotte Pomerantz, Michael Rosen, Dennis Lee, and Anonymous.

GERM: Not only is this a beautiful and joyous book to share aloud, over and over, it's a perfect present to give to the wee ones in your life, for it speaks to children about childhood, without being cloying or too adult.

RELATED TITLES: Crews, Nina. *The Neighborhood Mother Goose.* Greenwillow, 2004. / Denton, Kady MacDonald, comp. *A Child's Treasury of Nursery Rhymes.* Kingfisher, 1998. / DePaola, Tomie. *Tomie dePaola's Mother Goose.* Putnam, 1985. / Hoberman, Mary Ann. *The Llama Who Had No Pajama: 100 Favorite Poems.* Harcourt, 1998. / Hoberman, Mary Ann. *You Read to Me, I'll Read to You: Very Short Stories to Read Together.* Little, Brown, 2001. / Hopkins, Lee Bennett, comp. *Climb into My Lap: First Poems to Read Together.* Simon & Schuster, 1998. / Kennedy, Dorothy M., and X. J. Kennedy, comps. *Talking Like the Rain: A First Book of Poems.* Little, Brown, 1992. / Moore, Lillian, comp. *Sunflakes: Poems for Children.* Clarion, 1992. / Rosen, Michael, comp. *Poems for the Very Young.* Kingfisher, 1993.

SUBJECTS: POETRY—ANTHOLOGIES.

[J*] |A| | | |

How to Paint the Portrait of a Bird. Prévert, Jacques. Illus. by Mordicai Gerstein. Roaring Brook, 2007. {ISBN
    978-1-59643-215-4; unp.} 841 (Gr. K-6)

Waked by the singing of a bluebird on his windowsill, a dark-haired boy sets up a huge canvas and prepares to paint its portrait. First he paints a huge cage with an open door. Taking the unfinished picture to a park, he props the canvas against a tree and waits oh so patiently for the bird to enter the cage. From a poem written in 1949 by French poet Jacques Prévert, Caldecott Award–winning artist Gerstein has fashioned a most delectable picture book about imagination and dedication and creativity and the artistic process. In the original French, Prévert's poem rhymes, giving advice and step-by-step instructions to you, the painter. Gerstein's translation turns it into lyrical free verse and makes it more literal, with boy and bird portrayed in delicate pen and ink and watercolor paintings framed against a white background.

GERM: This book will get you looking at that procedural writing assignment with new eyes. How do you make a painting, compose a song, write a poem? Is the creative process anything like making a sandwich, building a birdhouse, or fixing a leaky faucet? If it's more birds you're looking for, there are 22 different types profiled in terrific and quirky poems and lighthearted full-page watercolors by Joan Rankin in Deborah Ruddel's ***Today at the Bluebird Café: A Branchful of Birds.***

RELATED TITLES: Beaumont, Karen. *I Ain't Gonna Paint No More.* Harcourt, 2005. / DePaola, Tomie. *The Art Lesson.* Putnam, 1989. / Franco, Betsy. *Birdsongs.* McElderry, 2007. / Gerstein, Mordicai. *Carolinda Clatter.* Roaring Brook, 2005. / Gerstein, Mordicai. *The Man Who Walked between the Towers.* Roaring Brook, 2003. / Gerstein, Mordicai. *What Charlie Heard: The Story of the Composer Charles Ives.* Farrar, 2002. / LaMarche, Jim. *The Raft.* HarperCollins, 2000. / Raczka, Bob. *Art Is . . . .* Millbrook, 2003. / Raczka, Bob. *No One Saw: Ordinary Things Through the Eyes of an Artist.* Millbrook, 2002. / Reynolds, Peter. *The Dot.* Candlewick, 2003. / Reynolds, Peter. *Ish.* Candlewick, 2004. / Ruddel, Deborah. *Today at the Bluebird Café: A Branchful of Birds.* McElderry, 2007. / Schwartz, Amy. *Begin at the Beginning: A Little Artist Learns About Life.* HarperCollins, 2005. / Sweet, Melissa. *Carmine: A Little More Red.* Houghton Mifflin, 2005.

SUBJECTS: BIRDS. CREATIVITY. PAINTING. POETRY—SINGLE AUTHOR. PROCEDURAL WRITING.

[J*] | | | | |

Knock, Knock! Illus. by Saxton Freymann and others. Dial, 2007. {ISBN 978-0-8037-3152-3; unp.} 818 (Gr.
    PreK-5)

Poetry employs language in surprising and innovative ways, one of which is clever wordplay. Don't be so quick to dismiss the silly stuff—jokes and riddles, puns, and tongue twisters. For children, these are their first taste of humor. If you can't understand a simple knock-knock joke, how will you ever get Shakespeare? In a companion volume to last year's ***Why Did the Chicken Cross the Road?***, 14 children's book artists were asked to supply and illustrate their favorite knock-knock jokes, with farcical results. Peter Reynolds offers "Lionel who?" Turn the page and there's a massive lion watching a boy trying to get inside: "Lion-el eat me if you don't open that door!" Contributors include Brett Helquist ("Ima who?"), Tomie dePaola ("Gorilla who?"), and Laurie Keller ("Impatient cow . . . MOO!").

GERM: At the back is an author's page (titled "Who do these artists want knocking at their doors?") with photos or self-portraits and a bit of info on each one. Use the book to ratchet up the humor level in your library, to introduce the joke and riddle sections, to look up biographical data on and locate books by each illustrator, and to perform or write your own knock-knock jokes for each other. Keep the wordplay coming with Gene Barretta's engaging ***Dear Deer: A Book of Homophones***, with cheerful watercolors illustrating sentences like, "The DOE KNEADED the DOUGH because she NEEDED the DOUGH."

RELATED TITLES: *The Art of Reading: Forty Illustrators Celebrate RIF's 40th Anniversary.* Dutton, 2005. / Barretta, Gene. *Dear Deer: A Book of Homophones.* Henry Holt, 2007. / Rosenbloom, Joseph. *The Funniest Knock-Knock Book Ever.* Sterling, 1986. / Rosenbloom, Joseph. *Knock Knock! Who's There?* Sterling, 1984. / *Why Did the Chicken Cross the Road?* Dial, 2006. / *Wings of an Artist: Children's Book Illustrators Talk About Their Art.* Abrams, 1999.

SUBJECTS: ARTISTS. JOKES. KNOCK-KNOCK JOKES. ILLUSTRATORS. PICTURE BOOKS FOR ALL AGES. RIDDLES.

[j] |A| | | |

Let It Shine: Three Favorite Spirituals. **Bryan, Ashley. Illus. by Ashley Bryan. Atheneum, 2007. {ISBN 978-0-689-84732-5; unp.} 782.25 (Gr. PreK-5) Coretta Scott King Illustrator Award**

Large, double-page, brightly colored cut paper collage illustrations accompany the verses of three spirituals: "This Little Light of Mine," "Oh, When the Saints Go Marching In," and "He's Got the Whole World in His Hands." Silhouettes of children and dramatic, almost psychedelic swirls of color pulse with energy. At the back, A Note from Ashley provides a bit of background on Spirituals, and the music is appended, too.

GERM: Sing the songs, of course. Then take a closer look, deconstructing each picture, looking at what Bryan chose to portray in the illustration of each song. Children can choose a new song and illustrate it. Meet the Jubilee Singers, a nineteenth century African American gospel group revered for their performances of spirituals, in Deborah Hopkinson's picture book, A Band of Angels.

RELATED TITLES: Bryan, Ashley. *All Night, All Day: A Child's First Book of African-American Spirituals.* Atheneum, 1991. / Bryan, Ashley. *Beautiful Blackbird.* Atheneum, 2003. / Cox, Judy. *My Family Plays Music.* Holiday House, 2003. / Hamilton, Virginia. *The People Could Fly: The Picture Book.* Knopf, 2004. / Hopkinson, Deborah. *A Band of Angels: A Story Inspired by the Jubilee Singers.* Atheneum,1999. / Krull, Kathleen. *M Is for Music.* Harcourt, 2003. / Levine, Ellen. *Henry's Freedom Box: A True Story.* Scholastic, 2007. / Ringgold, Faith. *Aunt Harriet's Underground Railroad in the Sky.* Crown, 1992. / Weatherford, Carole Boston. *Moses: When Harriet Tubman Led Her People to Freedom.* Hyperion/Jump at the Sun, 2006. / Winter, Jeannette. *Follow the Drinking Gourd.* Knopf, 1989. / Woodson, Jacqueline. *Show Way.* Putnam, 2005.

SUBJECTS: AFRICAN AMERICANS. HYMNS. MULTICULTURAL BOOKS. MUSIC. SONGS. SPIRITUALS.

[j] |A| | |S|

Little Red Riding Hood. **Pinkney, Jerry. Illus. by the author. Little, Brown, 2007. {ISBN 978-0-316-01355-0; unp.} 298.2 (Gr. PreK-2)**

In Pinkney's latest gorgeously illustrated folk tale, reset in a colder clime, Mama sends her sweet little girl to grandmother's house with a basket of chicken soup and raisin muffins. Snow is falling when Little Red Riding Hood encounters the wolf, and he suggests she gather kindling for her grandmother's fire (instead of the usual flowers). The rest of the story goes as we know it, with the big eyes and ears and teeth dialogue, and Little Red getting gobbled up. The sumptuous full bleed pencil, watercolor, gouache, and ink illustrations depicting a dark-haired brown-skinned girl in her sturdy red-hooded cloak will make this a new favorite with your older editions of the tale, including the one that won Trina Schart Hyman a Caldecott Honor way back when.

GERM: Compare the styles of illustrations in various versions of the story, including Trina Schart Hyman's Caldecott Honor-winning *Little Red Riding Hood,* James Marshall's lighthearted *Red Riding Hood,* and Andrea Wisnewski's *Little Red Riding Hood,* set in 19th-century New England. Ask children which ones they prefer and why. Pull in versions from other countries, too, such as Niki Daly's *Pretty Salma: A Little Red Riding Hood Story from Africa* and Ed Young's *Lon Po Po: A Red-Riding Hood Story from China.* Lighten up the mood with some U.S.-based parodies, traveling from Louisiana with Mike Artell's *Petite Rouge: A Cajun Red Riding Hood,* to Boston with Michael Emberley's *Ruby,* to the prairie with Lisa Campbell Ernst's *Little Red Riding Hood: A Newfangled Prairie Tale,* and to Texas with Susan Lowell's *Little Red Cowboy Hat.*

RELATED TITLES: Artell, Mike. *Petite Rouge: A Cajun Red Riding Hood.* Dial, 2001. / Daly, Niki. *Pretty Salma: A Little Red Riding Hood Story from Africa.* Clarion, 2007. / Emberley, Michael. *Ruby.* Little, Brown, 1990. / Ernst, Lisa Campbell. *Little Red Riding Hood: A Newfangled Prairie Tale.* Simon & Schuster, 1995. / Harper, Wilhelmina. *The Gunniwolf.* Dutton, 2003. / Hyman, Trina Schart. *Little Red Riding Hood.* Holiday House, 1983. / Lowell, Susan. *Little Red Cowboy Hat.* Henry Holt, 1997. / Marshall, James. *Red Riding Hood.* Dial, 1987. / Wisnewski, Andrea. *Little Red Riding Hood.* Godine, 2006. / Young, Ed. *Lon Po Po: A Red-Riding Hood Story from China.* Philomel, 1989.

SUBJECTS: FOLKLORE—GERMANY. GRANDMOTHERS—FOLKLORE. OBEDIENCE—FOLKLORE. WOLVES—FOLKLORE.

[J] |A| | | |

Martina the Beautiful Cockroach: A Cuban Folktale. Deedy, Carmen Agra. Illus. by Michael Austin. Peachtree, 2007. {ISBN 978-1-56145-399-3; unp.} 398.2 (Gr. 1-6) Belpré Honor (Author)

At the ripe old age of 21 days, Martina Josefina Catalina Cucaracha, a beautiful cockroach, is ready to give her leg in marriage. Abuela, her Cuban grandmother, gives her "un consejo increíble, some shocking advice." She tells Martina to spill coffee on each of her suitor's shoes to make him angry. Then she will know how he will behave when he loses his temper. Abuela says, "The Coffee Test never fails." Sure enough, each time Martina tries it on a potential husband—Don Gallo the rooster, Don Cerdo the pig, and Don Lagarto the lizard—she realizes they'd make terrible mates. It's not until she meets Pérez, a kind little mouse, that she finds her perfect match. Huge glossy acrylics portray that cockroach as the most delectable of creatures.

GERM: Don't you just love that Coffee Test? Ask children what other ways they can use to tell if someone is just right for them. For a Puerto Rican version of the same story, read Pura Belpre's classic picture book, *Perez and Martina*. You'll find it retold as "Martina Martínez and Pérez the Mouse" in the terrific collection of Hispanic folktales, *Tales Our Abuelitas Told* by F. Isabel Campoy and Alma Flor Ada.

RELATED TITLES: Belpre, Pura. *Perez and Martina: A Puerto Rican Folktale.* Viking, 1991. / Bernier-Grand, Carmen T. *Juan Bobo: Four Folktales from Puerto Rico.* HarperCollins, 1994. / Campoy, F. Isabel, and Alma Flor Ada. *Tales Our Abuelitas Told: A Hispanic Folktale Collection.* Atheneum, 2006. / González, Lucie M. *The Bossy Gallito: A Traditional Cuban Folktale.* Scholastic, 1994. / González, Lucia M. *Señor Cat's Romance and Other Favorite Stories from Latin America.* Scholastic, 1997. / Montes, Marisa. *Juan Bobo Goes to Work: A Puerto Rican Folktale.* HarperCollins, 2000. / Pitre, Felix. *Juan Bobo and the Pig: A Puerto Rican Folktale.* Lodestar, 1993. / Pitre, Felix. *Paco and the Witch: A Puerto Rican Folktale.* Dutton, 1995. / Sacre, Antonio. *The Barking Mouse.* Albert Whitman, 2003. / Simms, Laura. *The Squeaky Door.* Crown, 1991.

SUBJECTS: FOLKLORE—CUBA. FOLKLORE—LATIN AMERICA. MULTICULTURAL BOOKS.

[j] |A| |H| |

Tap Dancing on the Roof: Sijo (Poems). Park, Linda Sue. Illus. by Istvan Banyai. Clarion, 2007. {ISBN 978-0-618-23483-7; unp.} 811 (Gr. 3-7)

There are 27 quirky and gently ironic poems, some rhyming, some not, in this unique collection by Newbery Medal author Linda Sue Park. Sijo is a traditional form of poetry from Korea that contains three lines, each with 14 to 16 syllables. She writes about ordinary occurrences like breakfast, laundry, or brushing your teeth, and makes gently humorous observations about pockets, crocuses, and playing tennis. The digital black lined and pastel illustrations on the stark white square pages are a bit too hip and studiously whimsical for my taste, with a disconnect between the wacky little kids portrayed and the thoughtful poems, but your kids probably won't mind.

GERM: These poems are trickier to write than haiku, as they employ a twist in the final line, using "humor or irony, an unexpected image, a pun, or a play on words." There's a very good Author's Note with concrete tips for writing sijo. You'll want to hand out copies of Parks's poems for students to reread and tease out the meaning. Then set them loose to try writing and illustrating some of their own.

RELATED TITLES: Clements, Andrew. *Dogku.* Simon & Schuster, 2007. / Demi, comp. *In the Eyes of the Cat: Japanese Poetry for All Seasons.* Henry Holt, 1992. / Mora, Pat. *Yum! Mmmm! Que Rico!: Americas' Sproutings.* Lee & Low, 2007. / Park, Linda Sue. *The Kite Fighters.* Clarion, 2000. / Park, Linda Sue. *Seesaw Girl.* Clarion, 1999. / Park, Linda Sue. *A Single Shard.* Clarion, 2002. / Park, Linda Sue. *When My Name Was Keoko.* Clarion, 2002. / Prelutsky, Jack. *If Not for the Cat.* Greenwillow, 2004. / Sidman, Joyce. *This Is Just to Say: Poems of Apology and Forgiveness.* Houghton Mifflin, 2007.

SUBJECTS: KOREAN POETRY. POETRY—SINGLE AUTHOR. SIJO. MULTICULTURAL BOOKS.

[J] | | | |S|

This Is Just to Say: Poems of Apology and Forgiveness. **Sidman, Joyce. Illus. by Pamela Zagarenski. Houghton Mifflin, 2007. {ISBN 978-0-618-61680-0; 48p.} 811 (Gr. 4-7)**

Inspired by the "Sorry" poems in Kenneth Koch's seminal poetry guide, ***Rose, Where Did You Get That Red: Teaching Great Poetry to Children***, and by the poems she and a group of fourth graders composed to her own mother, author Sidman began thinking about apology and forgiveness. "What if all those sorry poems were actually sent to the people they were written to? What if all those people wrote back?" Starting off this fresh and often poignant collection of 16 poems ("Apologies") and their subsequent replies ("Responses") is the ultimate apology poem, "This Is Just to Say," by William Carlos Williams. The poems are written by a fictional sixth grade class as part of their poetry unit with teacher Mrs. Merz. There's Thomas who apologizes to Mrs. Garcia in the office for stealing the jelly doughnuts in the teacher's room; Alyssa who still feels guilty over stabbing her sister's hand with a pencil; and Jewel, who writes to her Dad who has left home, promising to be perfect if he just comes back. The kooky mixed media illustrations on snippets of notebook paper fit each poem and personality.

GERM: What's so welcome here are the eloquent responses, also written as poems—some funny, some wrenching, all forgiving. You'll be writing and illustrating your own poems in response, no doubt. Also read together Sharon Creech's free verse novel, ***Love That Dog***, which also uses that "plums in the icebox" poem to great effect. For another book that fools around with famous poems, ***I Must Go Down to the Beach Again and Other Poems*** by Karen Jo Shapiro parodies and mirrors 23 classics. Though your students will not know many of the originals, you can locate them online and in collections and compare and contrast them with the humorous new versions.

RELATED TITLES: Cleary, Brian P. *Rainbow Soup: Adventures in Poetry.* Carolrhoda, 2004. / Creech, Sharon. *Love That Dog.* HarperCollins, 2001. / Janeczko, Paul B. *How to Write Poetry.* Scholastic, 1999. / Janeczko, Paul B., comp. *A Kick in the Head: An Everyday Guide to Poetic Forms.* Candlewick, 2005. / Janeczko, Paul B. *Poetry from A to Z: A Guide for Young Writers.* Simon & Schuster, 1994. / Janeczko, Paul B. *Seeing the Blue Between: Advice and Inspiration for Young Poets.* Candlewick, 2002. / Koch, Kenneth. *Rose, Where Did You Get That Red: Teaching Great Poetry to Children.* Random House, 1988. / Shapiro, Karen Jo. *I Must Go Down to the Beach Again and Other Poems.* Charlesbridge, 2007. / Woodson, Jacqueline. *Locomotion.* Putnam, 2003.

SUBJECTS: APOLOGIES. FORGIVENESS. POETRY. TEACHERS.

[j] |A| | | |

Yum! Mmmm! Que Rico!: Americas' Sproutings. **Mora, Pat. Illus. by Rafael Lopez. Lee & Low, 2007. {ISBN 978-1-58430-271-1; unp.} 811 (Gr. K-4)**

Here's an interesting hodgepodge of 14 haiku, facts, and exuberantly bright full-bleed acrylic paintings all about foods indigenous to the Americas. Each double-page spread showcases one tasty food: blueberries, chiles, chocolate, corn, cranberries, papaya, peanuts, pecans, pineapples, prickly pears, potatoes, pumpkins, tomatoes, and vanilla. The haiku describes it poetically, while the supporting paragraph explains the foods origins, uses, and other tempting facts. (Interesting to note: four of the foods start with the letter "C," and seven with "P.")

GERM: In the Dear Reader letter at the back of the book, the author "gathers all of these foods into a fast-clapping or jump-rope rhyme" which you can recite. It would be fun and tasty, too, to make a mini-feast with the ingredients in the book. Then children can write and illustrate new haiku for foods they favor.

RELATED TITLES: Abrams, Pam. *Now I Eat My ABC's.* Scholastic, 2004. / Aston, Dianna. *A Seed Is Sleepy.* Chronicle, 2007. / Clements, Andrew. *Dogku.* Simon & Schuster, 2007. / Coy, John. *Two Old Potatoes and Me.* Knopf, 2003. / Ehlert, Lois. *Eating the Alphabet: Fruits and Vegetables from A to Z.* Harcourt, 1989. / Ehlert, Lois. *Growing Vegetable Soup.* Harcourt, 1987. / Gibbons, Gail. *From Seed to Plant.* Holiday House, 1991. / Hall, Zoe. *It's Pumpkin Time!* Scholastic, 1994. / Mora, Pat. *Doña Flor: A Tall Tale About a Giant Woman with a Great Big Heart.* Knopf, 2005. / Mora, Pat. *Let's Eat! A Comer!* HarperCollins, 2008. / Pfeffer, Wendy. *From Seed to Pumpkin.* HarperCollins, 2004. / Prelutsky, Jack. *If Not for the Cat.* Greenwillow, 2004. / Schaefer, Lola M. *Pick, Pull, Snap!: Where Once a Flower Bloomed.* HarperCollins, 2003.

BOOKS JUDY CHOSE NOT TO REVIEW
FOR THIS PROGRAM

NOTE: There's no sane way to review 180+ children's books in a one-day workshop, so I had to omit those titles I felt we could live without. Although many of these titles are worth buying for a library collection, none were on my personal "Best of the Year" list. Since the ***Winners!*** Conference is geared to books for grades K-6, I also omitted most of the Young Adult titles for grades 7 and up. (See that list on page 58.)

[j] | |B| | | ***Animal Poems.*** Worth, Valerie. Illus. by Steve Jenkins. Farrar, 2007. {ISBN 978-0-374-38057-1; 48p.} 811 (Gr. 3-8)

[j] | |B| | | ***The Apple Pie That Papa Baked.*** Thompson, Lauren. Illus. by Jonathan Bean. Simon & Schuster, 2007. {ISBN 978-1-41691-240-8; unp.} E (Gr. PreK-2)

[j] | | | |S| ***Artist to Artist: 23 Major Illustrators Talk to Their Children about Their Art.*** Philomel, 2007. {ISBN 978-0-399-24600-5; 105p.} 741.6 (Gr. 3-8)

[j] | | |H| | ***At Night.*** Bean, Jonathan. Illus. by the author. Farrar, 2007. {ISBN 978-0-374-30446-1; unp.} E (Gr. PreK-2)

[j] | | |H| | ***Becca at Sea.*** Baker, Deirdre. Groundwood, 2007. {ISBN 978-0-88899-737-1; 165p.} FIC (Gr. 4-6)

[j] | |B| | | ***Candyfloss.*** Wilson, Jacqueline. Roaring Brook, 2007. {ISBN 978-1-59643-241-3; 339p.} FIC (Gr. 4-7)

[_] |A| | | | ***The Cat: Or How I Lost Eternity.*** Richter, Jutta. Illus. by Rotraut Susanne Berner. Tr. by Anna Brailovsky. Milkweed Editions, 2007. {ISBN 978-1-571-31676-9; 63p.} FIC (Gr. 4-6) Batchelder Honor

[_] |A| | | | ***Chess Rumble.*** Neri, G. Illus. by Jesse Joshua Watson. Lee & Low, 2007. {ISBN 978-1-58430-279-7; 62p.} FIC (Gr. 5-7)

[j] | | | |S| ***Fox.*** Banks, Kate. Illus. by Georg Hallensleben. Farrar/Frances Foster, 2007. {ISBN 978-0-374-39967-2; unp.} E (Gr. PreK-1)

[j] |A| | | | ***Global Babies.*** Ajmera, Maya. Illus. with photos. Charlesbridge, 2007. {ISBN 978-1-58089-174-5; unp.} E (Gr. PreK)

[j] |A| | | | ***The Golden Dream of Carlo Chuchio.*** Alexander, Lloyd. Henry Holt, 2007. {ISBN 978-0-8050-8333-0; 306p.} FIC (Gr. 5-8)

[j] | |B| | | ***The Golden Rule.*** Cooper, Ilene. Illus. by Gabi Swiatowska. Abrams, 2007. {ISBN 978-0-8109-0960-1; unp.} E (Gr. K-5)

[j] |A| | | | *Good Enough to Eat.* Cole, Brock. Illus. by Brock Cole. Farrar, 2007. {ISBN 978-0-374-32737-8; unp.} E (Gr. K-3)

[j] |A| | | | *Good Sports.* Prelutsky, Jack. Illus. by Chris Raschka. Knopf, 2007. {ISBN 978-0-375-83700-5; 33p.} 811 (Gr. 3-5)

[j] | |B| | | *Half a World Away.* Gleeson, Libby. Scholastic/Arthur A. Levine, 2007. {ISBN 978-0-439-88977-3; unp.} FIC (Gr. PreK-2)

[j] | | | |S| *Heat Wave.* Spinelli, Eileen. Illus. by Betsy Lewin. Harcourt, 2007. {ISBN 978-0-15-216779-0; unp.} E (Gr. K-2)

[j] | | | |S| *How It Happened in Peach Hill.* Jocelyn, Marthe. Random House/Wendy Lamb, 2007. {ISBN 978-0-375-93701-9; 232p.} FIC (Gr. 5-8)

[j] | | | |S| *I Am Not Joey Pigza.* Gantos, Jack. Farrar, 2007. {ISBN 978-0-374-39941-2; 215p.} FIC (Gr. 5-8)

[j] | | | |S| *Into the Woods.* Gardner, Lyn. Illus. by Mini Grey. Random House/David Fickling, 2007. {ISBN 978-0-15-205817-3; 427p.} FIC (Gr. 4-6)

[j] | | | |S| *Jabberwocky: The Classic Poem from Lewis Carroll's Through the Looking-glass, and What Alice Found There.* Carroll, Lewis. Illus. by Christopher Myers. Hyperion/Jump at the Sun, 2007. {ISBN 978-1-4231-0372-1; unp.} 821 (Gr. 4-12)

[j] | |B| | | *Jack Plank Tells Tales.* Babbitt, Natalie. Scholastic/Michael di Capua, 2007. {ISBN 978-0-545-00496-1; 128p.} FIC (Gr. 4-6)

[j] | |B| | | *The Land of the Silver Apples.* Farmer, Nancy. Atheneum, 2007. {ISBN 978-1-41690-735-0; 496p.} FIC (Gr. 6-9)

[j] | | | |S| *Leaves.* Stein, David Ezra. Illus. by the author. Putnam, 2007. {ISBN 978-0-399-24636-4; unp.} E (Gr. PreK-K)

[j] | | | |S| *Lenny's Space.* Banks, Kate. Farrar/Frances Foster, 2007. {ISBN 978-0-374-34575-4; 151p.} FIC (Gr. 3-5)

[j] |A| | | | *Little Night.* Morales, Yuyi. Illus. by Yuyi Morales. Roaring Brook/Neal Porter, 2007. {ISBN 978-1-59643-088-4; unp.} E (Gr. PreK-1)

[j] |A| | | | *Marie Curie. (Giants of Science series.)* Krull, Kathleen. Illus. by Boris Kulikov. Viking, 2007. {ISBN 978-0-670-05894-5; 142p.} B (Gr. 5-8)

[j] |A| | | | *Middle School is Worse Than Meatloaf.* Holm, Jennifer. Illus. by Elicia Castaldi. Atheneum/Ginee Seo, 2007. {ISBN 978-0-689-85281-7; unp.} FIC (Gr. 5-7)

[j] |A| | | | *Mother Goose Numbers on the Loose.* Dillon, Leo, and Diane Dillon. Illus. by Leo Dillon and Diane Dillon. Harcourt, 2007. {ISBN 978-0-15-205676-6; 50p.} 398.8 (Gr. PreK-1)\

[j] |A| | | | *My Name Is Gabito: The Life of Gabriel García Márquez/Me llamo Gabito: La vida de Gabriel García Márquez.* Brown, Monica. Illus. by Raúl Colón. Rising Moon, 2007. {ISBN 978-0-87358-934-5; 32p.} B (Gr. 2-4) Pura Belpré Illustrator Honor Book

[j] |A| | | | *Nicholas and the Gang.* Goscinny, René. Trans. by Anthea Bell. Illus. by Jean-Jacques Sempé. Phaidon, 2007. {ISBN 978-0-7148-4788-7; 112p.} FIC (Gr. 4-6) Batchelder Honor

[j] |A| | | | *Nothing.* Agee, Jon. Illus. by the author. Hyperion, 2007. {ISBN 978-0-7868-3694-9; unp.} E (Gr. K-2)

[j] | |B| | *One City, Two Brothers.* Smith, Chris. Illus. by Aurélia Fronty. Barefoot, 2007. {ISBN 978-1-84686-042-3; unp.} 398.2 (Gr. K-4)

[j] |A| | | | *One Thousand Tracings: Healing the Wounds of World War II.* Judge, Lita. Hyperion, 2007. {ISBN 978-1-42310-008-9; 36p.} 940.53 (Gr. 3-6)

[j] | |B| | *Pink.* Gregory, Nan. Illus. by Luc Melanson. Groundwood, 2007. {ISBN 978-0-88899-781-4; unp.} E (Gr. PreK-2)

[j] |A| | | | *Rex Zero and the End of the World.* Wynne-Jones, Tim. Farrar/Melanie Kroupa, 2007. {ISBN 978-0-374-33467-3; 186p.} FIC (Gr. 5-8)

[j] | |B| | *Snow Baby: The Arctic Childhood of Admiral Robert E. Peary's Daring Daughter.* Kirkpatrick, Katherine. Holiday House, 2007. {ISBN 978-0-8234-1973-9; 50p.} B (Gr. 4-8)

[j] |A| | | | *Tracking Trash: Flotsam, Jetsam, and the Science of Ocean Motion.* Burns, Loree Griffin. Houghton Mifflin, 2007. {ISBN 978-0-618-58131-3; 56p.} 551.46 (Gr. 5-8)

[j] | | | |S| *Velma Gratch and the Way Cool Butterfly.* Madison, Alan. Illus. by Kevin Hawkes. Schwartz & Wade, 2007. {ISBN 978-0-375-93597-8; unp.} E (Gr. PreK- 3)

[j] | |B| | *Way Down Deep.* White, Ruth. Farrar, 2007. {ISBN 978-0-374-38251-3; 197p.} FIC (Gr. 5-7)

[j] | |B| | | *What Happens on Wednesdays.* Jenkins, Emily. Illus. by Lauren Castillo. Farrar/Frances Foster, 2007. {ISBN 978-0-374-38303-9; unp.} E (Gr. PreK-1)

[_] | | | |S| *Why War Is Never a Good Idea.* Walker, Alice. Illus. by Stefano Vitale. HarperCollins, 2007. {ISBN 978-0-06-075386-3; unp.} E (Gr. 3-12)

[j] |A| | | | *Yo, Jo!* Isadora, Rachel. Illus. by Rachel Isadora. Harcourt, 2007. {ISBN 978-0-15-205783-1; unp.} E (Gr. PreK-1)

YOUNG ADULT BOOKS FOR GRADES 7 AND UP
THAT WERE ON THIS YEAR'S LISTS

(With a couple of exceptions, "WINNERS!" only covers books
for Grades PreK through 6)

| | |H|S| *The Absolutely True Diary of a Part-Time Indian.* Alexie, Sherman. Illus. by Ellen Forney. Little, Brown, 2007. {ISBN 978-0-316-01368-0; 229p.} FIC (Gr. 8-12) National Book Award

| |B| | | *Before I Die.* Downham, Jenny. Random House/David Fickling, 2007. {ISBN 978-0-385-75155-1; 326p.} FIC (Gr. 9-12)

| | | |S| *Bone by Bone by Bone.* Johnston, Tony. Roaring Brook, 2007. {ISBN 978-1-59643-113-3; 184p.} FIC (Gr. 6-9)

| | | |S| *Book of a Thousand Days.* Hale, Shannon. Bloomsbury, 2007. {ISBN 978-1-59990-051-3; 305p.} FIC (Gr. 7-10)

|A| | | | *Brave Story.* Miyabe, Miyuki. Trans. by Alexander O. Smith. VIZ Media, 2007. {ISBN 978-1-571-31676-9; 816p.} 895.6 (Gr. 7-9) Batchelder Award

| |B| | | *Cures for Heartbreak.* Rabb, Margo. Delacorte, 2007. {ISBN 978-0-385-90414-8; 238p.} FIC (Gr. 9-12)

| | |H| | *A Darkling Plain.* Reeve, Philip. HarperCollins/EOS, 2007. {ISBN 978-0-06-089056-8; 559p.} FIC (Gr. 7-10)

| | | |S| *Dragon's Keep.* Carey, Janet Lee. Harcourt, 2007. {ISBN 978-0-15-205926-2; 302p.} FIC (Gr. 7-10)

| |B| | | *Dreamquake.* Knox, Elizabeth. Farrar/Frances Foster, 2007. {ISBN 978-0-374-31854-3; 449p.} FIC (Gr. 9-12)

| | | |S| *Epic.* Kostick, Conor. Viking, 2007. {ISBN 978-0-670-06179-2; 364p.} FIC (Gr. 8-12)

| |B| | | *Every Crooked Pot.* Rosen, Renee. St. Martin's/Griffin, 2007. {ISBN 978-0-312-36543-1; 227p.} FIC (Gr. 9-12)

| | | |S| *Evil Genius.* Jinks, Catherine. Harcourt, 2007. {ISBN 978-0-15-205988-0; 486} FIC (Gr. 7-10)

| |B| | | *The Falconer's Knot.* Hoffman, Mary. Bloomsbury, 2007. {ISBN 978-1-59990-056-8; 297p.} FIC (Gr. 7-10)

| | | |S| *Freak Show.* St. James, James. Dutton, 2007. {ISBN 978-0-525-47799-0; 297p.} FIC (Gr. 9-12)

|A|B| | | *Frida: Viva la Vida! = Long Live Life!* Bernier-Grand, Carmen T. Illus. with photos. and reprods. Marshall Cavendish, 2007. {ISBN 978-0-761-45336-9; 48p.} 811 (Gr. 7-12) Belpre Author Honor

|A| | |S| *An Inconvenient Truth: The Crisis of Global Warming.* Gore, Al. Adapted by Jane O'Connor. Illus. with photos. and reprods. Viking/Rodale, 2007. {ISBN 978-0-670-06271-3; 191p.} 363.738 (Gr. 7-10)

| | | |S| *The Lion Hunter.* Wein, Elizabeth E. Viking, 2007. {ISBN 978-0-670-06163-1; 223p.} FIC (Gr. 7-10)

|A| | | | *Miss Crandall's School for Young Ladies & Little Misses of Color: Poems.* Alexander, Elizabeth, and Nelson, Marilyn. Illus. by Floyd Cooper. Boyds Mills/Wordsong, 2007. {ISBN 978-1-59078-456-3; 47p.} 811 (Gr. 7-12)

|A| | | | *Muckrakers: How Ida Tarbell, Upton Sinclair, and Lincoln Steffens Helped Expose Scandal, Inspire Reform, and Invent Investigative Journalism.* Bausum, Ann. National Geographic, 2007. {ISBN 978-1-426-30137-7; 111p.} 070.4 (Gr. 6-10)

| | | |S| *My Mother the Cheerleader.* Sharenow, Robert. HarperCollins/Laura Geringer, 2007. {ISBN 978-0-06-114897-2; 288p.} FIC (Gr. 8-10)

|A| |H|S| *The New Policeman.* Thompson, Kate. Greenwillow, 2007. {ISBN 978-0-06-117428-5; 442p.} FIC (Gr. 7-10)

| |B| | | *Peak.* Smith, Roland. Harcourt, 2007. {ISBN 978-0-15-202417-8; 246p.} FIC (Gr. 7-12)

|A| | | | *The Poet Slave of Cuba: A Biography of Juan Francisco Manzano.* Engle, Margarita. Illus. by Sean Qualls. Henry Holt, 2007. {ISBN 978-0-8050-7706-3; 183p.} B (Gr. 7-10) Belpré Author Award

| |B| | | *Powers.* Le Guin, Ursula K. Harcourt, 2007. {ISBN 978-0-15-205770-1; 502p.} FIC (Gr. 8-12)

| |B| | | *Re-Gifters.* Carey, Mike. DC Comics/Minx, 2007. {ISBN 978-1-40120-371-9; 148p.} 741.5 (Gr. 7-9)

| | | |S| *The Real Benedict Arnold.* Murphy, Jim. Clarion, 2007. {ISBN 978-0-395-77609-4; 264p.} B (Gr. 7-12)

| | | |S| *Red Glass.* Resau, Laura. Delacorte, 2007. {ISBN 978-0-385-90464-3; 275p.} FIC (Gr. 8-10)

|A|B| |S| *Red Moon at Sharpsburg.* Wells, Rosemary. Viking, 2007. {ISBN 978-0-670-03638-7; 236p.} FIC (Gr. 7-10)

| | |H| | *Red Spikes.* Lanagan, Margo. Knopf, 2007. {ISBN 978-0-375-84320-4; 167p.} FIC (Gr. 9-12)

| |B| |S| *Slam.* Hornby, Nick. Putnam, 2007. {ISBN 978-0-399-25048-4; 309p.} FIC (Gr. 9-12)

| | |H| | *Someday This Pain Will Be Useful to You.* Cameron, Peter. Farrar/Frances Foster, 2007. {ISBN 978-0-374-30989-3; 229p.} FIC (Gr. 9-12)

| |B| |S| *Tamar.* Peet, Mal. Candlewick, 2007. {ISBN 978-0-7636-3488-9; 424p.} FIC (Gr. 8-12)

|A|B| |S| *Tasting the Sky: A Palestinian Childhood.* Barakat, Ibtisam. Farrar/Melanie Kroupa, 2007. {ISBN 978-0-374-35733-7; 176p.} B (Gr. 7-12)

| | | |S| *Tough Boy Sonatas.* Crisler, Curtis L. Illus. by Floyd Cooper. Boyds Mills/Wordsong, 2007. {ISBN 978-1-932425-77-2; 86p.} 811 (Gr. 8-12)

| | | |S| *Undercover.* Kephart, Beth. HarperFestival/Laura Geringer, 2007. {ISBN 978-0-06-123894-9; 278p.} FIC (Gr. 9-12)

| |B| | | *Useful Fools.* Schmidt, C. A. Dutton, 2007. {ISBN 978-0-525-47814-0; 262p.} FIC (Gr. 9-12)

| |B| |S| *What They Found: Love on 145th Street.* Myers, Walter Dean. Random House/Wendy Lamb, 2007. {ISBN 978-0-375-93709-5; 243p.} FIC (Gr. 9-12)

| | | |S| *When I Crossed No-Bob.* McMullan, Margaret. Houghton Mifflin, 2007. {ISBN 978-0-618-71715-6; 209p.} FIC (Gr. 6-9)

| |B| | | *The White Darkness.* McCaughrean, Geraldine. HarperCollins, 2007. {ISBN 978-0-06-089036-0; 373p.} FIC (Gr. 7-12)

| |B| | | *Your Own, Sylvia: A Verse Portrait of Sylvia Plath.* Hemphill, Stephanie. Knopf, 2007. {ISBN 978-0-375-83799-9; 261p.} 811 (Gr. 8-12)

The 100 Top-Rated Children's Books of 2007

AUTHOR and TITLE INDEX

The Absolutely True Diary of a Part-Time Indian. Alexie, Sherman. FIC (Gr. 8-12) *58*

Agee, Jon. *Nothing.* E (Gr. K-2) *56*

Ajmera, Maya. *Global Babies.* E (Gr. PreK) *54*

Alexander, Elizabeth, and Nelson, Marilyn. *Miss Crandall's School for Young Ladies & Little Misses of Color: Poems.* 811 (Gr. 7-12) *59*

Alexander, Lloyd. *The Golden Dream of Carlo Chuchio.* FIC (Gr. 5-8) *54*

Alexie, Sherman. *The Absolutely True Diary of a Part-Time Indian.* FIC (Gr. 8-12) *58*

The All-I'll-Ever-Want Christmas Doll. McKissack, Patricia A. E (Gr. PreK-3) *1*

Animal Poems. Worth, Valerie. 811 (Gr. 3-8) *54*

The Apple Doll. Kleven, Elisa. E (Gr. PreK-2) *2*

The Apple Pie That Papa Baked. Thompson, Lauren. E (Gr. PreK-2) *54*

Applegate, Katherine. *Home of the Brave.* FIC (Gr. 5-8) *27*

The Arrival. Tan, Shaun. FIC (Gr. 6-12) *21*

Artist to Artist: 23 Major Illustrators Talk to Their Children about Their Art. 741.6 (Gr. 3-8) *54*

Aston, Dianna. *A Seed Is Sleepy.* 581.4 (Gr. PreK-4) *43*

At Gleason's Gym. Lewin, Ted. 796.83 (Gr. K-5) *36*

At Night. Bean, Jonathan. E (Gr. PreK-2) *54*

Babbitt, Natalie. *Jack Plank Tells Tales.* FIC (Gr. 4-6) *55*

Baker, Deirdre. *Becca at Sea.* FIC (Gr. 4-6) *54*

Ballerina Dreams. Thompson, Lauren. 618.92 (Gr. K-4) *36*

Bang-Campbell, Monika. *Little Rat Makes Music.* E (Gr. K-3) *11*

Banks, Kate. *Fox.* E (Gr. PreK-1) *54*

Banks, Kate. *Lenny's Space.* FIC (Gr. 3-5) *55*

Barakat, Ibtisam. *Tasting the Sky: A Palestinian Childhood.* B (Gr. 7-12) *60*

Bausum, Ann. *Muckrakers: How Ida Tarbell, Upton Sinclair, and Lincoln Steffens Helped Expose Scandal, Inspire Reform, and Invent Investigative Journalism.* 070.4 (Gr. 6-10) *59*

Bean, Jonathan. *At Night.* E (Gr. PreK-2) *54*

The Bearskinner: A Tale of the Brothers Grimm. Schlitz, Laura Amy. 398.2 (Gr. 3-6) *46*

Becca at Sea. Baker, Deirdre. FIC (Gr. 4-6) *54*

Before I Die. Downham, Jenny. FIC (Gr. 9-12) *58*

Beowulf: A Hero's Tale Retold. Rumford, James. 398.2 (Gr. 3-8) *46*

Berlin, Eric. *The Puzzling World of Winston Breen.* FIC (Gr. 4-6) *32*

Bernier-Grand, Carmen T. *Frida: Viva la Vida! = Long Live Life!* 811 (Gr. 7-12) *59*

Bertholf, Bret. *The Long Gone Lonesome History of Country Music.* 781.642 (Gr. 3-6) *41*

Bishop, Nic. *Nic Bishop Spiders.* 595.4 (Gr. K-6) *42*

The Black Book of Secrets. Higgins, F. E. FIC (Gr. 5-7) *21*

Blue Lipstick: Concrete Poems. Grandits, John. 811 (Gr. 5-9) *47*

Blume, Lesley M. M. *The Rising Star of Rusty Nail.* FIC (Gr. 4-7) *33*

Bone by Bone by Bone. Johnston, Tony. FIC (Gr. 6-9) *58*

Book of a Thousand Days. Hale, Shannon. FIC (Gr. 7-10) *58*

Brave Story. Miyabe, Miyuki. 895.6 (Gr. 7-9) *58*

Broach, Elise. *When Dinosaurs Came with Everything.* E (Gr. PreK-2) *20*

Brown, Monica. *My Name Is Gabito: The Life of Gabriel García Márquez/Me llamo Gabito: La vida de Gabriel García Márquez.* B (Gr. 2-4) *56*

Bruel, Nick. *Poor Puppy.* E (Gr. PreK-2) *15*

Bryan, Ashley. *Let It Shine: Three Favorite Spirituals.* 782.25 (Gr. PreK-5) *51*

Bunting, Eve. *Hurry! Hurry!* E (Gr. PreK-1) *9*

Burns, Loree Griffin. *Tracking Trash: Flotsam, Jetsam, and the Science of Ocean Motion.* 551.46 (Gr. 5-8) *56*

Calmenson, Stephanie. *May I Pet Your Dog?: The How-to Guide for Kids Meeting Dogs (and Dogs Meeting Kids).* E (Gr. PreK-2) *12*

Cameron, Peter. *Someday This Pain Will Be Useful to You.* FIC (Gr. 9-12) *60*

Candyfloss. Wilson, Jacqueline. FIC (Gr. 4-7) *54*

Captain Raptor and the Space Pirates. O'Malley, Kevin, and Patrick O'Brien. E (Gr. K-3) *2*

Carey, Janet Lee. *Dragon's Keep.* FIC (Gr. 7-10) *58*

Carey, Mike. *Re-Gifters.* 741.5 (Gr. 7-9) *59*

AUTHOR and TITLE INDEX, cont.

AUTHOR and TITLE INDEX, cont.

AUTHOR and TITLE INDEX, cont.

The 100 Top-Rated Children's Books of 2007

SUBJECT INDEX

ADVENTURE AND ADVENTURERS
Lehman, Barbara. *Rainstorm.* E (Gr. PreK-2) *16*
Michael, Livi. *City of Dogs.* FIC (Gr. 4-7) *22*
O'Malley, Kevin, and Patrick O'Brien. *Captain Raptor and the Space Pirates.* E (Gr. K-3) *2*
Ray, Deborah Kogan. *Down the Colorado: John Wesley Powell, the One-Armed Explorer.* 917.91 (Gr. 3-5) *38*
Rowling, J. K. *Harry Potter and the Deathly Hallows.* FIC (Gr. 5-12) *26*
Stewart, Trenton Lee. *The Mysterious Benedict Society.* FIC (Gr. 4-7) *31*
Rumford, James. *Beowulf: A Hero's Tale Retold.* 398.2 (Gr. 3-8) *46*

AFRICAN AMERICANS
Applegate, Katherine. *Home of the Brave.* FIC (Gr. 5-8) *27*
Bryan, Ashley. *Let It Shine: Three Favorite Spirituals.* 782.25 (Gr. PreK-5) *51*
Curtis, Christopher Paul. *Elijah of Buxton.* FIC (Gr. 5-8) *24*
Harrington, Janice N. *The Chicken-Chasing Queen of Lamar County.* E (Gr. PreK-3) *5*
Levine, Ellen. *Henry's Freedom Box: A True Story.* E (Gr. 2-6) *8*
McKissack, Patricia A. *The All-I'll-Ever-Want Christmas Doll.* E (Gr. PreK-3) *1*
Rex, Adam. *The True Meaning of Smekday.* FIC (Gr. 4-8) *35*
Woodson, Jacqueline. *Feathers.* FIC (Gr. 4-7) *26*

ALABAMA
Miller, Sarah Elizabeth. *Miss Spitfire: Reaching Helen Keller.* FIC (Gr. 5-8) *30*

ALLITERATION
Bruel, Nick. *Poor Puppy.* E (Gr. PreK-2) *15*

ALPHABET
Bruel, Nick. *Poor Puppy.* E (Gr. PreK-2) *15*

AMERICA—DISCOVERY AND EXPLORATION
Freedman, Russell. *Who Was First?: Discovering the Americas.* 970.01 (Gr. 5-9) *45*

ANIMALS
Bishop, Nic. *Nic Bishop Spiders.* 595.4 (Gr. K-6) *42*
Henkes, Kevin. *A Good Day.* E (Gr. PreK-1) *8*
Jenkins, Steve. *Living Color.* 591.47 (Gr. PreK-4) *41*
Kulka, Joe. *Wolf's Coming!* E (Gr. PreK-1) *20*
Lunde, Darrin. *Hello, Bumblebee Bat.* 599.4 (Gr. PreK-2) *39*
Seeger, Laura Vaccaro. *First the Egg.* 571.8 (Gr. PreK-1) *39*
Stevens, April. *Waking Up Wendell.* E (Gr. PreK-1) *19*

ANIMALS—INFANCY
Collard, Sneed B., III. *Pocket Babies and Other Marsupials.* 599.2 (Gr. 3-7) *43*
Dowson, Nick. *Tracks of a Panda.* E (Gr. PreK-2) *19*

APOLOGIES
Sidman, Joyce. *This Is Just to Say: Poems of Apology and Forgiveness.* 811 (Gr. 4-7) *53*

APPLES
Kleven, Elisa. *The Apple Doll.* E (Gr. PreK-2) *2*

APPRENTICES
Higgins, F. E. *The Black Book of Secrets.* FIC (Gr. 5-7) *21*

SUBJECT INDEX, cont.

SUBJECT INDEX, cont.

CARTOONS AND COMICS
O'Malley, Kevin, and Patrick O'Brien. *Captain Raptor and the Space Pirates.* E (Gr. K-3) *2*
Tan, Shaun. *The Arrival.* FIC (Gr. 6-12) *21*
Varon, Sara. *Robot Dreams.* 741.5 (Gr. 2-6) *34*

CATS
Bruel, Nick. *Poor Puppy.* E (Gr. PreK-2) *15*
Jenkins, Steve. *Dogs and Cats.* 636.7 (Gr. 1-5) *37*
Lobel, Anita. *Nini Here and There.* E (Gr. PreK-2) *14*

CAUSE AND EFFECT
Henkes, Kevin. *A Good Day.* E (Gr. PreK-1) *8*
LaRochelle, David. *The End.* E (Gr. PreK-3) *7*
Seeger, Laura Vaccaro. *First the Egg.* 571.8 (Gr. PreK-1) *39*
Stevens, April. *Waking Up Wendell.* E (Gr. PreK-1) *19*

CEREBRAL PALSY
Thompson, Lauren. *Ballerina Dreams.* 618.92 (Gr. K-4) *36*

CHARACTERS IN LITERATURE
Graham, Bob. *Dimity Dumpty: The Story of Humpty's Little Sister.* E (Gr. PreK-2) *6*

CHAUCER, GEOFFREY
Williams, Marcia, retel. *Chaucer's Canterbury Tales.* 821 (Gr. 4-8) *22*

CHEESE
Palatini, Margie. *The Cheese.* E (Gr. PreK-2) *4*

CHICKENS
Bunting, Eve. *Hurry! Hurry!* E (Gr. PreK-1) *9*
Harrington, Janice N. *The Chicken-Chasing Queen of Lamar County.* E (Gr. PreK-3) *5*
Seeger, Laura Vaccaro. *First the Egg.* 571.8 (Gr. PreK-1) *39*

CHINA
Compestine, Ying Chang. *Revolution Is Not a Dinner Party: A Novel.* FIC (Gr. 5-8) *33*

CHRISTMAS
McKissack, Patricia A. *The All-I'll-Ever-Want Christmas Doll.* E (Gr. PreK-3) *1*

CINDERELLA STORIES
Fleischman, Paul. *Glass Slipper, Gold Sandal: A Worldwide Cinderella.* 398.2 (Gr. K-6) *48*

CIRCULAR STORIES
Henkes, Kevin. *A Good Day.* E (Gr. PreK-1) *8*
Stevens, April. *Waking Up Wendell.* E (Gr. PreK-1) *19*

CIRCUS
Graham, Bob. *Dimity Dumpty: The Story of Humpty's Little Sister.* E (Gr. PreK-2) *6*

COLOR
Gonzalez, Maya Christina. *My Colors, My World/Mis Colores, Mi Mundo.* E (Gr. PreK-2) *13*
Jenkins, Steve. *Living Color.* 591.47 (Gr. PreK-4) *41*

COLORADO RIVER—DISCOVERY AND EXPLORATION
Ray, Deborah Kogan. *Down the Colorado: John Wesley Powell, the One-Armed Explorer.* 917.91 (Gr. 3-5) *38*

COMMUNICATION
Clements, Andrew. *No Talking.* FIC (Gr. 3-6) *31*

SUBJECT INDEX, cont.

SUBJECT INDEX, cont.

DESERTS
Gonzalez, Maya Christina. *My Colors, My World/Mis Colores, Mi Mundo.* E (Gr. PreK-2) *13*

DEVIL—FOLKLORE
Schlitz, Laura Amy. *The Bearskinner: A Tale of the Brothers Grimm.* 398.2 (Gr. 3-6) *46*

DIARIES
Kinney, Jeff. *Diary of a Wimpy Kid: Greg Heffley's Journal.* FIC (Gr. 5-8) *23*

DINOSAURS
Broach, Elise. *When Dinosaurs Came with Everything.* E (Gr. PreK-2) *20*
O'Malley, Kevin, and Patrick O'Brien. *Captain Raptor and the Space Pirates.* E (Gr. K-3) *2*

DIVORCE
Coffelt, Nancy. *Fred Stays with Me!* E (Gr. K-3) *7*

DOGS
Bruel, Nick. *Poor Puppy.* E (Gr. PreK-2) *15*
Calmenson, Stephanie. *May I Pet Your Dog?: The How-to Guide for Kids Meeting Dogs (and Dogs Meeting Kids).* E (Gr. PreK-2) *12*
Coffelt, Nancy. *Fred Stays with Me!* E (Gr. K-3) *7*
Jenkins, Steve. *Dogs and Cats.* 636.7 (Gr. 1-5) *37*
Michael, Livi. *City of Dogs.* FIC (Gr. 4-7) *22*
O'Connor, Barbara. *How to Steal a Dog.* FIC (Gr. 4-7) *27*
Seeger, Laura Vaccaro. *Dog and Bear: Two Friends, Three Stories.* E (Gr. PreK-1) *6*
Varon, Sara. *Robot Dreams.* 741.5 (Gr. 2-6) *34*

DOGS—POETRY
Clements, Andrew. *Dogku.* 811 (Gr. PreK-4) *48*

DOLLS
Kleven, Elisa. *The Apple Doll.* E (Gr. PreK-2) *2*
McKissack, Patricia A. *The All-I'll-Ever-Want Christmas Doll.* E (Gr. PreK-3) *1*

DOMESTIC ANIMALS
Bunting, Eve. *Hurry! Hurry!* E (Gr. PreK-1) *9*

DREAMS
Lobel, Anita. *Nini Here and There.* E (Gr. PreK-2) *14*

EASTER
Wells, Rosemary. *Max Counts His Chickens.* E (Gr. PreK-1) *12*

ECONOMICS
Davies, Jacqueline. *The Lemonade War.* FIC (Gr. 2-5) *29*

EGGS
Bunting, Eve. *Hurry! Hurry!* E (Gr. PreK-1) *9*
Graham, Bob. *Dimity Dumpty: The Story of Humpty's Little Sister.* E (Gr. PreK-2) *6*
Seeger, Laura Vaccaro. *First the Egg.* 571.8 (Gr. PreK-1) *39*

ELEPHANTS
Willems, Mo. *I Am Invited to a Party!* E (Gr. PreK-1) *9*
Willems, Mo. *My Friend Is Sad.* E (Gr. PreK-1) *13*
Willems, Mo. *There Is a Bird on Your Head!* E (Gr. PreK-1) *17*
Willems, Mo. *Today I Will Fly!* E (Gr. PreK-1) *18*

SUBJECT INDEX, cont.

FARM LIFE
Harrington, Janice N. *The Chicken-Chasing Queen of Lamar County.* E (Gr. PreK-3) *5*

FATHERS AND DAUGHTERS
Tarshis, Lauren. *Emma-Jean Lazarus Fell Out of a Tree.* FIC (Gr. 5-7) *24*
Hest, Amy. *Remembering Mrs. Rossi.* FIC (Gr. 3-5) *32*
Kimmel, Elizabeth Cody. *The Top Job.* E (Gr. PreK-3) *18*

FIRST DAY OF SCHOOL
Kleven, Elisa. *The Apple Doll.* E (Gr. PreK-2) *2*

FLIGHT
Willems, Mo. *Today I Will Fly!* E (Gr. PreK-1) *18*

FLOWERS
Aston, Dianna. *A Seed Is Sleepy.* 581.4 (Gr. PreK-4) *43*

FOLKLORE—CUBA
Deedy, Carmen Agra. *Martina the Beautiful Cockroach: A Cuban Folktale.* 398.2 (Gr. 1-6) *52*

FOLKLORE—ENGLAND
Rumford, James. *Beowulf: A Hero's Tale Retold.* 398.2 (Gr. 3-8) *46*

FOLKLORE—GERMANY
Pinkney, Jerry. *Little Red Riding Hood.* 298.2 (Gr. PreK-2) *51*
Schlitz, Laura Amy. *The Bearskinner: A Tale of the Brothers Grimm.* 398.2 (Gr. 3-6) *46*

FOLKLORE—LATIN AMERICA
Deedy, Carmen Agra. *Martina the Beautiful Cockroach: A Cuban Folktale.* 398.2 (Gr. 1-6) *52*

FOOD—POETRY
Mora, Pat. *Yum! Mmmm! Que Rico!: Americas' Sproutings.* 811 (Gr. K-4) *53*

FORGIVENESS
Sidman, Joyce. *This Is Just to Say: Poems of Apology and Forgiveness.* 811 (Gr. 4-7) *53*

FRANCE
Selznick, Brian. *The Invention of Hugo Cabret: A Novel in Words and Pictures.* FIC (Gr. 4-7) *28*

FREEDOM
Curtis, Christopher Paul. *Elijah of Buxton.* FIC (Gr. 5-8) *24*

FRIENDSHIP
Blume, Lesley M. M. *The Rising Star of Rusty Nail.* FIC (Gr. 4-7) *33*
Kinney, Jeff. *Diary of a Wimpy Kid: Greg Heffley's Journal.* FIC (Gr. 5-8) *23*
Pennypacker, Sara. *The Talented Clementine.* FIC (Gr. 1-4) *34*
Scieszka, Jon. *Cowboy & Octopus.* E (Gr. PreK-2) *5*
Seeger, Laura Vaccaro. *Dog and Bear: Two Friends, Three Stories.* E (Gr. PreK-1) *6*
Tarshis, Lauren. *Emma-Jean Lazarus Fell Out of a Tree.* FIC (Gr. 5-7) *24*
Varon, Sara. *Robot Dreams.* 741.5 (Gr. 2-6) *34*
Willems, Mo. *I Am Invited to a Party!* E (Gr. PreK-1) *9*
Willems, Mo. *Knuffle Bunny Too: A Case of Mistaken Identity.* E (Gr. PreK-2) *10*
Willems, Mo. *My Friend Is Sad.* E (Gr. PreK-1) *13*
Willems, Mo. *There Is a Bird on Your Head!* E (Gr. PreK-1) *17*
Willems, Mo. *Today I Will Fly!* E (Gr. PreK-1) *18*

FRUIT
Gravett, Emily. *Orange Pear Apple Bear.* E (Gr. PreK-1) *14*

SUBJECT INDEX, cont.

FRUIT—POETRY
Mora, Pat. *Yum! Mmmm! Que Rico!: Americas' Sproutings.* 811 (Gr. K-4) *53*

GAMES
Bruel, Nick. *Poor Puppy.* E (Gr. PreK-2) *15*

GIANT PANDA
Dowson, Nick. *Tracks of a Panda.* E (Gr. PreK-2) *19*

GIFTS
McKissack, Patricia A. *The All-I'll-Ever-Want Christmas Doll.* E (Gr. PreK-3) *1*

GODS AND GODDESSES
Michael, Livi. *City of Dogs.* FIC (Gr. 4-7) *22*

GOOD AND EVIL
Rowling, J. K. *Harry Potter and the Deathly Hallows.* FIC (Gr. 5-12) *26*

GRAND CANYON
Ray, Deborah Kogan. *Down the Colorado: John Wesley Powell, the One-Armed Explorer.* 917.91 (Gr. 3-5) *38*

GRANDMOTHERS
Wells, Rosemary. *Max Counts His Chickens.* E (Gr. PreK-1) *12*

GRANDMOTHERS—FOLKLORE
Pinkney, Jerry. *Little Red Riding Hood.* 298.2 (Gr. PreK-2) *51*

GRAPHIC NOVELS
Tan, Shaun. *The Arrival.* FIC (Gr. 6-12) *21*
Varon, Sara. *Robot Dreams.* 741.5 (Gr. 2-6) *34*

GRIEF
Hest, Amy. *Remembering Mrs. Rossi.* FIC (Gr. 3-5) *32*

HAIKU
Clements, Andrew. *Dogku.* 811 (Gr. PreK-4) *48*
Mora, Pat. *Yum! Mmmm! Que Rico!: Americas' Sproutings.* 811 (Gr. K-4) *53*

HALLOWEEN
Montes, Marisa. *Los Gatos Black on Halloween.* E (Gr. 1-4) *11*

HAUNTED HOUSES
Montes, Marisa. *Los Gatos Black on Halloween.* E (Gr. 1-4) *11*

HISPANIC AMERICANS
Gonzalez, Maya Christina. *My Colors, My World/Mis Colores, Mi Mundo.* E (Gr. PreK-2) *13*

HISTORICAL FICTION
Blume, Lesley M. M. *The Rising Star of Rusty Nail.* FIC (Gr. 4-7) *33*
Compestine, Ying Chang. *Revolution Is Not a Dinner Party: A Novel.* FIC (Gr. 5-8) *33*
Curtis, Christopher Paul. *Elijah of Buxton.* FIC (Gr. 5-8) *24*
Levine, Ellen. *Henry's Freedom Box: A True Story.* E (Gr. 2-6) *8*
McKissack, Patricia A. *The All-I'll-Ever-Want Christmas Doll.* E (Gr. PreK-3) *1*
Miller, Sarah Elizabeth. *Miss Spitfire: Reaching Helen Keller.* FIC (Gr. 5-8) *30*

HOMELESS PERSONS
O'Connor, Barbara. *How to Steal a Dog.* FIC (Gr. 4-7) *27*

HOPE
Applegate, Katherine. *Home of the Brave.* FIC (Gr. 5-8) *27*

SUBJECT INDEX, cont.

SUBJECT INDEX, cont.

SUBJECT INDEX, cont.

SUBJECT INDEX, cont.

PICTURE BOOKS FOR OLDER READERS
Sís, Peter. *The Wall: Growing Up Behind the Iron Curtain.* 943.7 (Gr. 4-12) *45*

PIGS
Stevens, April. *Waking Up Wendell.* E (Gr. PreK-1) *19*
Willems, Mo. *I Am Invited to a Party!* E (Gr. PreK-1) *9*
Willems, Mo. *My Friend Is Sad.* E (Gr. PreK-1) *13*
Willems, Mo. *There Is a Bird on Your Head!* E (Gr. PreK-1) *17*
Willems, Mo. *Today I Will Fly!* E (Gr. PreK-1) *18*

PIRATES
O'Malley, Kevin, and Patrick O'Brien. *Captain Raptor and the Space Pirates.* E (Gr. K-3) *2*

PLANTS
Aston, Dianna. *A Seed Is Sleepy.* 581.4 (Gr. PreK-4) *43*

PLAY
Cowell, Cressida. *That Rabbit Belongs to Emily Brown.* E (Gr. PreK-2) *17*
Lehman, Barbara. *Rainstorm.* E (Gr. PreK-2) *16*

PLAYS
Schlitz, Laura Amy. *Good Masters! Sweet Ladies!: Voices from a Medieval Village.* 812.6 (Gr. 5-9) *49*
Schmidt, Gary D. *The Wednesday Wars.* FIC (Gr. 6-8) *35*

POETRY
Clements, Andrew. *Dogku.* 811 (Gr. PreK-4) *48*
Florian, Douglas. *Comets, Stars, the Moon, and Mars: Space Poems and Paintings.* 811 (Gr. K-6) *47*
Grandits, John. *Blue Lipstick: Concrete Poems.* 811 (Gr. 5-9) *47*
Mora, Pat. *Yum! Mmmm! Que Rico!: Americas' Sproutings.* 811 (Gr. K-4) *53*
Park, Linda Sue. *Tap Dancing on the Roof: Sijo (Poems).* 811 (Gr. 3-7) *52*
Prévert, Jacques. *How to Paint the Portrait of a Bird.* 841 (Gr. K-6) *50*
Schlitz, Laura Amy. *Good Masters! Sweet Ladies!: Voices from a Medieval Village.* 812.6 (Gr. 5-9) *49*
Sidman, Joyce. *This Is Just to Say: Poems of Apology and Forgiveness.* 811 (Gr. 4-7) *53*
Yolen, Jane, and Andrew Fusek Peters, eds. *Here's a Little Poem: A Very First Book of Poetry.* 811.008 (Gr. PreK-1) *49*

POINT OF VIEW
Grandits, John. *Blue Lipstick: Concrete Poems.* 811 (Gr. 5-9) *47*
Schlitz, Laura Amy. *Good Masters! Sweet Ladies!: Voices from a Medieval Village.* 812.6 (Gr. 5-9) *49*

POWELL, JOHN WESLEY, 1834-1902
Ray, Deborah Kogan. *Down the Colorado: John Wesley Powell, the One-Armed Explorer.* 917.91 (Gr. 3-5) *38*

PRINCES AND PRINCESSES
LaRochelle, David. *The End.* E (Gr. PreK-3) *7*

PRINCIPALS
Pennypacker, Sara. *The Talented Clementine.* FIC (Gr. 1-4) *34*

PROBLEM SOLVING
Tarshis, Lauren. *Emma-Jean Lazarus Fell Out of a Tree.* FIC (Gr. 5-7) *24*

PROCEDURAL WRITING
Calmenson, Stephanie. *May I Pet Your Dog?: The How-to Guide for Kids Meeting Dogs (and Dogs Meeting Kids).* E (Gr. PreK-2) *12*
O'Connor, Barbara. *How to Steal a Dog.* FIC (Gr. 4-7) *27*
Prévert, Jacques. *How to Paint the Portrait of a Bird.* 841 (Gr. K-6) *50*

PUZZLES
Berlin, Eric. *The Puzzling World of Winston Breen.* FIC (Gr. 4-6) *32*

SUBJECT INDEX, cont.

RABBITS
Cowell, Cressida. *That Rabbit Belongs to Emily Brown.* E (Gr. PreK-2) *17*
Wells, Rosemary. *Max Counts His Chickens.* E (Gr. PreK-1) *12*
Willems, Mo. *Knuffle Bunny Too: A Case of Mistaken Identity.* E (Gr. PreK-2) *10*

RACE RELATIONS
Woodson, Jacqueline. *Feathers.* FIC (Gr. 4-7) *26*

RAILROAD STATIONS
Selznick, Brian. *The Invention of Hugo Cabret: A Novel in Words and Pictures.* FIC (Gr. 4-7) *28*

RAIN AND RAINFALL
Lehman, Barbara. *Rainstorm.* E (Gr. PreK-2) *16*

RATS
Bang-Campbell, Monika. *Little Rat Makes Music.* E (Gr. K-3) *11*
Jonell, Lynne. *Emmy and the Incredible Shrinking Rat.* FIC (Gr. 3-6) *25*
Palatini, Margie. *The Cheese.* E (Gr. PreK-2) *4*

READER'S THEATER
Fleming, Candace. *The Fabled Fourth Graders of Aesop Elementary School.* FIC (Gr. 2-5) *25*
O'Malley, Kevin, and Patrick O'Brien. *Captain Raptor and the Space Pirates.* E (Gr. K-3) *2*
Palatini, Margie. *The Cheese.* E (Gr. PreK-2) *4*
Scieszka, Jon. *Cowboy & Octopus.* E (Gr. PreK-2) *5*
Willems, Mo. *My Friend Is Sad.* E (Gr. PreK-1) *13*

RELIGION
Woodson, Jacqueline. *Feathers.* FIC (Gr. 4-7) *26*

REVERE, PAUL
Giblin, James Cross. *The Many Rides of Paul Revere.* B (Gr. 4-7) *42*

RIDDLES
Knock, Knock! 818 (Gr. PreK-5) *50*

ROBOTS
Selznick, Brian. *The Invention of Hugo Cabret: A Novel in Words and Pictures.* FIC (Gr. 4-7) *28*
Varon, Sara. *Robot Dreams.* 741.5 (Gr. 2-6) *34*

RUSSIAN AMERICANS
Blume, Lesley M. M. *The Rising Star of Rusty Nail.* FIC (Gr. 4-7) *33*

SAFETY
Calmenson, Stephanie. *May I Pet Your Dog?: The How-to Guide for Kids Meeting Dogs (and Dogs Meeting Kids).* E (Gr. PreK-2) *12*

SCHOOLS
Applegate, Katherine. *Home of the Brave.* FIC (Gr. 5-8) *27*
Clements, Andrew. *No Talking.* FIC (Gr. 3-6) *31*
Fleming, Candace. *The Fabled Fourth Graders of Aesop Elementary School.* FIC (Gr. 2-5) *25*
Grandits, John. *Blue Lipstick: Concrete Poems.* 811 (Gr. 5-9) *47*
Kinney, Jeff. *Diary of a Wimpy Kid: Greg Heffley's Journal.* FIC (Gr. 5-8) *23*
Kleven, Elisa. *The Apple Doll.* E (Gr. PreK-2) *2*
Pennypacker, Sara. *The Talented Clementine.* FIC (Gr. 1-4) *34*
Rowling, J. K. *Harry Potter and the Deathly Hallows.* FIC (Gr. 5-12) *26*
Schmidt, Gary D. *The Wednesday Wars.* FIC (Gr. 6-8) *35*
Stewart, Trenton Lee. *The Mysterious Benedict Society.* FIC (Gr. 4-7) *31*
Tarshis, Lauren. *Emma-Jean Lazarus Fell Out of a Tree.* FIC (Gr. 5-7) *24*
Urban, Linda. *A Crooked Kind of Perfect.* FIC (Gr. 4-6) *23*
Willems, Mo. *Knuffle Bunny Too: A Case of Mistaken Identity.* E (Gr. PreK-2) *10*
Woodson, Jacqueline. *Feathers.* FIC (Gr. 4-7) *26*

SUBJECT INDEX, cont.

SUBJECT INDEX, cont.

SOCIAL STUDIES
Compestine, Ying Chang. *Revolution Is Not a Dinner Party: A Novel.* FIC (Gr. 5-8) *33*
Curtis, Christopher Paul. *Elijah of Buxton.* FIC (Gr. 5-8) *24*
Freedman, Russell. *Who Was First?: Discovering the Americas.* 970.01 (Gr. 5-9) *45*
Giblin, James Cross. *The Many Rides of Paul Revere.* B (Gr. 4-7) *42*
Levine, Ellen. *Henry's Freedom Box: A True Story.* E (Gr. 2-6) *8*
Ray, Deborah Kogan. *Down the Colorado: John Wesley Powell, the One-Armed Explorer.* 917.91 (Gr. 3-5) *38*
Schlitz, Laura Amy. *Good Masters! Sweet Ladies!: Voices from a Medieval Village.* 812.6 (Gr. 5-9) *49*
Sís, Peter. *The Wall: Growing Up Behind the Iron Curtain.* 943.7 (Gr. 4-12) *45*

SOLDIERS—FOLKLORE
Schlitz, Laura Amy. *The Bearskinner: A Tale of the Brothers Grimm.* 398.2 (Gr. 3-6) *46*

SONGS
Bryan, Ashley. *Let It Shine: Three Favorite Spirituals.* 782.25 (Gr. PreK-5) *51*

SPACE FLIGHT
O'Malley, Kevin, and Patrick O'Brien. *Captain Raptor and the Space Pirates.* E (Gr. K-3) *2*

SPANISH LANGUAGE
Gonzalez, Maya Christina. *My Colors, My World/Mis Colores, Mi Mundo.* E (Gr. PreK-2) *13*
Montes, Marisa. *Los Gatos Black on Halloween.* E (Gr. 1-4) *11*
Mora, Pat. *Yum! Mmmm! Que Rico!: Americas' Sproutings.* 811 (Gr. K-4) *53*

SPIDERS
Bishop, Nic. *Nic Bishop Spiders.* 595.4 (Gr. K-6) *42*

SPIRITUALS
Bryan, Ashley. *Let It Shine: Three Favorite Spirituals.* 782.25 (Gr. PreK-5) *51*

SPORTS
Cook, Sally, and James Charlton. *Hey Batta Batta Swing!: The Wild Old Days of Baseball.* 796.357 (Gr. 1-8) *40*
Gutman, Dan. *Casey Back at Bat.* E (Gr. K-8) *3*
Lewin, Ted. *At Gleason's Gym.* 796.83 (Gr. K-5) *36*
McCarthy, Meghan. *Strong Man: The Story of Charles Atlas.* B (Gr. 1-5) *44*

STATUE OF LIBERTY
Kimmel, Elizabeth Cody. *The Top Job.* E (Gr. PreK-3) *18*

STEPMOTHERS—FOLKLORE
Fleischman, Paul. *Glass Slipper, Gold Sandal: A Worldwide Cinderella.* 398.2 (Gr. K-6) *48*

STORIES IN RHYME
Gravett, Emily. *Orange Pear Apple Bear.* E (Gr. PreK-1) *14*
Gutman, Dan. *Casey Back at Bat.* E (Gr. K-8) *3*
Hutchins, Hazel. *A Second Is a Hiccup: A Child's Book of Time.* E (Gr. PreK-1) *16*
Kulka, Joe. *Wolf's Coming!* E (Gr. PreK-1) *20*
Montes, Marisa. *Los Gatos Black on Halloween.* E (Gr. 1-4) *11*
Wheeler, Lisa. *Jazz Baby.* E (Gr. PreK-1) *10*

STORIES WITHOUT WORDS
Lehman, Barbara. *Rainstorm.* E (Gr. PreK-2) *16*
Tan, Shaun. *The Arrival.* FIC (Gr. 6-12) *21*
Varon, Sara. *Robot Dreams.* 741.5 (Gr. 2-6) *34*

STORYTELLING
Williams, Marcia, retel. *Chaucer's Canterbury Tales.* 821 (Gr. 4-8) *22*

SUBJECT INDEX, cont.

STRONG MEN
McCarthy, Meghan. *Strong Man: The Story of Charles Atlas.* B (Gr. 1-5) *44*

STUFFED ANIMALS
Cowell, Cressida. *That Rabbit Belongs to Emily Brown.* E (Gr. PreK-2) *17*
Willems, Mo. *Knuffle Bunny Too: A Case of Mistaken Identity.* E (Gr. PreK-2) *10*

SULLIVAN, ANNIE, 1866-1936
Miller, Sarah Elizabeth. *Miss Spitfire: Reaching Helen Keller.* FIC (Gr. 5-8) *30*

SUMMER
Davies, Jacqueline. *The Lemonade War.* FIC (Gr. 2-5) *29*
Perkins, Lynne Rae. *Pictures from Our Vacation.* E (Gr. K-3) *15*

TALENT SHOWS
Pennypacker, Sara. *The Talented Clementine.* FIC (Gr. 1-4) *34*

TEACHERS
Clements, Andrew. *No Talking.* FIC (Gr. 3-6) *31*
Fleming, Candace. *The Fabled Fourth Graders of Aesop Elementary School.* FIC (Gr. 2-5) *25*
Hest, Amy. *Remembering Mrs. Rossi.* FIC (Gr. 3-5) *32*
Miller, Sarah Elizabeth. *Miss Spitfire: Reaching Helen Keller.* FIC (Gr. 5-8) *30*
Schmidt, Gary D. *The Wednesday Wars.* FIC (Gr. 6-8) *35*
Sidman, Joyce. *This Is Just to Say: Poems of Apology and Forgiveness.* 811 (Gr. 4-7) *53*
Willems, Mo. *Knuffle Bunny Too: A Case of Mistaken Identity.* E (Gr. PreK-2) *10*

TEDDY BEARS
Seeger, Laura Vaccaro. *Dog and Bear: Two Friends, Three Stories.* E (Gr. PreK-1) *6*

THIEBAUD, WAYNE
Rubin, Susan Goldman. *Delicious: The Life & Art of Wayne Thiebaud.* B (Gr. 5-12) *37*

TIME
Hutchins, Hazel. *A Second Is a Hiccup: A Child's Book of Time.* E (Gr. PreK-1) *16*

TOTALITARIANISM
Compestine, Ying Chang. *Revolution Is Not a Dinner Party: A Novel.* FIC (Gr. 5-8) *33*
Sís, Peter. *The Wall: Growing Up Behind the Iron Curtain.* 943.7 (Gr. 4-12) *45*

TOY AND MOVEABLE BOOKS
Seeger, Laura Vaccaro. *First the Egg.* 571.8 (Gr. PreK-1) *39*

TRANSFORMATIONS
Jonell, Lynne. *Emmy and the Incredible Shrinking Rat.* FIC (Gr. 3-6) *25*

TREES
Aston, Dianna. *A Seed Is Sleepy.* 581.4 (Gr. PreK-4) *43*

TURKEY VULTURES
Sayre, April Pulley. *Vulture View.* 598.9 (Gr. PreK-2) *44*

U.S.—HISTORY—1865-1898
Ray, Deborah Kogan. *Down the Colorado: John Wesley Powell, the One-Armed Explorer.* 917.91 (Gr. 3-5) *38*

U.S.—HISTORY—20TH CENTURY
Bertholf, Bret. *The Long Gone Lonesome History of Country Music.* 781.642 (Gr. 3-6) *41*

U.S.—HISTORY—REVOLUTION, 1775-1783
Giblin, James Cross. *The Many Rides of Paul Revere.* B (Gr. 4-7) *42*

SUBJECT INDEX, cont.

EVALUATING CHILDREN'S BOOKS

THINGS TO CONSIDER WHEN READING AND DISCUSSING BOOKS

Adapted from *Books Kids Will Sit Still For 3*
(Libraries Unlimited, 2006) by Judy Freeman.

Here is my personal list of evaluative guideposts that I use when pondering the strengths and weaknesses of a new book.

PLOT — Plan of action; holds story together; how the story is arranged. Encompasses exposition, problem, rising action, conflict, climax, falling action (dénouement), resolution.

SETTING — Past, present, or future. Specific place, generic or universal setting; vital to the story (integral setting), or an unimportant backdrop.

CHARACTERIZATION — What types of protagonists and antagonists? (Flat, stereotyped, fully developed, round, etc.) How presented? (Through narration, character's conversations with self or others, character's thoughts, character's actions, physical description.) Major and minor; static (unchanging) or dynamic (changing).

POINT OF VIEW — How the reader learns of the events, character motivation, and climax. Told in first person, second person (rare), third person; omniscient, limited omniscient, objective.

THEME — Author's purpose in writing the story, going beyond the general plot; the underlying truths or lessons to be learned about life, stated explicitly or implicitly.

STYLE — What makes writing memorable. Smooth, fast-paced, full of vivid description of action; or stilted, moralistic, sentimental, didactic, and patronizing to the child reader. How is the story arranged: chronological, with flashbacks, episodic.

FORMAT — Shape, size, design of book; special features (pop-up, gatefold or die-cut pages; unusual cover or dust jacket design)

ILLUSTRATIONS — How do they complement / extend text? What style / medium is used?

COMPARISONS — With other books of same topic, theme, genre, style, author, etc.

20 BASIC QUESTIONS TO ASK YOURSELF WHEN EVALUATING A NEW BOOK

Adapted from *Books Kids Will Sit Still For 3* (Libraries Unlimited, 2006) by Judy Freeman.

1. Is the plot original or groundbreaking or surprising? Or is it predictable or preachy or overdone.

2. How is the plot presented? (Flashback, chronological, episodic, etc.) Could you follow the thread of the story throughout?

3. Do all of the events and supporting details make sense and work, within the context of the story? Are the facts accurate, even in a fantasy?

4. Does the author have a recognizable narrative style? What is distinctive about it? Does it flow naturally with interesting language, varied sentence structure, and appeal to the reader, or does it feel clunky or choppy or soporific? What tone does the author use?

5. Point of view: Who narrates the book? Is the narration believable? Were you able to lose yourself in the story and experience a willing suspension of disbelief?

6. Are the main characters worth getting to know? Can you visualize them? Do you feel you got to know them well?

7. Does the setting play an important part? If so, is it visually vivid, as in sci fi and fantasy, which may take place in an unfamiliar world?

8. Are there any parts that you feel are very well or very poorly written? Did you want to keep reading without stopping, or did you keep putting the book down? As author James Patterson would say, does this book have Narrative Power that propels the book and makes you keep turning the pages?

9. Is the ending satisfying, or does the story fall apart midway? Is it an open or closed ending?

10. What is the theme? Is it intuitive to the reader or thought-provoking, or didactic or moralistic? Will children grasp what the author wanted to say?

11. Do the illustrations fit the story? Do they extend the story or just restate it?

12. Is there anything remarkable about the format?

13. Does the cover work? Will it turn kids on, off, or leave them cold?

14. When you think of the book, which scene or character first comes to mind? Will you think about this book in a week? A month? A year? Forever?

15. What did you enjoy most/least about the book?

16. What grades/age levels does this book best fit?

17. What types of children will want to read this book and why?

18. Do you agree with the published reviews (*Booklist*, *Hornbook*, *School Library Journal*, *Publishers Weekly*, *Kirkus*, *The New York Times*, etc.)? Do the published reviews agree with each other?

19. How can you use / present this book with children?

20. What other books do you have on this topic or theme, or in this style, to which you can link this title for readers? How will this book strengthen your collection?

WINNERS & LOSERS

The "Experts" liked this book a lot. They are grown-ups. You are a kid. Kids are the ones who are going to read this book. The "Experts" are not always right. Sometimes they forget or misjudge what kids will like. When you read this book, give an honest opinion of what you think of it.

*AUTHOR*_____

TITLE _____

After completing your book, write a paragraph or more explaining exactly what you thought of it. You do not need to give a summary of the plot. Instead, consider these points:

THE ILLUSTRATIONS

THE STORY

TO WHOM WOULD YOU RECOMMEND THIS? WHY?

DOES THIS BOOK DESERVE TO BE CONSIDERED A "WINNER" OR A "LOSER"? EXPLAIN WHY.

BE VERY HONEST.

_____
_____
_____
_____
_____
_____
_____
_____
_____
_____
_____
_____
_____
_____
_____

10 Reasons to Befriend a Book

Laughter, friendship, and empathy are just a few

by Judy Freeman

An article for *Curriculum Connections*
(A Supplement to *School Library Journal*), Fall, 2007 issue.
Reprinted with permission from *School Library Journal/Curriculum Connections*,
October 2007, Reed Business Information, copyright 2007.

It seems commonsensical to say that the more you read, the smarter you get. That's a reasonable justification for hitting the books. One study says the more education you have, the more money you make. Another tells us that poor readers die earlier. The research seems clear: if you want to be healthy, wealthy, and wise—read. It's a start, anyway. Ask your students: What's so important about being a reader? What is it about a great book that is so enticing?

In my title, *Books Kids Will Sit Still For 3* (Libraries Unlimited, 2006), I wrote a chapter with "10 Reasons to Befriend a Great Book." Here, then, is an updated list to share with children, with one memorable new read-aloud book for each reason.

1. Books can make you laugh out loud as you fool around with words.
"Once upon a time, in a grand castle, there lived a rat named Bob, who was fond of baking and wild about reading." I was smitten with that first sentence of Mary Hanson's *How to Save Your Tail: If You Are a Rat Nabbed by Cats Who Really Like Stories about Magic Spoons, Wolves with Snout-Warts, Big, Hairy Chimney Trolls . . . and Cookies Too* (Schwartz & Wade, 2007; Gr 2-5). Hey, me, too! I thought. I love baking and reading, too! A captivating first sentence in a children's fiction book is a gift. I continued: "Now, baking can be dangerous for a rat. Paws get burned and tails get caught in eggbeaters all the time. But it was his love of books that almost killed…." (Killed who?) Eagerly, I turned the page. "Bob."

On page two, there was also the first of John Hendrix's genial black-and-white pen-and-ink illustrations, with my new friend Bob lounging on a pot holder, his head resting on a rolling pin, a bandanna tied around his neck. On page four, Bob is snared by the Queen's cats, Brutus and Muffin, but he bribes his way out with warm butter cookies and a story.

Luckily, Bob is a storyteller, though it takes him five tales to save his own neck from those hungry but not-so-swift-witted cats. If you know your fairy tales, you'll recognize elements of "Jack and the Beanstalk," "The Three Pigs," "Rumpelstiltskin," "Toads and Diamonds," and "Cinderella," retold in short, rat-themed chapters just begging to be read aloud with a plate of cookies and a glass of milk.

Don't assume your students are familiar with the tales on which Bob's stories are based; read them in tandem. With older children, follow up on the rat versus Cinderella theme with Philip Pullman's *I Was a Rat* (Knopf, 2000; Gr 4-7). For a writing tie-in Bob would appreciate, have children read other well-known fairy tales and rewrite them, putting Bob's relatives in major roles. (Refer to the book's chart of his extensive family tree for inspiration.)

2. With books, you get to make new friends who will always be there for you.
In Derek Landy's *Skulduggery Pleasant* (HarperCollins, 2007; Gr 5-8), readers meet Stephanie Edgley, a 12-year-old girl described by her Uncle Gordon as "strong willed, intelligent, sharp-tongued, [and] doesn't suffer fools gladly," who has just inherited the bulk of her late uncle's estate in Ireland. He was a best-selling author whose tales of horror and magic Stephanie always assumed were fiction, but that was before she teams up with her uncle's good friend, Skulduggery Pleasant, an enigmatic figure in a tan overcoat and gloves, his face obscured by his scarf, hat, and sunglasses.

93.

In his prime, Skulduggery was an Elemental, a type of sorcerer or mage, but ever since his murder, oh, several hundred years back, he's been a walking, talking, wisecracking, mystery-solving skeleton, trying to save the world from rogue magicians. It's entirely possible Uncle Gordon was murdered because he had knowledge of the legendary Scepter of the Ancients, and Stephanie might unwittingly possess the key that the bad guys need to find it.

Be forewarned: there are lots of fireballs and car crashes and violence and blood in this breezy but suspenseful fantasy. Still, readers will get quite fond of the girl and the living skeleton, which is good, as this is the first in a series of seven and a booktalker's dream.

3. Books let you hear another person's voice in your head.

The singular voices of all of the main characters in Christopher Paul Curtis's books are what pull you into his novels. Joining my favorite narrators, Kenny from *The Watsons Go to Birmingham, 1963* (1995) and Bud from *Bud, Not Buddy* (1999, both Delacorte), is 11-year-old Elijah Freeman in *Elijah of Buxton* (Scholastic, 2007; Gr 4-8).

In this latest masterpiece, set in 1859 in Buxton, Ontario, a Canadian village founded by freed slaves, Elijah knows he is considered special. He was the first child to be born free in the Settlement and, as an infant, the one who threw up all over visiting dignitary, Frederick Douglass.

He's all boy, sneaking a toady-frog in his Ma's knitting basket with predictable results, but is "terrorfied" and cries himself silly when Ma retaliates by putting a snake in the cookie jar for him to discover. She wants him to be less "fra-gile," as she puts it, but he is naive and often bamboozled by a fast-talking con man known as the Preacher.

For all Elijah's gut-busting stories and observations about his best friend Cooter, school days, and attending a Carnival of Oddities, this extraordinary novel has a serious component. After newly freed slaves make it to Buxton, bad news comes from America, and Elijah finds out firsthand the difference between slavery and freedom. The book is an eye-opener as a read-aloud, and a sterling example of personal narrative and voice. It ties into the social studies curriculum in its look at the realities of slavery.

4. Books let us know how other people feel.

"The day I decided to steal a dog was the same day my best friend, Luanne Godfrey, found out I lived in a car." That first sentence of Barbara O'Connor's *How to Steal a Dog* (Farrar, 2007; Gr 3-7) will get your children talking.

Live in a car? How can you live in a car? Daddy's deserted them, Mama's working two jobs, and, after school each day, Georgina and her little brother Toby wait outside the Chevrolet for Mama to meet them. It's been a week now. Luanne says, "No offense, Georgina. But you're starting to look unkempt." Seeing a missing dog sign with its offer of a five hundred dollar reward tacked to a telephone pole, the desperate girl hatches a plan, recording in her notebook lists of the rules and steps she needs to carry it out.

Read aloud the first chapter, and scrutinize the cute little black-and-white dog on the book's cover. Set up a debate. Would it be OK for Georgina to abduct that little dog if the reward money could help her family find a place to live? What should she do? Mind you, Georgina does steal that dog.

What's compelling about this fast-moving novel is the utter realism of it for children. Georgina is a sympathetic character, but as you read, you find yourself talking to her in your head: Don't do it, Georgina! Why doesn't someone help them? Does this really happen to people? What would I do if it happened to me? Mookie, a homeless older man Georgina encounters, and the conscience of the story, has a relevant motto, which you can discuss: "Sometimes the trail you leave behind you is more important than the path ahead of you."

5. Books allow you to go places you might never get to visit on your own.

Preteens get to have so much fun in fiction books. Look at 11-year-old Theodosia Throckmorton in *Theodosia and the Serpents of Chaos* by R. L. LaFevers (Houghton, 2007; Gr 4-7). Theodosia often sleeps in a sarcophagus at the Museum of Legends and Antiquities in London, where her preoccupied and clueless father is the head curator. Clueless? Although Father is an expert in Egyptian antiquities, and Mother is off at a dig in Egypt, neither parent has any idea that the artifacts they bring back to the museum are dripping with ancient, evil curses. Theodosia not only detects the black magic clinging to each object, but has educated herself in how to remove each curse. That's one smart kid.

When Mother returns home with a priceless scarab, Thutmose III's Heart of Egypt, and it's stolen, Theodosia, aided by her younger brother, Henry, and a street urchin named Sticky Will, must find it before its curse brings down the British Empire. And the plucky girl must stow away on a ship bound for Cairo to do it. So not only do readers have the pleasure of a vicarious jaunt through the foggy London streets of 1906, but they also take a hazardous expedition through a pharaoh's tomb in the Valley of the Kings.

Pull out your books on ancient Egypt, hieroglyphics, and mummies and invite your students on an online tour of the British and Cairo Museums. There are all sorts of wonderful links, contests, facts, and even a blog where they can write to Theodosia and she'll respond at <**www.theodosiathrockmorton.com**>.

6. Books let you travel in time and vicariously experience adventures.

Recently, I was working in my attic study late at night and heard a scritch, scritch, scritch behind me. I turned around to see a brown bat, sitting on a folder two feet from my head. Believe it or not, before I bolted down the stairs, I thought of Kenneth Oppel and my favorite bat novel, *Silverwing* (S & S, 1997), which gave me such bat empathy a decade ago. I perceived my little adventure as a sign to pick up Oppel's sweeping prehistorical fantasy *Darkwing* (Eos, 2007; Gr 4-8), set 65 million years ago in the days before bats could fly.

Dusk is a chiropter, a fictional batlike creature, but he has only two claws on each hand instead of three, and weak legs, which makes climbing the sequoia where he lives an exhausting undertaking. There are two things Dusk can do that set him apart from the others: he can flap his wings and fly like a bird, not just glide, and he has night vision. These differences make him an outcast at a time when his father, Icaron, the leader of the colony, finds his authority being challenged. The peace the animals have enjoyed for years is now being threatened by a furry felid named Carnassial who has decided to become a predator. What's real and what's fantasy? An "Author's Note" clarifies some of that; the Web site, <**www.darkwing.ca**>, adds more detail and is filled with sound and pictures.

7. Books help you cope with problems you have in your own life.

All children come to school with emotional baggage; good books can help them deal with difficult issues. The toughest one of all is the death of a parent. In Amy Hest's wistful chapter book, *Remembering Mrs. Rossi* (Candlewick, 2007; Gr 2-4), illustrated by Heather Maione, third-grader Annie Rossi and her professor dad are finding their way together after Mrs. Rossi, a school teacher, dies unexpectedly. They're not the only ones affected; Mrs. Rossi's sixth-grade class invites Annie and her dad to the school's Winter Assembly to present them with a special book of students' essays about their beloved teacher.

What the two discover is that somehow, in spite of bouts of tears and sadness and anger and missing Mommy, there's joy, too. Somehow, life continues. There's a snow day when Annie sits in on her father's college English class and a summer at the beach when she and her friend Helen walk to town alone, without permission.

Told in present tense, the omniscient narrator shepherds us tenderly but carefully through what could be risky terrain for children-What if my mom died?-and lets us see how a family copes with tragedy. The book of heartfelt essays by Mrs. Rossi's students, appended at the back, is a huge help to Annie and will be a source of writing ideas to use with your kids, too. Go to <**www.candlewick.com**>, type the title in the search bar, and you can download a good teacher's guide.

8. Books let us find out facts we never knew before.

Mac's number one goal is to be the best fourth-grade scientist ever in Frances O'Roark Dowell's *Phineas L. MacGuire...Gets Slimed!* (2007; Gr 1-4), illustrated by Preston McDaniels. If you read the first book, *Phineas L. MacGuire...Erupts!; The First Experiment* (2006, both Atheneum), you'll recall Mac and his new best friend, Ben, only got an honorable mention for their science-fair entry, a volcano. Currently, Mac is thinking scientifically about mold.

What's so terrific about this chapter-book series for younger readers is the melding of Mac's comic and insightful left-brained observations about his friends and family, social issues that all children deal with-artistic genius Ben wants to run for class president to please his divorced dad-and pure science. Mac plans to put together a mold museum in the school basement. As he says, "There's probably nothing more beautiful on the whole planet Earth than a colorful slime mold."

Turn to Mac's three science experiments at the back of the book for directions on how to grow some, and make a class project out of it. Have your students come up with topics Mac might want to tackle in his next book and write sample chapters, incorporating science facts into the narrative.

9. Books are beautiful.

James Rumford's pen-and-ink and watercolor illustrations in *Beowulf: A Hero's Tale Retold* (Houghton, 2007; Gr 3-8) are a visual feast, inspired by the works of Arthur Rackham and Edmond Dulac. Perhaps they're not beautiful in the classic sense, infused as they are with two pretty creepy green monsters that rise up from the marshes and an orange dragon that lurks outside of the page borders, children will find them satisfyingly scary.

Rumford's skillful retelling and distillation of the ninth-century hero poem is elemental enough for even third graders to comprehend. And what a saga it is. With his bare hands, the stalwart young knight Beowulf rips off the arm of the ogre Grendel, kills Grendel's evil mother ("Then up through the gore-red waves came Beowulf, unharmed!"), and, many years later, as King of the Geats, meets his end fighting and defeating a flying fire-snake. Talk about testosterone!

In an appended note, Rumford explains how, with the exception of three Old Norse words-they, their, and them-he used only words that can be traced back to the Old English, a language also called Anglo-Saxon. Online, you'll find many bits of side-by-side translations you can print out and audio clips of readings in Anglo-Saxon, including those on Ben Slade's site, **<www.beowulftranslations.net/benslade.shtml>**. Children will be amazed to find they can't understand a word of it.

10. Books inspire us to write or tell our own stories.

In Barbara Kerley's *Greetings from Planet Earth* (Scholastic, 2007; Gr 4-7), sixth-grader Theo says, "My science teacher asked our class if what we do is the same as what we are....I think sometimes we do things that aren't who we are at all. And the more that happens, the harder it is to find yourself again."

It's 1977 and NASA is preparing to launch *Voyager 1* and *2*. Each spacecraft will carry a golden record with images of Earth recorded in it. Mr. Meyer poses a question for his students to answer in a recording: what would be most important for someone from another planet to know about earthlings? Theo has enough questions about his own world and place in it. Foremost in his mind are questions about his dad. He was supposed to return from Vietnam when Theo was five, but never did. Theo needs the truth.

Interspersed between each chapter are Theo's tape recordings to his dad, with his observations about space and family and how he fits in. From this introspective novel, children will think about who they are, too. Ask them to put together a small box containing clues to themselves and a list of questions they'd like to see answered, both scientific and personal.

As S. I. Hayakawa, former U.S. Senator from California, said, "It is not true that we have only one life to live; if we can read, we can live as many more lives and as many kinds of lives as we wish."

Ask your students about the lives they've lived through books. They can then make their own lists of 10 Reasons to Read and include the titles, contemporary to classic, that they've befriended. Post the assignments in a prominent spot so everyone can find some new books to love.

JUDY FREEMAN (www.JudyReadsBooks.com) is a consultant, writer, and speaker on children's literature. She is the author of *Books Kids Will Sit Still For 3* (2006) and *Once Upon a Time: Using Storytelling, Creative Drama, and Reader's Theater with Children, Grades PreK-6* (2007; both Libraries Unlimited).

Judy Freeman's
LIST OF MEMORABLE AUTHORS & ILLUSTRATORS

Updated Spring, 2008

In *Books Kids Will Sit Still For*, I drew up a list of authors and illustrators who had made a lasting contribution to children's literature and had accumulated a significant body of work. I broke the lists into suggested grade levels to assist teachers and librarians looking to institute monthly or weekly author/illustrator studies, either for reading aloud or having students familiarize themselves with an author's books.

I update this list every year, and while it is in no way comprehensive, I hope you can use it as a way to familiarize yourself with some of the best in the children's literature field and to introduce new and worthy writers and artists to your media-dazed students. For additional suggestions, be sure to look at the lists one grade level above and below your students', depending on their reading and maturity levels.

(Key: Author = A, Illustrator = I, Author/Illustrator = A/I)

PRESCHOOL, KINDERGARTEN, AND GRADE 1:

Jose Aruego (A/I), Frank Asch (A/I), Jim Aylesworth (A), Molly Bang (A/I), Byron Barton (A/I), Robert J. Blake (A/I), Harry Bliss (I), Barbara Bottner (A), Jan Brett (A/I), Norman Bridwell (A/I), Marc Brown (A/I), Anthony Browne (A/I), Nick Bruel (A/I), Denise Brunkus (I), Janell Cannon (A/I), Nancy Carlson (A/I), Eric Carle (A/I), Judith Caseley (A/I), Denys Cazet (A/I), Victoria Chess (I), Lauren Child (A/I), Eileen Christelow (A/I), Henry Cole (I), Joy Cowley (A), Donald Crews (A/I), Doreen Cronin (A), Katie Davis (A/I), Demi (A/I), Ariane Dewey (A/I), Arthur Dorros (A/I), Olivier Dunrea (A/I), Pamela Duncan Edwards (A), Tim Egan (A/I), Richard Egielski (A/I), Lois Ehlert (A/I), Ian Falconer (A/I), Cathryn Falwell (A/I), Jules Feiffer (A/I), Denise Fleming (A/I), Mem Fox (A), Marla Frazee (A/I), Don Freeman (A/I), Dick Gackenbach (A/I), Bob Graham (A/I), Kevin Henkes (A/I), Amy Hest (A), Mary Ann Hoberman (A), Syd Hoff (A/I), Arthur Howard (A/I), Shirley Hughes (A/I), Pat Hutchins (A/I), Satomi Ichikawa (A/I), Simon James (A/I), Steve Jenkins (A/I), Dolores Johnson (A), Ann Jonas (A/I), G. Brian Karas (A/I), Keiko Kasza (A/I), Ezra Jack Keats (A/I), Holly Keller (A/I), Eric A. Kimmel (A), Jarrett J. Krosoczka (A/I), Kathryn Lasky (A), Loreen Leedy (A/I), Barbara Lehman (A/I), Helen Lester (A), Betsy Lewin (A/I), Grace Lin (A/I), Leo Lionni (A/I), Jean Little (A) Arnold Lobel (A/I), Anita Lobel (A/I), Jonathan London (A), Suse MacDonald (A/I), James Marshall (A/I), Bill Martin, Jr. (A), Petra Mathers (A/I), Mercer Mayer (A/I), Barbara McClintock (A/I), Gerald McDermott (A/I), Patricia C. McKissack (A), Bruce McMillan (A/I), Kate McMullan (A) and James McMullan (I), David McPhail (A/I), Holly Meade (I/I), Margaret Miller (A/I), Barry Moser (A/I), Bernard Most (A/I), Mother Goose (A), Robert Munsch (A), Lynn Munsinger (I), Laura Numeroff (A), Helen Oxenbury (A/I), Margie Palatini (A/I), Dav Pilkey (A/I), Daniel Pinkwater (A/I), Beatrix Potter (A/I), Giselle Potter (I), Robin Pulver (A), Chris Raschka (A/I), Peggy Rathmann (A/I), Eric Rohmann (A/I), Barry Root (I), Marisabina Russo (A/I), Carole Lexa Schaefer (A/I), Amy Schwartz (A/I), Laura Vaccaro Seeger (A/I), Maurice Sendak (A/I), David Shannon (A/I), Nancy Shaw (A/I), Marc Simont (A/I), Peter Sís (A/I), Joseph Slate (A), Gary Soto (A), Alexander Stadler (A/I), Janet Stevens (A/I), Simms Taback (A/I), Jean Van Leeuwen (A), Martin Waddell (A/I), Eileen Stoll Walsh (A/I), Nicki Weiss (A/I), Rosemary Wells (A/I), Nadine Bernard Westcott (A/I), David Wiesner (A/I), Mo Willems (A/I), Vera B. Williams (A/I), Kay Winters (A), Audrey and Don Wood (A/I), Ed Young (A/I), Harriet Ziefert (A)

A LIST OF MEMORABLE AUTHORS & ILLUSTRATORS, cont.

GRADE 2:

Mary Jane Auch (A/I), Caralyn Buehner (A) and Mark Buehner (I), Eve Bunting (A), Stephanie Calmenson (A), Peter Catalanotto (I), Lynne Cherry (A/I), R. Gregory Christie (I), Brock Cole (A/I), Joanna Cole (A), Barbara Cooney (A/I), Pat Cummings (A/I), Bruce Degen (I), Demi (A/I), Tomie dePaola (A/I), David Diaz (I), Henrik Drescher (A/I), Tim Egan (A/I), Susan Middleton Elya (A), Lisa Campbell Ernst (A/I), Candace Fleming (A), Debra Frasier (A/I), Stephen Gammell (I), Gail Gibbons (A/I), Patricia Reilly Giff (A), James Howe (A), Tony Johnston (A), William Joyce (A/I), Steven Kellogg (A/I), Loreen Leedy (A/I), Elizabeth Levy (A), Ted Lewin (I), Thomas Locker (A/I), Margaret Mahy (A), Rafe Martin (A), Meghan McCarthy (A/I), Emily Arnold McCully (A/I), Susan Meddaugh (A/I), Eve Merriam (A), Tololwa M. Mollel (A), Pat Mora (A), Kevin O'Malley (A/I), Kadir Nelson (I), Mary Pope Osborne (A), Peggy Parish (A), Barbara Park (A), Bill Peet (A/I), Brian Pinkney (I), Jerry Pinkney (I), Patricia Polacco (A/I), Gloria Rand (A) and Ted Rand (I), Joanne Ryder (A), Robert Sabuda (A/I), Allen Say (A/I), S. D. Schindler (I), Jon Scieszka (A), Dr. Seuss (A/I), Marjorie Weinman Sharmat (A), Carol Diggory Shields (A), Judy Sierra (A), David Small (I), Lane Smith (A/I), Chris K. Soenpiet (I), William Steig (A/I), Sarah Stewart (A), James Stevenson (A/I), Mark Teague (A/I), Chris Van Allsburg (A/I), Judith Viorst (A), Bernard Waber (A/I), James Warhola (A/I), Jane Yolen (A), Paul O. Zelinsky (A/I)

GRADES 3 AND 4: (All (A) unless noted)

David A. Adler, Jon Agee, Hans Christian Andersen, Caroline Arnold, Lynne Barasch, Barbara Bash (A/I), Michael Bond, Franklyn M. Branley, Don Brown (A/I), Joseph Bruchac, Robert Burleigh, Ann Cameron, Beverly Cleary, Ellen Conford, Roald Dahl, Paula Danziger, Leo & Diane Dillon (A/I), Betsy Duffey, Margaret Early (A/I), Barbara Juster Esbensen, Leonard Everett Fisher (A/I), Douglas Florian (A/I), Jean Fritz, Kristine O'Connell George, Mordicai Gerstein (A/I), Paul Goble (A/I), Mary Grandpré (I), Nikki Grimes, Jacob and William Grimm, Brenda Guiberson (A/I), Kevin Hawkes (I), E. W. Hildick, Lee Bennett Hopkins, Deborah Hopkinson, James Howe, Johanna Hurwitz, Trina Schart Hyman (I), Eva Ibbotson, Maira Kalman (A/I), X. J. Kennedy, Eric A. Kimmel, Dick King-Smith, Rudyard Kipling, Suzy Kline, Kathryn Lasky, Patricia Lauber, Julius Lester, J. Patrick Lewis, Jean Little, Myra Cohn Livingston, David Macaulay (A/I), Ann M. Martin, Jacqueline Briggs Martin, Marianna Mayer (A/I), Megan McDonald, A. A. Milne, Marissa Moss (A/I), Christopher Myers (I), Barbara Park, Robert Newton Peck, P. J. Petersen, Andrea Davis Pinkney, Brian Pinkney (I), Daniel Pinkwater (A/I), Jack Prelutsky, James Ransome (I), Peter H. Reynolds (A/I). Pam Muñoz Ryan, Louis Sachar, Robert D. San Souci, Alvin Schwartz, Jon Scieszka, Brian Selznick (I), Aaron Shepard, Diane Siebert, Shel Silverstein, Seymour Simon, Peter Sís (A/I), Robert Kimmel Smith, Donald J. Sobol, Judith St. George, Diane Stanley (A/I), Jean Van Leeuwen, E. B. White, Laura Ingalls Wilder, David Wisniewski (A/I), Elvira Woodruff

GRADE 5 and 6: (All (A))

Arnold Adoff, Lloyd Alexander, David Almond, Jennifer Armstrong, Avi, Joan Bauer, Marion Dane Bauer, Rhoda Blumberg, Bill Brittain, Joseph Bruchac, Eve Bunting, Betsy Byars, Andrew Clements, Jane Leslie Conley, Bruce Coville, Sharon Creech, Lynn Curlee, Christopher Paul Curtis, Karen Cushman, Cynthia deFelice, Kate DiCamillo, Nancy Farmer, John D. Fitzgerald, Paul Fleischman, Sid Fleischman, Russell Freedman, Jack Gantos, Jean Craighead George, Patricia Reilly Giff, Dan Gutman, Mary Downing Hahn, Virginia Hamilton, Kevin Henkes, Karen Hesse, Michael Hoeye, Jennifer L. Holm, Diana Wynne Jones, E. L. Konigsburg, Gordon Korman, Kathleen Krull, Janet Taylor Lisle, Lois Lowry, Michael Morpurgo, Jim Murphy, Donna Jo Napoli, Phyllis Reynolds Naylor, Linda Sue Park, Katherine Paterson, Gary Paulsen, Richard Peck, Philip Pullman, Lynne Reid Banks, Adam Rex, Rick Riordan, J. K. Rowling, Pam Muñoz Ryan, Cynthia Rylant, Louis Sachar, Marilyn Sachs, Laura Amy Schlitz, Carol Diggory Shields, Jan Slepian, Lemony Snicket, Zilpha Keatley Snyder, Jerry Spinelli, Mildred Taylor, Vivian Vande Velde, Wendelin Van Draanen, Cynthia Voigt, Jacqueline Woodson, Valerie Worth, Laurence Yep, Jane Yolen

FREEMAN'S FAVORITES, 1998–2007

Every year, as I finish compiling my list of best books, I apply my own 50-item selection criteria (see the "50 Ways To Recognize a Read-Aloud" chapter in **More Books Kids Will Sit Still For**, page 7), and select my very favorite picture book, fiction, and nonfiction read-aloud for that year. Looking to single out the books that I found most successful, provocative, fresh, child friendly, beloved, and pleasurable to read aloud, I deem it an instructive and amusing exercise.

Coming up with just one book per category can be agonizing. You can tell a lot about a person by the books he or she loves. Your own list would most likely be vastly different; I urge you to try it for yourself, and then ask your students to come up with lists of their past favorite books.

My choices from the past decade, are as follows:

1998:
Picture Book: *I Lost My Bear* by Jules Feiffer (Morrow) Gr. PreK-5
Fiction: *Harry Potter and the Sorcerer's Stone* by J. K. Rowling (Scholastic) Gr. 4-7
Holes by Louis Sachar (Farrar) Gr. 5-8
Nonfiction: *Snowflake Bentley* by Jacqueline Briggs Martin, illus. by Mary Azarian (Houghton) Gr. 1-4

1999:
Picture Book: *Joseph Had a Little Overcoat* by Simms Taback (Viking) Gr. PreK-1
Fiction: *Bud, Not Buddy* by Christopher Paul Curtis (Delacorte) Gr. 4-7
Nonfiction: *William Shakespeare and the Globe* by Aliki (HarperCollins) Gr. 1-6

2000:
Picture Book: *Olivia* by Ian Falconer (Simon & Schuster) All Ages
Fiction: *A Year Down Yonder* by Richard Peck (Dial) Gr. 5-8
Nonfiction: *So You Want to Be President* by Judith St. George (Philomel) Gr. 2-Adult

2001:
Picture Book: *And the Dish Ran Away with the Spoon* by Janet Stevens (Harcourt) Gr. PreK-1
Fiction: *Goose Chase* by Patrice Kindl (Houghton Mifflin) Gr. 5-8
Nonfiction: *The Dinosaurs of Waterhouse Hawkins* by Barbara Kerley, illus. by Brian Selznick (Scholastic) Gr. 2-6

2002:
Picture Book: *I Stink* by Kate McMullan (HarperCollins) Gr. PreK-1
Fiction: *Time Stops for No Mouse* by Michael Hoeye (Putnam) Gr. 4-8
Nonfiction: *Fireboat: The Heroic Adventures of the John J. Harvey* by Maira Kalman (Putnam) Gr. 1-12

FREEMAN'S FAVORITES, cont.

2003:

Picture Book: *Don't Let the the Bus Pigeon Drive* by Mo Willems (Hyperion) Gr. K-Adult

Fiction: *The Tale of Despereaux* by Kate DiCamillo, illus. by Timothy Basil Ering (Candlewick) Gr. 4-8

Nonfiction: *The Man Who Walked between the Towers* by Mordicai Gerstein (Roaring Brook) Gr. K-12

2004:

Picture Book: *Knuffle Bunny* by Mo Willems (Hyperion) Gr. PreK-1

Fiction: *Al Capone Does My Shirts* by Gennifer Choldenko (Putnam) Gr. 5-8

Nonfiction: *Actual Size* by Steve Jenkins (Houghton Mifflin) Gr. PreK-6

2005:

Picture Book: *Bad Kitty* by Nick Bruel (Roaring Brook) Gr. PreK-2

Fiction: *The Lightning Thief* by Rick Riordan (Miramax/Hyperion) Gr. 5-8

Nonfiction: *Encyclopedia Prehistorica: Dinosaurs* by Robert Sabuda and Matthew Reinhart, illus. by Robert Sabuda (Candlewick) All Ages

2006:

Picture Book: *John, Paul, George & Ben* by Lane Smith. (Hyperion) Gr. 2-Adult

Fiction: *The Miraculous Journey of Edward Tulane* by Kate DiCamillo (Candlewick Press) Gr. 3-8

Nonfiction: *The American Story* by Jennifer Armstrong, illus. by Roger Roth (Knopf) (Gr. 3-8)

2007:

Picture Book: *Knuffle Bunny Too: A Case of Mistaken Identity* by Mo Willems (Hyperion) Gr. PreK-2

Fiction: *The Invention of Hugo Cabret* by Brian Selznick (Scholastic) Gr. 4-8

Nonfiction: *Nic Bishop Spiders* by Nic Bishop (Scholastic) (Gr. K-6)

JUDY FREEMAN'S BEST OF THE DECADE:

If I had to pick my one favorite picture book in the past decade, it would have to be Mo Willems's insouciant Caldecott Honor winner, ***Don't Let the Pigeon Drive the Bus***, in which children young and old talk back to that persistent Pigeon.

For fiction, my top pick is still ***Harry Potter and the Sorcerer's Stone***, the first in a series which has changed adults' reactions to children's books forever, we hope. What a decade it has been, thanks to Harry and his friends and enemies at Hogwarts.

For nonfiction, ***Actual Size*** is a book I love to use with children when I do school visits and assemblies and it never fails to wow 'em.

THE ROBERT F. SIBERT INFORMATIONAL BOOK AWARD

The information below is available from the Web site of the Association for Library Service to Children (ALSC), a division of the American Library Association. It is reprinted here with permission of ALSC. Go to: **http://www.ala.org/ala/alsc/awardsscholarships/literaryawds/sibertmedal/Sibert_Medal.htm**

The Robert F. Sibert Informational Book Award, established by the Association for Library Service to Children in 2001 with support from Bound to Stay Bound Books, Inc., is awarded annually to the author(s) and illustrator(s) of the most distinguished informational book published in English during the preceding year. The award is named in honor of Robert F. Sibert, the long-time President of Bound to Stay Bound Books, Inc. of Jacksonville, Illinois. ALSC administers the award.

PURPOSE

The Sibert Award honors the most distinguished informational book published in English in the preceding year for its significant contribution to children's literature. The award is presented to the author, author/illustrator, co-authors, or author and illustrator named on the title page of that book. Honor Books may be named with recognition again going to the author, author/illustrator, co-authors, or author and illustrator named on the title page of that book.

TERMS

The Sibert Award is presented annually to the author, author/illustrator, co-authors, or author and illustrator named on the title page of the most distinguished informational book for children published in the United States during the preceding year. Terms include:
* Poetry and traditional literature (e.g., folktales) are not eligible. There are no other limitations as to the character of the book providing it is an original work.
* Honor Books may be named. They are books that are also truly distinguished.
* The award is restricted to authors, author/illustrators, co-authors, or author and illustrator named on the title page who are citizens or residents of the United States.
* The award is restricted to original work first published in the United States.
* The committee is to consider in its deliberations only books eligible for the award as specified in the terms.
* The award may be given posthumously.

DEFINITIONS

Informational books are defined as those written and illustrated to present, organize, and interpret documentable, factual material.

Significant contribution is gauged by how well the work elucidates, clarifies and enlivens its subject. The committee considers overall accuracy, documentation and organization.

Children's literature is defined as the body of books published for a potential child audience. Such books display respect for children's understanding, abilities, and appreciation. Children range from birth through age fourteen. Books for the entire range are to be considered.

Distinguished is defined as noted for significant achievement; marked by quality, excellence, or eminence; distinctive.

THE ROBERT F. SIBERT INFORMATIONAL BOOK AWARD

DEFINITIONS, cont.

Author may include co-authors or author-illustrators. Illustrator may include persons credited on the title page for visual material.

Original work means that books reprinted or compiled from other sources are not eligible.

First published in the United States means that books originally published in other countries are not eligible.

In English means that the committee considers only books published in English. This requirement DOES NOT limit the use of words or phrases in another language where appropriate in context.

Published in the preceding year means that the book has a publication date in the year under consideration, was available for purchase in that year, and has a copyright date no later than that year. An eligible book may have a copyright date prior to the year under consideration if it was not published until the year under consideration. The intent: that every eligible book be considered, but that no book be considered in more than one year.

Resident is defined as someone who maintains a home in the United States rather than someone who just visits.

The phrase only the books eligible for the award specifies that the committee is to consider only eligible books, not an author's body of work or previous accolades.

CRITERIA

1. In identifying the most distinguished informational book for children from the preceding year, committee members consider important elements and qualities:

    a. Excellent, engaging, and distinctive use of language.
    b. Excellent, engaging, and distinctive visual presentation.
    c. Appropriate organization and documentation.
    d. Clear, accurate, and stimulating presentation of facts, concepts, and ideas.
    e. Visual material and book design.
    f. Appropriate style of presentation for subject and for intended audience.
    g. Supportive features (index, table of contents, maps, timelines, etc).
    h. Respectful and of interest to children.

2. Not every book relies equally on every element. The committee need not find excellence in every element listed above but only in those relevant to the book.
3. The book must be a self-contained entity, not dependent on other media for enjoyment.
4. The Sibert Award is presented to honor distinguished informational books for children. The award is not presented for didactic intent or for popularity.

Adopted by the ALSC Board, January 2000; revised January 2002; January 2005.

All Robert F. Sibert Medal Winners and Honor Books, 2001-Present

2008 Medal Winner

***The Wall: Growing Up Behind the Iron Curtain* by Peter Sís (Farrar/Frances Foster)**
In his deeply felt memoir set in mid-20th century Prague, Sís contrasts the constrictive walls of the communist state with his personal quest for artistic freedom. Black & white drawings accentuated with sharp punches of red are brightened with splashes of color as hope gradually takes hold. Sís takes us from his childhood, when fear, suspicion and lies permeated everyday life, to the "Prague Spring" of 1968 and beyond, a time when "everything seemed possible."

"Sís combines the personal and the political in a feat of visual and verbal storytelling," said Sibert Chair Caroline Parr. "Young readers will learn about an extraordinary time through the detailed, intricate art and the simple but powerful text."

2008 Honor Books

***Lightship* written and illustrated by Brian Floca (Simon & Schuster/Richard Jackson)**
In simple, stately prose that perfectly complements his luminous watercolors, Floca introduces the lightship Ambrose, its crew and cat. Masterful use of the historical present tense, deft, humorous touches and detailed endpapers engage young children while acknowledgments and notes in the book, fore and aft, provide context.

***Nic Bishop Spiders* written and illustrated by Nic Bishop (Scholastic Nonfiction)**
Even the squeamish will be awed by Bishop's oversized, dramatic and vibrant up-close color photographs of more than a dozen types of spiders in *Nic Bishop Spiders*. His compelling, conversational and knowledgeable text provides basic information and startling facts which all ages will relish.

2007 Medal Winner:
Team Moon: How 400,000 People Landed Apollo 11 *on the Moon* by Catherine Thimmes (Houghton)

Honor Books:
Freedom Riders: John Lewis and Jim Zwerg on the Front Lines of the Civil Rights Movement by Ann
   Bausum (National Geographic)
Quest for the Tree Kangaroo: An Expedition to the Cloud Forest of New Guinea written by Sy
   Montgomery, photographs by Nic Bishop (Houghton Mifflin)
To Dance: A Ballerina's Graphic Novel written by Siena Cherson Siegel, artwork by Mark Siegel (Simon
   & Schuster/Richard Jackson)

2006 Medal Winner:
Secrets of a Civil War Submarine: Solving the Mysteries of the H.L. Hunley by Sally M. Walker
   (Carolrhoda Books)

Honor Book:
Hitler Youth: Growing Up in Hitler's Shadow by Susan Campbell Bartoletti (Scholastic Nonfiction)

2005 Medal Winner:
The Voice that Challenged a Nation: Marian Anderson and the Struggle for Equal Rights by Russell Freedman (Clarion Books)

Honor Books:
Walt Whitman: Words for America written by Barbara Kerley, illustrated by Brian Selznick (Scholastic Press)
The Tarantula Scientist written by Sy Montgomery, photographs by Nic Bishop (Houghton Mifflin Company)
Sequoyah: The Cherokee Man Who Gave His People Writing written by James Rumford, translated into Cherokee by Anna Sixkiller Huckaby (Houghton Mifflin)

2004 Medal Winner:
An American Plague: The True and Terrifying Story of the Yellow Fever Epidemic of 1793 by Jim Murphy (Clarion Books/Houghton Mifflin)

Honor Book:
I Face the Wind written by Vicki Cobb, illustrated by Julia Gorton (HarperCollins)

2003 Medal Winner:
The Life and Death of Adolf Hitler by James Cross Giblin (Clarion)

Honor Books:
Six Days in October: The Stock Market Crash of 1929 by Karen Blumenthal (Atheneum)
Hole in My Life by Jack Gantos (Farrar, Strauss & Giroux)
Action Jackson written by Jan Greenberg and Sandra Jordan, illustrated by Robert Andrew Parker (Roaring Brook Press)
When Marian Sang written by Pam Munoz Ryan, illustrated by Brian Selznick (Scholastic)

2002 Medal Winner:
Black Potatoes: The Story of the Great Irish Famine, 1845-1850 by Susan Campbell Bartoletti (Houghton Mifflin)

Honor Books:
Surviving Hitler: A Boy in the Nazi Death Camps by Andrea Warren (HarperCollins)
Vincent van Gogh by Jan Greenberg and Sandra Jordan (Delacorte Press)
Brooklyn Bridge by Lynn Curlee (Atheneum Books for Young Readers)

2001 Medal Winner:
Sir Walter Ralegh and the Quest for El Dorado by Marc Aronson (Clarion Books)

Honor Books:
The Longitude Prize by Joan Dash; illustrated by Dusan Petricic (Frances Foster Books/ Farrar)
Blizzard! The Storm That Changed America by Jim Murphy (Scholastic Press)
My Season with Penguins: An Antarctic Journal by Sophie Webb (Houghton Mifflin)
Pedro and Me: Friendship, Loss, and What I Learned by Judd Winick (Henry Holt)

JUDY'S POST ON LM_NET
AFTER ALA MIDWINTER IN PHILADELPHIA,
JANUARY 15, 2008

Hey everyone--

After 4 exhilarating days in my hometown, Philadelphia, meeting fellow librarians from all over the country, looking at all the new books on display at each publisher's booth at the exhibits, going to lots of receptions and cocktail parties, and eating lots of great dinners and way too many good desserts, I came home to NJ last night and fell into bed, but the excitement lingers. I'm back in my attic today with the cat snoring at my feet, but the hubbub of ALA is still reverberating in my head. The ALA Conference is a fabulous experience, if you've never been there. And if you haven't thought about it, maybe it's time to join ALA and ALSC and volunteer to serve on a committee. You'll never forget it. Go to <**www.ala.org**> to check it out.

This year I was one of the lucky ones to get elected to the Sibert Committee that chooses the most distinguished informational book for children. For some dumb reason, it never gets mentioned in all the press releases, even though, like the Newbery & Caldecott, you can only serve on one of those 3 committees every 5 years. I guess there are so many awards nowadays, the Sibert gets overlooked.

So 5 years after I served on my first committee, the Newbery, choosing ***Bud, Not Buddy*** (and what an amazing experience that was--I wrote a chapter about it in ***Books Kids Will Sit Still For 3***, if you want to see what it's like), I got asked to run for Sibert. Eight people ran, with the top 4 vote-getters getting on the committee, and four others—mostly folks who have already been on lots of committees—were appointed. Our chair, Caroline Parr, was so warm and funny and organized and delightful—she made it all so much fun. The nine of us came from NJ, MD, IN, CA, MA, NY, TX, KS, and OH, and we had a great time discussing and comparing and championing our choices. It's a real talker's marathon, picking a winner.

We'd been reading all year, and boy-o-boy do I know a lot of random facts from all my nonfiction perusing. What's the biggest spider of the 38,000 kinds in the world? That would be the Goliath Birdeater Tarantula. When was Prague Spring? That one's easy—I was around in the '60s. It was 1968. I could tell you more facts, but then you'd know what books we considered, and we're never allowed to tell you that. We read hundreds, though. You'll never see a list of books from any of the committees except the Notables Committee, and you can find their list at <**www.ala.org/alsc**> if you noodle around in the website.

I am allowed to tell you all my favorite nonfiction books for the year, though, and if you look up my BER lists on <**www.TitleWave.com**>, you'll see ***Spider*** and ***The Wall*** and lots more of my "bests" listed there. (Log in, click the CURRICULUM tab at the top, then go to POPULAR SUBJECT LISTS and you'll find it under J for Judy Freeman.)

Anyway, it took us several days to make our decision. Locked in a room at the top floor of the under-construction Embassy Suites Hotel, we supplied ourselves with water, chocolate, tangerines, and cookies. We discussed each of the 6 books each of us had nominated, and then balloted. Our gold medal was ***The Wall*** by Peter Sís, an absolutely extraordinary picture book memoir about his childhood as a budding artist, growing up in Prague in the mid-20th century, leading up to the Prague Spring of 1968 and its aftermath. It's a book you'll want to share with children from third grade through high school. It also won a Caldecott Honor, which we found most gratifying.

Our Sibert Honor books were *Nic Bishop Spiders* by Nic Bishop and *Lightship* by Brian Floca, two riveting nonfiction picture books you can use with preschoolers through early elementary, which is an interesting change for the usual Sibert Medal books which often skew way older.

Just wanted to toot the horn for nonfiction, though this year's Newbery, *Good Masters, Sweet Ladies*, is a glorious choice and this year's Caldecott, *The Invention of Hugo Cabret*, is simply spectacular—a book for middle graders (grades 3-7) that I have been vociferously touting all year. What a revolutionary choice for Caldecott. I was so worried it wasn't going to win anything—I thought it wouldn't be eligible for Caldecott and that the Newbery Committee would think the writing wasn't as strong as the pictures (which is true). When they announced it as this year's gold medal winner at the Announcements meeting in the Philly Convention Center, everyone just started shouting and cheering. Oh, well, maybe everyone wasn't shouting—I was too busy jumping up and down and screaming to notice.

It was so thrilling being at the announcements. We Sibert Committee folks got to sit together in reserved seats in the third row, near all the other committees, and I cheered until I was hoarse and clapped until my palms were red and singing. I had made predictions for all the winners, and this year I predicted every Caldecott and every Newbery except Woodson's *Feathers*. My best record ever! I've been using all of the winners except for Newbery Honors *Feathers* and *The Wednesday Wars* in my workshops all year, so it was pretty exciting to see all my favorites clean up like that. Newbery Honor winner *Elijah of Buxton* was one of my most treasured books of the year and it also won the Coretta Scott King Author Award. And *Henry's Freedom Box*, a Caldecott Honor book, is simply stunning. I met a librarian who said she read it to rambunctious 14- and 15-year-old boys after school and even they were riveted!

Last spring I even got to write Hyperion's Activity Guide for another Caldecott Honor, *Knuffle Bunny Too*, which is downloadable on their website <**www.hyperionbooksforchildren.com**>, on the *Knuffle Bunny Too* homepage. And same goes for the Elephant & Piggy books, for which I wrote the activity guide, since *There Is a Bird on My Head* just won the Geisel Medal. Both guides have lots of very cute reproducibles and ideas. (By the way—if you want the great egg-turns-into-chicken prop I've been showing in my workshops, go to <**www.mimismotifs.com**>. It's great to use with *First the Egg*, for which Laura Vaccaro Seeger just won her first Caldecott Honor and a Geisel Honor, too! I LOVE that book!)

There aren't a lot of authors speaking or autographing at ALAS Midwinter. For that, you need to go to the Annual Conference in June, which is in Anaheim this year. I'll be there! The Sibert Medal doesn't get a big dinner like the Newbery-Caldecott dinner, worse luck, but there will be a ceremony, and we'll get to meet the very hunky Peter Sís, also a past recipient of a MacArthur Genius Award, which is pretty doggone special. (You get up to 1/2 a million dollars just for being a genius. Not a bad thing.) My favorite thing of all is The Big Dinner, where Brian Selznick and Amy Schlitz will be giving their Big Speeches. (Hmmm. I know Brian's related to the movie mogul; I wonder if Amy Schlitz is related to the guy who started the beer company.) It is indeed like the Librarian Academy Awards. We librarians clean up nicely that night. I already have my fancy dress and shoes. I am READY!

Have a great time sharing the award winners with your kids. These are books they will love. Whew. You can't ask for more than that!

Judy

CELEBRATING CHILDREN'S BOOKS

♫♪♪♪♪♪♪ **Judy Freeman's Songbook** ♫♪♪♪♪♫

HI HO LIBRARIO

(Words by Jane Scherer, ©1980; Tune: "The Farmer in the Dell")

The author writes the book, the author writes the book;
Hi ho librario, the author writes the book.

The illustrator draws, the illustrator draws;
Hi ho librario, the illustrator draws.

The publisher puts it together, the publisher puts it together;
Hi ho librario, the publisher puts it together.

The copyright tells us when they made the book, and then,
Hi ho librario, let's sing it once again.

MOTIONS: The author writes the book *(pantomime writing)*
            The illustrator draws *(pantomime painting)*
            The publisher puts it together *(hold hands out as if you are holding a book, and then slap them closed)*
            The copyright tells us when . . . *(draw a great big letter C in the air and a circle around it, like the sign for copyright: ©)*

MISS MARY MACK
(Traditional)

Miss Mary Mack-Mack-Mack all dressed in black-black-black
With silver buttons-buttons-buttons all down her back-back-back

She asked her mother-mother-mother
For fifty cents-cents-cents
To see the elephants-elephants-elephants
Jump the fence-fence-fence

They jumped so high-high-high
That they reached the sky-sky-sky
And they didn't come back-back-back
Till the fourth of July-ly-ly.

108.

CLEMENTINE

(Traditional)

1. In a cavern, in a canyon, excavating for a mine,
    Dwelt a miner, forty-niner, and his daughter Clementine.

    CHORUS:
    Oh my darling, oh my darling, oh my darling Clementine
    You are lost and gone forever, dreadful sorry, Clementine.

2. Light she was, and like a fairy, and her shoes were number nine,
    Herring boxes without topses, sandals were for Clementine.

3. Walking lightly as a fairy, though her shoes were number nine,
    Sometimes tripping, lightly skipping, lovely girl, my Clementine.

4. Drove she ducklings to the water, ev'ry morning just at nine,
    Hit her foot against a splinter, fell into the foaming brine.

5. Ruby lips above the water, blowing bubbles soft and fine,
    But alas, I was no swimmer, neither was my Clementine.

6. In a churchyard near the canyon, where the myrtle doth entwine,
    There grow rosies and some posies, fertilized by Clementine.

7. Then, the miner, forty-niner, soon began to fret and pine,
    Thought he oughter join his daughter, so he's now with Clementine.

8. I'm so lonely, lost without her, wish I'd had a fishing line,
    Which I might have cast about her, might have saved my Clementine.

9. In my dreams she still doth haunt me, robed in garments soaked with brine,
    Then she rises from the waters, and I kiss my Clementine.

10. Listen fellers, heed the warning of this tragic tale of mine,
    Artificial respiration could have saved my Clementine.

11. How I missed her, how I missed her, how I missed my Clementine,
    Til I kissed her little sister, and forgot my Clementine.

CLEMENTINE, REVISITED

An all-new version, based on Sara Pennypacker's book, *Clementine* (Hyperion, 2006), written by Erica Patente's Third Grade Class, Old York School, Branchburg, New Jersey.

In an apartment, in a city, supervising all the time,
Lived a pigeon pooper scooper, and his daughter Clementine.

    CHORUS:
    Pay attention, pay attention, pay attention Clementine!
    You are silly and get in trouble, thanks for helping, Clementine.

Orange her hair was, like a pumpkin, and shiny like a dime.
Kitten boxes, holes in topses, Moisturizer for Clementine. CHORUS

And you sit there in the office, cause you never listen well;
Margaret glued it, then you ruined it, why'd you do it, Clementine? CHORUS

She's the hard one, even harder, causing trouble all the time,
But, alas, they didn't trade her, so they kept their Clementine. CHORUS

How we liked it, how we liked it, how we liked the book Clementine,
But we finished, our hopes diminished, until the next book, Clementine!

NOTE: Your students may want to compose all-new verses based on the second book in the series,
    The Talented Clementine (2007).

OH I HAD A LITTLE CHICKEN
(To the tune of "Turkey in the Straw")

Oh I had a little chicken and she couldn't lay an egg,
So I poured hot water up and down her leg,
And the little chicken cried, and the little chicken begged,
And the little chicken laid a hard-boiled egg.

Oh I went to Cincinnati and I walked around the block,
And I walked right into a bakery shop,
And I picked two doughnuts out of the grease,
And I handed the lady a five cent piece.
Well, she looked at the nickel and she looked at me,
She said, "This nickel's no good to me;
There's a hole in the middle and it's all the way through."
Said I, "There's a hole in the doughnut, too.
Thanks for the doughnut. Goodbye."

APPLES AND BANANAS

I like to eat, eat, eat, eat, I like to eat apples and bananas;
I like to eat, eat, eat, eat, I like to eat apples and bananas;

I like to ate, ate, ate, ate, I like to ate ay-ples and ba-nay-nays. (2X)

I like to eat, eat, eat, eat, I like to eat ee-ples and ba-nee-nees. (2X)

I like to ite, ite, ite, ite, I like to ite i-ples and ban-i-nis. (2X)

I like to ote, ote, ote, ote, I like to ote o-ples and ba-no-nos. (2X)

I like to ute, ute, ute, ute, I like to ute u-ples and ba-nu-nus. (2X)

Now we're through, through, through, through, now we're through with A-E-I-O-U,
Now we're through, through, through, through, now we're through with A-E-I-O-U.

NOTE: Use this silly song with books like *The Apple Doll* by Elisa Kleven (Farrar, 2007) or *Orange Pear Apple Bear* by Emily Gravett (Simon & Schuster, 2007).

KNOCK-KNOCK
(Words and music by Judy Freeman, ©2000)

>**CHORUS:**
>**Knock knock, who's there?**
>**At the door, on the stair?**

Wooden shoe.
Wooden shoe who?
(Spoken): Wooden shoe like to know!

Needa Tish.
Needa Tish who?
(Spoken): Why? Is your nose running?

Lettuce.
Lettuce who?
(Spoken): Lettuce in—it's freezing out here!

I. Wub.
I Wub who?
(Spoken): I Wub 'oo, too!

WRITE AND SING NEW VERSES: Use any knock knocks you know, or write new ones.

WILL YOU REMEMBER ME?

(An old joke adapted by Judy Freeman, 2000)

Q: Will you remember me in a thousand years?
A: A millennium? YES.

Q: Good. Will you remember me in a hundred years?
A: A century? YES.

Q: Good. Will you remember me in ten years?
A: A decade? YES.

Q: Good. Will you remember me in 365 days or 12 months?
A: One year? YES.

Q: Good. Will you remember me in 30 days or 4 weeks?
A: A month? YES.

Q: Good. Will you remember me in 7 days?
A: A week? YES.

Q: Good. Will you remember me in 24 hours?
A: A day? YES.

Q: Good. Will you remember me in 60 minutes?
A: An hour? YES.

Q: Good. Will you remember me in 60 seconds?
A: A minute? YES.

Q: Good. Will you remember me in one second?
A: YES.

Q: KNOCK, KNOCK.
A: WHO'S THERE?
Q: YOU FORGOT ME ALREADY???!!!

NOTE: This is a fun extended knock-knock joke to use with a book about time, such as *A Second Is a Hiccup* by Hazel Hutchins (Scholastic / Arthur A. Levine, 2007).

THE FARMER IN THE DELL

The farmer in the dell, the farmer in the dell
Hi-ho the dairy-o, the farmer in the dell

The farmer takes a wife, the farmer takes a wife
Hi-ho the dairy-o, the farmer takes a wife

The wife takes a child, the wife takes a child
Hi-ho the dairy-o, the wife takes a child

The child takes a dog, the child takes a dog
Hi-ho the dairy-o, the child takes a dog

The dog takes a cat, the dog takes a cat
Hi-ho the dairy-o, the dog takes a cat

The cat takes a rat, the cat takes a rat
Hi-ho the dairy-o, the cat takes a rat

The rat takes the cheese, the rat takes the cheese
Hi-ho the dairy-o, the rat takes the cheese

The cheese stands alone, the cheese stands alone
Hi-ho the dairy-o, the cheese stands alone

NOTE: You'll want to sing this song with your children before reading aloud Margie Palatini's hilarious picture book, *The Cheese* (Katherine Tegan Books/HarperCollins, 2007).

THROW IT OUT THE WINDOW

Old Mother Hubbard went to her cupboard to fetch her poor dog a bone;
But when she got there, the cupboard was bare,
So she threw it out the window, the window, the second story window;
But when she got there, the cupboard was bare, so she threw it out the window.

Little Miss Muffett sat on her tuffet, eating her curds and whey;
Along came a spider, and sat down beside her,
And threw it out the window, the window, the second story window;
Along came a spider, and sat down beside her, and threw it out the window.

Humpty Dumpty sat on a wall, Humpty Dumpty had a great fall;
All the king's horses and all the king's men
They threw him out the window, the window, the second story window;
All the king's horses and all the king's men, they threw him out the window.

OTHER VERSES: Old King Cole / Jack and Jill / Little Bo Peep / Yankee Doodle

NOTE: Try this nonsense song with nursery rhyme parodies like Bob Graham's *Dimity Dumpty: The Story of Humpty's Little Sister* (Candlewick, 2007).

TAKE ME OUT TO THE BALLGAME

(By Jack Norworth and Harry Von Tilzer, 1907. For the score and to listen to the music, go to: <http://sniff.numachi.com/pages/tiTAKEBALL;ttTAKEBALL.html>)

Katie Casey was baseball mad
Had the fever and had it bad.
Just to root for the home town crew,
Every sou, Katie blew;
On a Saturday, her young beau
Called to see if she'd like to go
To see a show, but Miss Kate said "No
I'll tell you what you can do:"

>   CHORUS:
>   Take me out to the ball game
>   Take me out with the crowd,
>   Buy me some peanuts and Cracker Jack
>   I don't care if I never get back.
>   Let me root, root, root for the home team,
>   If they don't win, it's a shame;
>   For it's one, two, three strikes you're out
>   At the old ball game.

Katie Casey saw all the games,
Knew the players by their first names;
Told the umpire he was wrong
All along, good and strong.
When the score was just two to two
Katie Casey knew what to do,
Just to cheer up the boys she knew
She made the gang sing this song: (CHORUS)

LOOK FOR 398.2
(©1983 by Judy Freeman)

If you want a good story, let me tell you what to do:
Look for 398.2

Ogres, leprechauns and goblins all are waiting there for you:
Look for 398.2

Prince or princess in hot water, trouble with a witch's brew:
Look for 398.2

Fierce and fire-breathing dragons, shiny scales of green and blue:
Look for 398.2

Find a tale from every country, from Australia to Peru:
Look for 398.2

JUDY FREEMAN'S TEACHER'S GUIDE FOR

A GOOD DAY
by Kevin Henkes (Greenwillow, 2007)

Used with with permission of the publisher, HarperCollins.

JUDY FREEMAN (www.JudyReadsBooks.com), children's literature consultant and workshop presenter, is the book review columnist for *School Library Media Activities Monthly* and the author of *Books Kids Will Sit Still For 3* (Libraries Unlimited, 2006; www.LU.com).

For more about Kevin Henkes and his wonderful books, go to his website, <**www.kevinhankes.com**>. You'll find this guide in the teacher's guide, "The World of Kevin Henkes," written by Judy Freeman, which you can download at <**www.harpercollinschildrens.com**>. To find it, click on "Teachers & Librarians" and type Henkes in the Search Bar.

It's a bad day for a little yellow bird who loses his favorite tail feather, a little white dog whose leash gets tangled, a little orange fox who can't find his mother, and a little brown squirrel who drops her nut. But then, something good happens to each of them, turning a bad day into a good one. The most elemental of texts and handsome brown bordered watercolors make this lost-and-found story just right for toddler and preschool story hours.

PRE-READING DISCUSSION
Ask your listeners if they're having a good day. If they say they are, ask them what has made it good. If anyone is having a bad day, ask what made it bad. Talk over what they think it would take to turn a bad day into a good one or vice versa. Have you ever had a bad day that turned into a good day? What happened to perk up your day?

CAUSE AND EFFECT
It takes no more than a minute to read the book aloud, and it's one you'll probably want to read several times so your group can point out details and connections they may have missed. After reading the story aloud the first time, go back and have children retell it, using as many of the actual words as they can recall. Then have children retell the story through dialogue from the point of view of each of the animals.

DISCUSSION POINTS:
All four animals have something in common? What is it? (They've all lost something: the bird lost his feather, the dog lost her freedom, the fox lost his mother, and the squirrel lost her nut.)
What did each animal do to turn a bad day into a good one?
Why was each item or thing important to the animal that lost it?
What important things have you lost? Did you find it? Which of your things is most important to you?
What have you found that someone else may have lost?
What does "Finders keepers, losers weepers" mean? Is it fair?

SEEING THE WHOLE PICTURE

The final illustration ties the whole story together and gives it context. It incorporates the good fortune of all four animals and the little girl. Like a camera, it zooms out to show where each animal is in relation to the others in the story and puts each in perspective. When we looked at each animal's saga close up, we focused on that animal alone. On the final spread, where the little girl runs to her house, we see the big picture, with the dog in the yard, the bird flying above, the squirrel in the tree, and the fox and his mother on the other side of the nearby stream.

You could stage this story in an open space, setting up the scene with props and simple scenery. Each of the five actors would be in his or her different spot. Each of the four animals could then use invented dialogue. Over to one side, Little Bird, pretending to perch in her tree, could say, "Oh, no. I lost my favorite feather!" Little white dog, in the front left corner of the space would get herself tangled in her leash. Highlight each animal in sequence with the beam from a flashlight.

Choose another natural scene or place or biome--perhaps the beach or the desert. Have children draw pictures of one animal they'd find in that biome. Then make a mural of the whole scene, incorporating their pictures.

OPPOSITES

A bad day can turn into a good day. Look at other opposites for writing and illustrating prompts:
A HOT DAY, A COLD DAY
A WET DAY, A DRY DAY
A CLOUDY DAY, A SUNNY DAY
AN INSIDE DAY, AN OUTSIDE DAY

PATTERNS AND COLORS

In math, when you're talking about patterns, take a good look at the patterns in the illustrations of *A Good Day*. Have children list the sequence of the story—bird, dog, fox, squirrel—and see if it is repeated in the second half. They'll see that it goes in reverse sequence—squirrel, fox, dog bird. That's one pattern.

Look at the striped pattern page on the back cover, the first page, and midway through the story. Have children count the watercolor pastel stripes of color and determine if there is a repeating pattern. (There is; the colors, interspersed with brown lines, are: red, yellow, green, blue, violet, and orange.) Are all three pages the same or different? (They're the same.)

They will probably observe that the stripes look like rainbow colors. Show the colors of the rainbow (ROY G. BIV is the mnemonic device you can teach them to recall those colors: red, orange, yellow, green, blue, indigo, and violet.) Are they in rainbow sequence? Are all the colors there? (No, they are in a different sequence, and indigo is missing.)

About the colored stripes--why did Henkes use those colors? Sharp-eyed ones will notice that those are all the colors used in the illustrations. And one observant child will see that the little girl's sleeves are stripes as well. Are they in the same pattern? (Yes, they are.)

REPEATING PATTERNS

Using watercolors, children can then paint their own repeating striped patterns of colors. Then, using those same colors, they can paint a picture.

Bring out colored beads and make colored patterns with them. Have children label their patterns with letters. Say their pattern is red-green-yellow-red-green-yellow. If red = A, green = B, and yellow = C, the pattern would be: ABC ABC. Have them rearrange their bead patterns and come up with new ones.

Picking a pattern that pleases them, children can string the beads and make patterned necklaces to wear. They can reveal their chosen pattern sequences to the rest of the group, explaining, for instance, "My repeating sequence is ABCCBA—blue, red, yellow, yellow, red, blue." Look at other stripes in shirts and fabrics and have children discern the patterns.

ALL ABOUT FEATHERS

Since losing and finding a feather is a pivotal element in *A Good Day*, use the opportunity to do a mini-lesson on feathers.

You can introduce the six types of feathers (flight, contour, down, semiplume, filoplume, and bristle), the five parts of a feather (shaft, vane, barb, barbule, barbicel), and talk about the ways birds use their feathers. Bring in a peacock feather or a goose quill for students to examine.

Ask your librarian for bird books and encyclopedias that will be useful. Explore the excellent KidWings website <**www.kidwings.com**>, where you'll find simple information, experiments, games, and more than 100 color photographs of birds in the wild.

Make feather paintings, using a feather as your brush. (Your crafts store will have feathers.) Or have children paint or draw a picture and incorporate an actual feather into it.

FOUND ART

A Good Day is a book about nature. Ask your viewers to pick out all the natural elements in the illustrations—there are flowers, grass, trees, a stream, the sky, clouds, and the sun, and the animals, of course. Using some of these elements, you can try some interesting art projects.

ACORNS

Little Brown Squirrel lost and found an acorn. Make a colorful Jackson Pollack-style painting with a handful of nuts. Using washable paint, pour one color per plastic bowl. Put one acorn in each bowl. Lay a piece of paper in the bottom of a box lid. (The tops to those big boxes of photocopy paper work well.)

Carefully, with a spoon, a child will lift out the acorn from one of the colors, and place it on the paper. As he slowly rolls the acorn in the lid, back and forth, the paint-covered acorn will skitter from side to side, making a blue pattern on the paper as it turns.

Next, the child will lift out the blue acorn with the blue spoon and put it back in the blue paint bowl. Selecting an acorn from another bowl—a purple one, perhaps—he can repeat the rolling process. When he finishes with his three or four selected colors, he'll lift out his paint-coated painting and place it on newspaper to dry. Behold: a lovely piece of abstract art. You can use more than one box lid so more than one child can paint simultaneously.

NATURAL ART
Go outside with your group and gather found objects from nature such as twigs, leaves, flowers, and pebbles which they can then incorporate into mixed media pictures.

BUT THEN . . .
Make that text-to-life connection. Starting with the story-starters below, with the first sentence on the left side of the page, and the second on the right side, have children create new scenarios. They can write about animals or about themselves, and illustrate each side of the page to show the transition from bad day to good one. Then they can share, reading their stories aloud and showing the corresponding pictures.

It was a bad day . . . BUT THEN . . . _____.

SCIENCE: COMPARING AND CONTRASTING
Look at the four animals on the cover of the book. What do they have in common? How are they different? With your group, brainstorm a list of different aspects and features of the animals. Make up a chart and, as children compare and contrast each characteristic, record the information. For example:

CHARACTERISTICS	BIRD	DOG	FOX	SQUIRREL
COLOR	yellow	white	orange/white	brown
COLLAR	no	yes	no	no
TAIL	yes	yes	yes	yes
COAT	feathers	fur	fur	fur
WINGS	yes	no	no	no
LEGS	2 legs	4 legs	4 legs	4 legs
EARS	none	pointy	pointy	rounded
WHISKERS	none	not visible	yes	yes
FEET	claws	paws	paws	paws
LOCOMOTION	flies	stands	stands	stands
TYPE	wild	pet	wild	wild
ANIMAL FAMILY	bird	mammal	mammal	mammal

You can also make a large Venn diagram, comparing aspects of two of the animals, such as the dog and the fox or the squirrel and the bird.

Judy Freeman's Activity Guide for

Mo Willems's "Elephant and Piggie" series

I Am Invited to a Party!
My Friend Is Sad
There Is a Bird on Your Head!
Today I Will Fly!

by Mo Willems
Hyperion Books for Children, 2007

Used with permission of the publisher, Hyperion Books for Children.

Go to <www.hyperionbooksforchildren.com> to download the activity pages for this guide. Type "Mo Willems" in the Search Bar, click on one of the above titles, and go to its home page, where you'll find the guide listed.

JUDY FREEMAN (www.JudyReadsBooks.com), children's literature consultant and workshop presenter, writes the "Wild About Books" column for *School Library Media Activities Monthly*, teaches children's literature and storytelling courses at Pratt Institute in New York City, and is the author of **Books Kids Will Sit Still For 3** (Libraries Unlimited, 2006) and **Once Upon a Time: Using Storytelling, Creative Drama, and Reader's Theater with Children in Grades PreK-6** (2007).

Elephant and Piggie are two best friends. Elephant, also known as Gerald, is cautious, nervous at times, a worrier, and a bit of a pessimist. Piggie is more of a risk taker, and shows her joy easily, with abandon. The four books in this exuberant and funny series are told entirely in dialogue, with speech bubbles in gray (for Elephant) and pink (for Piggie). Since they are very short, you can read all four of them together, or read one aloud and have children reread it with you. These easy readers work as read-alouds, read-alones, and read-togethers. Older children can write new adventures of Elephant and Piggie. Pre-readers can act out the stories in pairs and celebrate Elephant and Piggie's very special friendship. All will welcome two very special new characters to the children's books scene.

GENERAL ACTIVITIES AND IDEAS

FINGER PUPPETS:

Design a set of finger puppets of Elephant and Piggie that children can use to help act out each story. These could be simple paper doll-like puppets that children can cut out and color. Puppets can fit on their fingers or be glued on popsicle sticks. In pairs, children can act out each story's situation and dialogue between the two friends Elephant and Piggie.

ELEPHANT AND PIGGIE FINGERPLAYS AND SONGS

AN ELEPHANT GOES LIKE THIS AND THAT

An elephant goes like this and that. *(stomp from side to side)*
He's terribly big *(hold arms up in air)*
And he's terribly fat. *(hold arms up and out to the sides)*
He has no fingers *(wiggle fingers)*
And he has no toes, *(shake feet)*
But goodness gracious,
What a long nose! *(hold out two arms, joined at hands to make a great long trunk)*

ONE GRAY ELEPHANT BALANCING

(If you don't know this tune, go to <**www.mystrands.com/album/470110**> to hear it, or you could sing it to the tune of "Five Little Ducks Went Out One Day")

One gray elephant balancing
Step by step on a piece of string,
Thought it was such a wonderful stunt
That he called for another elephant.

Two gray elephants balancing
Step by step on a piece of string,
Thought it was such a wonderful stunt
That they called for another elephant.

Three gray elephants balancing
Step by step on a piece of string,
Thought it was such a wonderful stunt
That they called for another elephant.

Four gray elephants balancing
Step by step on a piece of string,
Thought it was such a wonderful stunt
That they called for another elephant.

Five gray elephants balancing
Step by step on a piece of string,
All of a sudden the piece of string broke
And down came all the elephant folk.

NOTE: Act this out as you sing it, in groups of five. The leader of each group, swings her trunk (arms extended down, hands clasped) and pretends to balance on a string as she lumbers straight ahead. At end of each verse, the leader selects another child to join the line. Each time you start a new verse, another "elephant" joins the line, holding onto waist of the elephant in front. At the end of the song, everyone falls down.

PUNCTUATION AND READING WITH EXPRESSION:

Punctuation plays a big part in all of the Elephant and Piggie books. Use the books as a teaching device to read aloud with expression. Have children say each of the following titles of the Elephant and Piggie books in three different ways: first with a period at the end, then an exclamation point, and finally a question mark.

I Am Invited to a Party!
My Friend Is Sad.
There Is a Bird on Your Head!
Today I Will Fly!

Discuss how the punctuation makes a difference in how you read the words. Read aloud sections of each book together and have your children figure out how each line should be said.

WRITE NEW DIALOGUE FOR ELEPHANT AND PIGGIE:

Notice that all of the Elephant and Piggie stories are told entirely in dialogue, with gray speech balloons for elephant and pink speech balloons for Piggie. Working with a partner, write a new dialogue for the two friends.

You could set this up like a little graphic cartoon, with four panels on one page. Each page could show blank balloons for dialogue. Children can work in pairs to come up with a quick skit, drawing Elephant and Piggie in each of the panels, writing the dialogue in the balloons, and then reading it aloud to the rest of the group, with one child reading Piggie's lines and the other, Elephant's.

Or, you could just draw two dialogue balloons, and the kids can then draw Elephant and Piggie underneath and write one caption for each.

WHAT WILL ELEPHANT AND PIGGIE DO NEXT?:

What do you think Elephant and Piggie's next adventure should be? Look at the covers of the Elephant and Piggie books. You will see the title at the top, and a picture of the two friends that gives you a clue of what each the story will be about. Think of a good title for their next book and draw the cover.

ELEPHANT AND PIGGIE WORD SEARCH

Reinforce vocabulary from the book and word recognition. I formatted the puzzle using:
<http://puzzlemaker.school.discovery.com/WordSearchSetupForm.html>

Find the following words hidden in the puzzle below. Each word could be horizontal, vertical, diagonal, forwards, or backwards. Circle or highlight each word you find with a pencil, crayon, or highlighter marker.

```
A A A A A A A A A G G G H H H
H D R G N G H L N P S A E S R
S E P D N R P I P U P M L K E
P O A R A I Y I R P U O S C A
E Z M D O L H P Y T O P T I D
E T W E F B R C S P L I C H Y
H C O D W I L O T A E G L C G
C E R B S H C E S A M G O P F
E L R E O V E H M Y H I V P K
N E O B I R D R S F O E E L L
S P M P A R T Y E G A B Y E P
B H O N W O L C M E G N W H R
A A T G L A S S E S G E C O S
N N D G N I D L I U B O Y C
W T V D N E I R F T S E N I Z
```

HIDDEN WORDS:

AAAAAAAAAGGGHHH	EGGS	HEAD	READY
BIRD	ELEPHANT	HELP	ROBOT
BUILDING	FANCY	LOVE	SOMEWHERE
CHEEP	FLYING	NEST	SPLASH
CHICKS	FRIEND	PARTY	SURPRISE
CLOWN	GLASSES	PIGGIE	TOMORROW
COSTUME	HAPPY	POOL	
COWBOY	HATCHING	PROBLEM	

AN ELEPHANT & PIGGIE
FILL IN THE BLANK STORY

(Fill in the blanks of the Elephant and Piggie story below and draw pictures to go along it.)

One day, Piggie and Elephant went to _____

_____.

Piggie found _____.

Elephant found _____.

"Oh, no!" Elephant cried. "Look at this _____

_____!"

Piggie said, "Don't worry, Elephant. Now you can _____

_____!"

The two friends laughed.

Elephant asked, "_____

_____?"

"_____

_____!" said Piggie.

I AM INVITED TO A PARTY!
by Mo Willems (Hyperion, 2007)

Activity Guide by Judy Freeman

When Piggie gets a cool invitation to go to her first party, she is thrilled and invites Elephant (AKA Gerald) to go with her. Elephant says, "I know parties," and that, as it turns out, is very true.

DISCUSSION QUESTIONS TO ASK BEFORE OR WHILE READING THE STORY

What kinds of parties have you been to? What did you do there?
What happens at a party?
What are the most important parts of a party?

DISCUSSION QUESTIONS TO ASK AFTER READING THE STORY

How did Elephant know what to wear to the party?
What do you think Elephant and Piggie did at the fancy costume pool party? What did they eat? What games did they play?
What was the best party you ever attended? Why was it so great?

STORY TIME IDEAS

GETTING DRESSED:

After you read the story aloud, it would be fun to re-read it using props. Store them in a chest or suitcase or large sack. As you pull out each of the props, have two children, a boy and a girl, put them on. Props include: Elephant's top hat, bow tie, cane, giant swimming trunks, inner tube, black mask, cape, boots; Piggie's dress, gloves, earrings, flippers, water wings, goggles, cowboy hat and bandana.

WHAT KINDS OF PARTIES ARE THERE:

Elephant and Piggie went to a Fancy Pool Costume Party. What other kinds of parties are there?

With your children, make a large Party Chart of the different types of parties. (Possible types might include Halloween, Valentine's Day, Christmas, Hanukkah, Surprise, Birthday, Fourth of July, Come as You Are, Wedding, Graduation, Baby Showers, or Barbecues.) Fill in the components of each type of party as follows:

TYPE OF PARTY   WHAT TO WEAR   WHAT TO EAT   GAMES & ACTIVITIES

Or have children break into small groups. Have each group pick a type of party and plan all its components and then share their plan with the larger group.

IN MY SWIMMING POOL:

Elephant and Piggie are ready for a pool party. Don't have a pool handy? Sing the interactive "Swimming Pool" song with your children and you'll feel wonderfully waterlogged.

SWIMMING POOL SONG
(To the tune of "Sailing, Sailing, Over the Bounding Main")

Swimming, Swimming (arms do crawl)

In my swimming pool (make rectangle with index fingers)

When days are hot (fan face with hands)

When days are cold (Hug arms)

In my swimming pool (make rectangle with index fingers)

Side stroke (do side stroke with arms)

Breast stroke (do breast stroke with arms)

Fancy diving too (with hands together, dive up and down)

Don't you wish that you had (wag index finger)

Nothing else to do (hold palms open)

But....

The first time, sing the whole song as you do each motion. The second time, leave off the first line ("Swimming, swimming") and just do the pantomime. Each time you repeat the verse, leave off one more line, and just pantomime the actions instead of singing them. By the time you sing it ten times, you will be pantomiming the entire song silently (except for all the giggles), and end with only one word spoken: **"BUT."**

BEAUTIFUL AND SILLY HATS:

Elephant wears a top hat to the party, and Piggie sports a cowboy hat. Make your own hats with foam or paper plates. Poke a hole on either side of each plate and thread a piece of ribbon in each side that can tie under a child's chin to keep the hat in place. Children can decorate their hats, attaching bows, ribbons, shiny strands of assorted paper, and found objects with glue-sticks.

Then sing this song:

SILLY HAT
(To the tune of "This Old Man")

On my head I wear a hat.
It is such a silly hat
That my head will wiggle,
Wiggle to and fro.
Where else should my silly hat go?

Each time you sing it, place the hat somewhere on your body--on your toe, your elbow, your ear, etc. Children will have lots of suggestions on where to put it next.

FINAL VERSE:

On the floor I put my hat.
It is such a quiet hat
That the floor won't wiggle,
It just stays flat.
I am glad I thought of that.

PARTY GAMES FOR AN ELEPHANT & PIGGIE PARTY

WHO AM I?:

When the children first come through the door, tape the name of an animal on each child's back. Through the course of the first few minutes of the party, they need to ask each other yes and no questions about what they are. You will want to demonstrate this with the name taped on your own back, modeling for them the kinds of questions they may ask. (Am I a wild animal? Am I a pet? Am I a farm animal? Do I have fur? Can I fly? And so on.) For children who get stumped, give them a good hint. When everyone has discovered his or her animal identity, have each child take a turn saying what they think they are.

ANIMAL TWINS:

This variation is similar to Who Am I?, but for this one, you whisper in each child's ear a name of an animal. (It's a good idea to keep a list of names and animals for when children forget which ones they are.) Tell them that there is at least one other person who is the same animal as they are. Have them ask each other yes or no questions to figure out what animals they are. (Are you a pet? Do you have feathers? Do you live in a cage?) When they locate their animal twin, they should sit together. Have everyone then reveal their animal identities.

DRAW AN ELEPHANT:

Break children into teams of four to six. Tell them each team is going to draw a big elephant on a large piece of chart paper affixed to an easel (or to the wall). At the easel, blindfold one child on the first team and hand him a crayon. As the rest of the children watch in silence, ask that child to draw the elephant's big body. When he finishes, he takes off his blindfold and the next child in the team steps to the easel to be blindfolded. That next player draws the head with ears and eyes, the third one draws the legs, and the fourth one does the trunk and the tail. (You can have up to six children on each team--the fifth and sixth can do the tail and the ears.)

The team whose drawing is the most accurate can be the winner, or just encourage everyone to laugh and enjoy seeing the final drawings.

MAKE ME LAUGH, PIGGIE:

Have your group break into pairs: Elephant and Piggie. When you give the starting signal, Piggie faces Elephant and has one minute to make him laugh. Elephant must keep his "serious" face and not smile or laugh at all. Piggie may use her hands and facial expressions to make Elephant laugh, and is only allowed to say one thing: "Oink, oink." Piggie is not permitted to make any other noises or to touch Elephant, or Elephant will be the automatic winner. If Elephant laughs, Piggie wins. If not, Elephant wins. Then have the pairs switch roles and do it again.

PIGGIE SAYS:

Play a game of "Simon Says" but use Piggie's name instead. "Piggie Says . . . 'Hop on one foot.'" When you leave off "Piggie Says" from your directions, the children who still perform that action are out. Possible directions include: Wave your hands in the air, stand on tiptoes, smile, jump up and down, clap your hands, wave good-bye, etc.

PIN THE NOSE ON ELEPHANT AND PIGGIE:

Make a large poster of Elephant and Piggie (but without their noses) and tape it to the wall. Make a template page with Elephant's trunk and Piggie's snout on it, and photocopy a page for each child. Children can write their names on their two noses and cut them out with scissors. Put a piece of double-stick tape on the back of each nose. Blindfold the first child, who is holding one nose in each hand, turn her around, and gently nudge her in the direction of the poster. The object, of course, is to put the noses on the proper faces.

WHAT ARE ELEPHANT AND PIGGIE WEARING TO THEIR NEXT PARTY?:

What kind of party will Elephant and Piggie attend next? Draw a picture of them at the party, dressed in their party clothes and having fun. Make sure your picture shows what kind of party it is.

PARTY TIME!:

Draw a picture of yourself all dressed up at a party you would love to attend. Draw the food or the games or the other guests and show why it is the most fun party ever.

PARTY FOODS, FAVORS, AND PREPARATIONS

INVITATIONS:

If you're throwing an Elephant and Piggie party, advertise it in the form of an invitation. Fill in the invitation with the time, date, and place.

It would be fun to format the page like an envelope that could actually be folded and mailed or handed out. A pink one, like Piggie's invitation in the book. It could have a picture on the front that says, "Elephant and Piggie invite you to a party!" or "Come as you are to an Elephant & Piggie Party!")

FOOD:

Easy finger foods include pretzel sticks, to represent elephant noses, red jellybeans, to represent pig snouts, or animal crackers.

Or you could have the children help you measure out the ingredients for a bowl of Party Mix. To four cups of Cheerios and/or Chex or Bugles, add a half cup each of Goldfish crackers, little round pretzels, raisins and dried cherries, M&M's, little marshmallows, and popcorn. To serve, scoop the mix into little cups.

Make Jungle Juice in your punch bowl: Pour in lemon-lime soda; when ready to serve, add scoops of lime sherbet to turn the juice green. Add a little pretzel stick as an elephant trunk, and a maraschino cherry as a pig snout.

NAME TAGS:

Make Elephant and Piggie name tag stickers. Write the children's names in block letters.

MY FRIEND IS SAD
by Mo Willems (Hyperion, 2007)

Activity Guide by Judy Freeman

Piggie does everything she can to cheer up Gerald (AKA Elephant), but nothing seems to work.

DISCUSSION QUESTIONS TO ASK BEFORE OR WHILE READING THE STORY

Why do you think Elephant is sad?
What makes you sad?
What cheers you up when you are sad?
What do you think Piggie might do to cheer up Elephant?

DISCUSSION QUESTIONS TO ASK AFTER READING THE STORY

Why was Elephant sad? Why couldn't Piggie cheer him up? How did she finally do it?
Why does Piggie say, "You need new glasses . . . "
Elephant's other name is Gerald. What do you think Piggie's other name might be?

STORY TIME IDEAS

READING WITH EXPRESSION AND BODY LANGUAGE:

In *My Friend Is Sad,* the dialogue between the two friends displays great use of expression, humor, and emotions. Have two children at a time come to the front of the group and read and act out the scene where Elephant explains to Piggie why he was sad and what made him happy again. Elephant's gray dialogue balloons are on the left side of the page, and Piggie's pink dialogue balloons are on the right. Have them use great expression in their voices and in their faces as they read.

LOTS OF EMOTIONS:

Page through the story again and have children name the many emotions they can see Elephant and Piggie experiencing. Make a chart of their words and add a few of their own. (Possible words: happy, sad, puzzled, excited, worried, concerned, upset, miserable, angry, disappointed, pleased, contented) After you finish the list, read it aloud, one word at a time, and have children act out the word with their facial expressions and body language.

READER'S THEATER:

The Reader's Theater script for *My Friend Is Sad* (see page 158) can be handed out to pairs of students to act out together. After they read it the first time, they can switch roles so each child has the chance to be both Elephant and Piggie. Be sure to explain how stage directions are written in parenthesis and in italics, to be followed by the actors but not to be read aloud. When you photocopy this script, be sure to run it single-sided. Double-sided scripts are confusing for children to follow.

HAPPY AND SAD: CAUSE AND EFFECT:

Draw one thing that makes you sad and then something that cheers you up and makes you happy again. At the bottom of the page, fill in the following sentences.

I am sad when _____.

I am happy when _____.

THERE IS A BIRD ON YOUR HEAD!
by Mo Willems (Hyperion, 2007)

Activity Guide by Judy Freeman

Elephant is not one bit happy when Piggie tells him there are two love birds building a nest on his head.

DISCUSSION QUESTIONS TO ASK BEFORE OR WHILE READING THE STORY

Look at the cover of the book. How does Elephant feel about having a bird on his head?
Why do you think that bird is sitting on Elephant's head?
If you had a bird sitting on your head, like Elephant does, how might you get that bird to leave?

DISCUSSION QUESTIONS TO ASK AFTER READING THE STORY

Why doesn't Elephant want those birds to hatch their eggs on his head?
How does Piggie's advice help Elephant?
Now how is Piggie going to get the birds to leave her head? What do you think Piggie will learn from this
     experience?
If someone does something that bothers you, what are good ways you can get that person to stop doing it?

STORY TIME IDEAS

TWO LITTLE BIRDS (FINGERPLAY)

Two little birds, *(hold both two thumbs up in front of you)*
Sitting on a hill.
One named Jack, *(lift one thumb higher)*
One named Jill. *(lift the other thumb higher)*
Fly away Jack, *(put first thumb behind you)*
Fly away Jill. *(put other thumb behind you)*
Come back Jack, *(bring back first thumb)*
Come back Jill. *(bring back other thumb)*

EGG HUNT:

Hide foil-wrapped chocolate eggs or plastic eggs around the room and have children search for them.

HOW MANY EGGS?:

Fill a glass jar with jelly beans. (Count them first.) Have children estimate and guess how many jelly beans (which you can tell them to pretend are really eggs) are in the jar.

WHAT KINDS OF BIRDS ARE THERE?:

Ask children to name all the types of birds they know and make a list. (By the way, though Piggie refers to the birds on Elephant's head as "love birds", the term "Love Bird" actually refers to nine species of small African parrots of the genus "Agapornis." Just in case you didn't know.) Show pictures of the birds they name from a bird book or encyclopedia. How many species of birds are there in the world today? Answers vary, but experts agree there are more than 8,000 species. That's a lot of birds!

CIRCLE TIME ACTIVITIES

HOMEMADE BINOCULARS:

Start collecting cardboard toilet paper rolls. To make your own binoculars, have each child glue together (or wrap masking tape around the outside of) two of the rolls. With a hole puncher, punch a hole in the side of each roll, and tie the ends of a long piece of string to each side.

When children put their homemade binoculars up to their eyes and look out, they will be able to focus on details. Have them use their binoculars to go bird-watching.

MAKE YOUR OWN BIRD'S NEST:

Talk about birds building nests. What are nests made of? If you have as birds nest, show it to the children. You can make your own bird's nests, though it's a bit on the messy side, so if there isn't a sink available for washing up dirty hands afterwards, you may not want to try this.

Gather your materials. You'll need a bag of small pliable sticks and twigs, pine needles, hay, leaves, and even bits of yarn or string. Children can construct and weave their own small nests and put in stones or pebbles to be their eggs.

To make less of a mess, have them construct their nests in paper bowls so they can bring them home in one piece.

TODAY I WILL FLY!
by Mo Willems (Hyperion, 2007)

Activity Guide by Judy Freeman

You know that old saying, "Pigs will fly"? Well, Piggie intends to do just that--fly. Elephant tells her, "YOU WILL NEVER FLY!" Does that stop Piggie? Not for a second. With the help of an obliging dog, a pelican, and a strategically-tied piece of string, Piggie takes to the air.

DISCUSSION QUESTIONS TO ASK BEFORE OR WHILE READING THE STORY

Look at the cover and the endpapers of the book *Today I Will Fly!* Why do you think Piggie wants to fly?
Do you think Piggie can fly? How might she do it?
What does Elephant think about Piggie's wish to fly?

DISCUSSION QUESTIONS TO ASK AFTER READING THE STORY

"If at first you don't succeed, try, try again." What does this old saying mean? How does it apply to Piggie
  when she wants to fly?
Why does Elephant say, "Tomorrow *I* will fly!"?
Piggie got help from her friend the pelican when she wanted to fly. What kind of help will Elephant need
  to fly?
How have your friends help you to do something you really wanted to do?
Piggie does not allow herself to get discouraged. What have you learned to do that was not easy but you
  kept on trying until you succeeded?

STORY TIME IDEAS

RHYMING WORDS:

Elephant shouts, "YOU WILL NEVER FLY!" Piggie says, "I will try. Good-bye." Your listeners may note that those words—fly, try, and good-bye—all rhyme. Brainstorm a longer list of rhyming words to go with the word "fly." Children can make up sentences using one of those rhyming words.

HOW FAR CAN YOU FLY?:

Well, all right. We all know we can't actually fly, at least not without help. But we CAN jump! So have a jumping contest to see how far your children can jump. Measure their jumps with a yardstick or tape measure, and record their distances on a chart.

IF I COULD FLY:

Draw a picture of what you would do or where you would go if you could fly.

If   I   could   fly,   I   would

_____ .

PIGGIE'S NEXT ADVENTURE:

Today Piggie flew. What adventure do you think she will try next? Draw a picture of what she might do tomorrow.

ELEPHANT CAN FLY!:

Draw a picture of Elephant and how he will try to fly.

ELEPHANT CAN FLY? WHAT ELSE CAN HE DO?

DIRECTIONS: Can you fill in the correct rhyming words?

(Children can write in the correct word, choosing from the list of rhyming words at the bottom of the page. It's a fun easy rhyming word activity for using context clues. Children can each select one sentence to illustrate, writing the words at the bottom of their papers. Sing the answers with the "Elephant Song" below.)

Elephant is looking up into the _____.

Elephant is baking a cherry _____.

Elephant was wet but now he is _____.

Elephant is wearing a hat and a _____.

Elephant feels sad. He is going to _____.

Elephant looked low and then he looked _____.

Elephant is singing a _____.

Elephant is waving and saying _____.

POSSIBLE ANSWERS:

dry   fry   good-bye   sky   cry   spy

lullaby   high   fly   pie   my   tie

ELEPHANT SONG
(To the tune of "I Know an Old Lady Who Swallowed a Fly")

NOTE: When you sing this song with children, leave off the final word of each first line so children can sing in the right word.

Elephant is looking up into the ___ (sky).
Piggie thinks Elephant is quite a guy.
Perhaps he'll fly.

Elephant is baking a cherry ___ (pie).
Piggie thinks Elephant is quite a guy.
Perhaps he'll fly.

Elephant was wet but now he is ___ (dry).
Piggie thinks Elephant is quite a guy.
Perhaps he'll fly.

Elephant is wearing a hat and a ___ (tie).
Piggie thinks Elephant is quite a guy.
Perhaps he'll fly.

Elephant feels sad. He is going to ___ (cry).
Piggie thinks Elephant is quite a guy.
Perhaps he'll fly.

Elephant looked low and then he looked ____ (high).
Piggie thinks Elephant is quite a guy.
Perhaps he'll fly.

Elephant is singing a _____ (lullaby).
Piggie thinks Elephant is quite a guy.
Perhaps he'll fly.

Elephant is waving and saying _____ (good-bye).
Piggie thinks Elephant is quite a guy.
Perhaps he'll fly.

Judy Freeman's Teacher's Guide for

Knuffle Bunny Too: A Case of Mistaken Identity by Mo Willems (Hyperion, 2007)

Used with permission of the publisher, Hyperion Books for Children.

JUDY FREEMAN (www.JudyReadsBooks.com), children's literature consultant and workshop presenter is the author of *Once Upon a Time: Using Storytelling, Creative Drama, and Reader's Theater with Children, Grades PreK-6* (Libraries Unlimited, 2007), and ***Books Kids Will Sit Still For 3*** (Libraries Unlimited, 2006). She writes the "Wild About Books" column for *School Library Media Activities Monthly*.

Go to <**www.hyperionbooksforchildren.com**> to download the activity pages for this guide. Type "Knuffle Bunny" in the Search Bar, click on the title, and go to its home page, where you'll find the guide listed.

Trixie and her daddy are heading to someplace really special—preschool—where Trixie can't wait to show all her friends her beloved stuffed rabbit, Knuffle Bunny. Unfortunately, another little girl, Sonja, has the same idea.

(A REMINDER: Note that there are many, many possible and interesting questions to ask your children before, during, and after reading this memorable story. Please don't ask them all. Pick just a couple that fit your group's mood and interests, and an activity or two that extends their knowledge and lets them delve deeper into the story.)

SNAPSHOTS

On the copyright and title page, there are five framed "photos" of major events in Trixie's family's life. Children familiar with the first book, ***Knuffle Bunny,*** will recognize the first four: Trixie's parents getting married; the proud couple holding up their red-faced, bawling newborn; smiling mom and dad in front of their Brooklyn brownstone, with Trixie peering out of Dad's baby carrier; and toddler Trixie in the laundromat, hugging her chartreuse-colored flop-eared stuffed rabbit, Knuffle Bunny, to whom she has just said her first words.

The fifth photo is a new one: Trixie and Knuffle Bunny hugging another little girl. Astute children will notice a second pair of bunny ears in that final photo, and will be eager to predict what might be coming up in the story and what important moment in Trixie's life is being pictured.

As you read the story, ask listeners to note the ways Trixie, no longer a toddler, has changed since the first book.

THIS IS YOUR LIFE

Have children bring in photographs chronicling important moments in their lives. They can describe to each other the significance of their photos. Make an "IMPORTANT MOMENTS" bulletin board. Children can write or dictate captions for each photo, such as: "CHRISTOPHER TAKES HIS FIRST STEP."

Children can also make time lines of their lives, using a sequential series of photos or drawings which they can hang on a line of string or yarn.

SOMEPLACE VERY SPECIAL

"Trixie was excited because she was taking her one-of-a-kind Knuffle Bunny someplace very special . . . school!"

Discussion Points: Why does Trixie love school? Why do you love school? How is Trixie's school the same as yours? How is it different?

Predictions: Trixie and her daddy are heading someplace special. Where do you think they are going? Why is she excited about going there?

Make a chart with two columns—ALIKE and DIFFERENT—and record children's comments as they compare and contrast their daily situations with Trixie's.

CONFLICTING EMOTIONS

"But just as her daddy kissed her good-bye, Trixie saw Sonja."

Trixie can't wait to get to preschool so she can show everybody her special Knuffle Bunny. We see her smiling contentedly as she walks into her classroom. And then the expression on her face changes dramatically. Before you turn the page, ask listeners to explain the downturn in her grin. Ask them to predict what Trixie sees, who Sonja is, and what Sonja might be doing that to upset Trixie.

Trixie careens through a wide range of emotions in this story. With your children, compile a list of adjectives—describing words—that categorize her many facial expressions. (They may say she looks happy, shocked, surprised, angry, jealous, and upset, to name but a few.) Then have them act out each state. Tell them, "You be Trixie. When I say each feeling, act out that emotion with your face and with your whole body."

Say, "Trixie was happy," and they'll all smile. Continue through the list, adding a few descriptors of your own, such as annoyed, distressed, or shocked.

Afterwards, have them finish and illustrate each sentence, such as:

Trixie was angry when ___.
Trixie was nervous when ___.
Trixie was delighted when ___.

CAN YOU SAY KNUFFLE BUNNY?

"Suddenly, Trixie's one-of-a-kind Knuffle Bunny wasn't so one-of-a-kind anymore."

Trixie and Sonja argue over the names of their virtually identical bunnies: "Kuh-nuffle!" "Nuffle!" What is the difference between the two stuffed animals? Though you, as an adult, may not notice any difference between the two toys, it's a pretty good bet that your children will. (HINT: Check out the ears.)

Discuss: Why were Trixie and Sonja arguing? Why did Mrs. Greengrove take away their bunnies? How do the girls feel when their rabbits are taken away?

What about the proper pronunciation of Knuffle Bunny? According to Mo Willems, the author, "'Knuffle' is Dutch for snuggle, and is, in Holland, pronounced with a hard K. But, this isn't Holland, so you can pronounce it however you like!"

In English, we don't usually pronounce the K—it is silent. (OK, knish is an exception . . .) Discuss this rule with your young linguists and have them make a list of all the words they can think of that start with "kn". (In case you can't think of many, look up KN words in the dictionary together.)

Then make a list of words that start with a hard K.

ON THE PLAYGROUND

"And the day got better."

Reunited with her beloved stuffed animal, Trixie rushes out to the playground. Have your children identify the types of playground equipment they see in the illustrations.

Ask them to describe their favorite playground games and how to play them, step by step. As they do, have other children pantomime the process of each game or activity, such as playing hopscotch, jumping rope, swinging, or sliding down the sliding board.

ROBOTS FROM THE PLANET SNURP

Trixie "tried to escape the Mommy and Daddy robots from planet Snurp!"

Before bedtime, Trixie plays a fun chasing game with her parents. Ask your group what they think the rules of this game are. Have them describe the special pretending games they play with their parents.

PIGEON AGAIN?

You know how Mo Willems always inserts a picture of Pigeon somewhere in each of his books? Ask children to be on the lookout for him, and for Leonardo the Terrible Monster, too. (They'll also love the picture on Trixie's bedroom wall of a pigeon sporting blonde curls, drawn by Trixie. Is it meant to be a self portrait? A picture of Pigeon's girlfriend? Hard to say.)

GETTING READY FOR BED

"At half-past bedtime, Trixie was tucked in."

Discussion Points: What does Trixie do to get ready for bed? How do you get ready for bed? What are your "bedtime rituals?"

Put together a list of these activities, including tooth brushing and changing into pajamas, and bedtime stories, of course, and have your children act them out, ending with a nice bit of snoring.

Make a class graph of everyone's bedtime traditions, including the times they go to sleep. (It may surprise you how late some of your children go to bed. This might be a good opportunity to talk about tooth brushing, bedtimes, and the importance of a good night's sleep.)

WIDE AWAKE

"That is *not* my bunny."

Now, your astute listeners may well have figured from the get-go what Trixie takes so long to realize as she wakes from her fitful sleep. The important question to ask here, simple, but not simplistic, is, what took her so long? Why didn't Trixie realize she had the wrong Knuffle Bunny? How did she know the difference? (And if you still haven't figured out the difference, Trixie's rabbit has blue ears, Sonya's rabbit's are pink.) Once Trixie knows it's not her rabbit, what will she do about it?

TELLING TIME, 2:30 a.m.

"Trixie's daddy tried to explain what '2:30 a.m.' means."

Quick questions: What does "2:30 a.m." mean? How do Trixie's parents react when she wakes them up in the middle of the night? Why can't Trixie wait until morning? Look at Trixie's face. She doesn't say a word. (And note that she never cries, either.) What do you think she is thinking? Why does Trixie's dad decide not to "deal with this in the morning"?

Text-to-life questions: Have you ever waked your parents up in the middle of the night? Why? What happened?

THE BIG EAR IS ON THE . . .

Notice Trixie's Knuffle Bunny clock above her bed. (The bunny ears are the hands of the clock!) We watch her, in a four panel layout, sleeping contentedly at 9:00, snoring at 10:00, waking at 1:00, and wide-eyed at 2:00.

Make your own Knuffle Bunny clock out of poster board and a brass fastener so your children can practice telling time.

BRIIIINGGG!

"We have your bunny."

We witness the little drama between Trixie and her parents at 2:30 a.m., and then, just as daddy heads off to call Sonja's house, the phone rings. It's obviously Sonja's daddy. We don't see what's been happening at Sonja's house, but we assume she also just discovered that her Nuffle Bunny has gotten himself switched.

After finishing the book, do some creative or interactive or shared writing. Children can describe what they envision must be happening at Sonja's house in the wee hours, but they can also retell the entire story from Sonja's point of view. You could call it *Nuffle Bunny Too*. If you're doing some shared writing, children can dictate sentences of their new story while you script it out on chart paper.

You could also have children tell the whole story from Knuffle Bunny's point of view. If Knuffle Bunny could talk, what would he have to say about his nocturnal adventure with Sonja?

Then type up your collaborative story in a nice big 18-point font, with one sentence at the bottom of each page, and run it off. Hand out one page of the story per child so they can then read their sentences and add an illustrate to their pages. When all the pictures are completed, have the class lay out the story in sequence in a long line across the floor. Gather up the pages in order, number them, and assemble them into a bound book for the class to read aloud as a companion story to *Knuffle Bunny*.

PICTURES WORTH A THOUSAND WORDS

"There was an exchange."

You'll love the views of the Arch in Brooklyn's Grand Army Plaza in the double-page black and white photograph taken at 3 a.m. on the top of the main branch of the Brooklyn Public Library. Let children study this picture until they notice Trixie and her daddy, in their jammies, heading across the street on the left, and Sonja and her daddy on the right. The illustration of the two daddies swapping bunnies, reminiscent of a prisoner exchange in a film noir scene, with their daughters peering fearfully around them, is simply priceless.

Ask children: How was this a life-changing moment for both Trixie and Sonja?

BEST FRIENDS AT LAST

"And that is how Trixie found her first best friend."

Discussion Points: Why do Trixie and Sonja decide to become best friends? And, when you read the Epilogue, ask why the daddies are not smiling in the illustration. (See if you can manage to ask that question without laughing a lot.) And don't forget to show the back cover, which is a perfect ending.

How did you find your own best friend? What things do you have in common?

Ask children to draw and tell their stories of finding best friends.

WHAT'S YOUR NAME?

Trixie knows the names of all the kids in her preschool class. This chant is perfect for getting to know everyone's name and getting your little ones to talk up with attitude. Standing in a big circle, each child gets a turn, going around the circle.

WHO TOOK THE COOKIES FROM THE COOKIE JAR?

GROUP:	Who took the cookies from the cookie jar?
LEADER:	Judy took the cookies from the cookie jar.
JUDY:	Who me?
GROUP:	Yes, you!
JUDY:	Couldn't be!
GROUP:	Then who?
JUDY:	Izzy took the cookies from the cookie jar.
IZZY:	Who me?
GROUP:	Yes, you!
IZZY:	Couldn't be!
GROUP:	Then who?

And so on until you go all around the circle, with each child as accused and accuser.
You can end it like this:

GROUP:	Our teacher took the cookies from the cookie jar!
TEACHER:	Who me?
GROUP:	Yes, you!
TEACHER:	Couldn't be!
GROUP:	Then who?
TEACHER:	All right! I admit it! I took all the cookies! And they were DELICIOUS!

(And if you want to, hand out a little cookie to each child. Or bake cookies together, and share Mo Willems' tale of a cookie-baking dinosaur, *Edwina, the Dinosaur Who Didn't Know She Was Extinct*.)

SING A SONG OF FRIENDSHIP

Try this children's hand-clapping game and song. Listen to this midi recording of the music online and have children sing along with the words below: <**www.grandpaschober.com/plamate.mid**>.

Oh little playmate, come out and play with me,
And bring your dollies three, climb up my apple tree;
Slide down my rain barrel, into my cellar door,
And we'll be jolly friends forever more.

I'm sorry playmate, I cannot play with you;
My dolly's got the flu, boo hoo hoo hoo hoo hoo.
I've got no rain barrel, I've got no cellar door;
But we'll be jolly friends
forever more.

TRIXIE'S NEIGHBORHOOD

Where does Trixie live? How is her house and neighborhood like yours? How is it different? Draw picture of your houses or neighborhood or bedrooms.

Take digital photographs of your classroom and school and print them out on computer paper. Using crayons, children can draw themselves in the pictures.

Make a large map of the neighborhood or of the school for your bulletin board.

KNUFFLE BUNNY'S NEXT ADVENTURE

Now that Knuffle Bunny has gone for a spin in the washing machine at the laundromat and experienced his first sleepover at Sonja's house, perhaps he's ready for another heart-stopping expedition. Where should he go this time? Draw Knuffle Bunny in his next exciting adventure.

Have children bring in a favorite toy or stuffed animal for show and tell and describe the adventures they have had together. Ask them what makes that toy special or one-of-a-kind.

Do you have a favorite toy or blanket that you can't sleep without? Draw a picture of yourself asleep with it here.

KNUFFLE BUNNY AND *KNUFFLE BUNNY TOO*

Here's a good higher level thinking skills question to ponder and evaluate: What do these two stories have in common? How are they alike and how are they different?

The short answer? In each book, Trixie loses her bunny and figures out how to get it back. But your children will find deeper issues to compare and contrast. Like how Trixie and Knuffle Bunny and daddy set off together in each story. And how each book uses the pivotal sentence " . . . Trixie realized something." In both books, Trixie and her daddy rush through the neighborhood—in the daytime in *Knuffle Bunny*, and in the middle of the night in *Knuffle Bunny Too*—to rescue the rabbit.

Will they see that the structure of the stories is similar? And that both stories end with the picture on the back cover? Will they notice daddy's new glasses? Or will they find things that you never even noticed?

MO WILLEMS' OTHER BOOKS

You'll find two video interviews with Mo Willems, plus information, teacher's guides, and activity pages you can download for all of his other books, including the Pigeon series, *Edwina the Dinosaur Who Didn't Know She Was Extinct*, *Leonardo the Terrible Monster*, and the Elephant & Piggie series at <**www.pigeonpresents.com**>.

Go to <**www.mowillems.com**> for Mo's bio, questions and Mo's own answers about his work, a message board (registration required), and the toons page, where you can watch some of the many cartoons Mo has done (which are mostly not for young kids, though you'll thoroughly enjoy them).

And then visit <**mowillemsdoodles.blogspot.com/**> to view his illustration-filled blog, "Mo Willems Doodles," which he subtitles "sketches, works in progress, blobs."

143.

Judy Freeman's Teachers Guide for

The Talented Clementine
by Sara Pennypacker
Hyperion Books for Children, 2007

It's so gratifying to see our new favorite third grader back in a sequel that is just as funny as her first fabulous first book, *Clementine*. Poor kid. Unlike her fourth grade friend and neighbor Margaret, who has a whole alphabet of talents to draw on for the upcoming school show—Talent-Palooza, Night of the Stars—Clementine can't think of even one thing she could do on stage. Sure, she's great at art and math, and her dad says she is the queen of noticing things and is very empathetic to boot. Her attempts at juggling and tap dancing don't quite pan out, and dad won't let her bring her little brother for her "Elvis and the Laughing Dog" act. Don't worry about Clementine. Her own talents help her big time on the night of the big show when assists her formidable but understanding principal, Mrs. Rice.

CHAPTERS 1-2

EXCITING AND BORING

Clementine begins her narrative with, "I have noticed the teachers get *exciting* confused with *boring* a lot. But when my teacher said, 'Class, we have an exciting project to talk about,' I listened anyway." (page 1)

Think about the projects you've done in school, the ones that were exciting, and others that were boring. Also think about projects you'd like to do and those you hope never to have to do. Make a list in two columns:

EXCITING PROJECTS   **BORING PROJECTS**

TALENT-PALOOZA
To help raise money for the big spring trip, the third and fourth graders in Clementine's school are putting on a talent show. Clementine claims not to have a talent. She can't even hop. Michael, her friend Margaret's older brother, says "Maybe you have a really great talent you just haven't figured out yet." Margaret has an entire alphabet of talents, and is trying to figure out how to do them all at once. Classmate Willy has only one talent—he can fit his entire lunch in his mouth at once. Her teacher says, "Everyone has a talent, Clementine. Everyone has something they're especially good at." (page 17-18)

Discussion Points:
What kinds of talents does Clementine have?
What talents do you have? If you were participating in Talent-Palooza, Night of the Stars, what would be your act?

Activity:
Teachers can have their students compile an alphabetical list of all their talents, both serious and silly. Hold an impromptu talent show to share them.

MOVING TO EGYPT

Trying to figure out a way to get out of being in the Talent-Palooza, Clementine tells her teacher her family might be moving this week—to Egypt. She says her father, an apartment building manager, might have to manage the Great Pyramid, especially if it goes condo. Clementine's teacher walks away laughing. "You are one in a million," he tells her (pages 20-25).

Discussion Points:
Why does she tell her teacher this story?
Why does he laugh?

CHAPTER 3:

THE RED SOX

In this chapter, Mitchell and Clementine's dad discuss baseball and the Red Sox, a natural (and inevitable) topic of conversation for two people who live in Boston. Mitchell would love to play for the Red Sox when he's older.

Research Idea:
For background, students can do some research on the Red Sox, perhaps investigating their long drought in pursuit of the World Series championship after their last win in 1918 until their triumphs in 2004 and 2007. (Baseball fans especially will enjoy finding out about the so-called "Curse of the Bambino.")

HAVING EMPATHY

Clementine's Dad tells her, "You're the most talented person I know" (page 36). Top on his list of attributes for Clementine is that she is very empathetic.

Discussion Points:
What does it mean to be empathetic?
How is Clementine empathetic? What are some of the things she's done that show empathy?
How have you been empathetic?

CHAPTERS 4-5:

MARGARET'S TALENTS

Margaret announces that her act for the talent show will be called "Dressing Fashionably." Clementine asks if she can use one of Margaret's extra talents. She picks tap dancing. Not having tap shoes, Clementine goes to the basement and her father's workbench to make a pair, supergluing 24 beer bottle caps to the bottom of her sneakers.

Discussion Point:
What is good and not so good about Clementine's solution to the tap shoes problem?

CHAPTER 6:

NOT-CHOOSING

After Clementine ruins her sneakers, her parents bargain over who will have to take her to the shoe store to buy new ones. Clementine always takes a really really long time in stores because she has a hard time choosing things. Or not-choosing things. As she says, "The problem is, whenever you have to choose something, that means you have to not-choose about a hundred other things. Which is not so easy" (page 68).

Writing Prompt:
Write about a time you had to choose between two or more good things. What did you pick? How did you decide?

BUYING WOW SHOES

At the shoe store, Clementine tries everything until she chooses the first ones she saw—a pair of lime green sneakers, size 3. Her mother buys herself a pair of not very sensible purple "WOW" shoes with tall skinny high heels and sparkly green dragonflies at the toes.

Writing/Drawing Prompt:
What kind of shoes would you pick out if you had to go to the shoe store today? Draw and describe a pair of "WOW" shoes you either have or would like to have.

BENEFITS OF BEING A GROWN-UP

Clementine's mom says buying the least sensible shoes in the store is "one of the benefits of being a grown up" (page 78).

Discussion Points:
What are some of the other benefits of being a grown-up?
What are the benefits of being a child?
Compare and contrast: Which one is better and why?

CHAPTER 7:

SUBSTITUTE KID PLANS

Clementine tells her principal Mrs. Rice she plans to send in a substitute kid in her place to the Talent-Palooza. Mrs. Rice says, "I'm sorry, but there are no substitute students" (page 83).

Project:
When teachers are going to be absent, they are expected to write lesson plans for their substitutes. Imagine if you could get a substitute kid to come to school for you for one whole day. What would you have your substitute kid do? Make a schedule—a day book, hour by hour, with plans for your substitute kid.

CHAPTER 8:

THE OLD STANDBY

Clementine is talented at making her little brother laugh. Her best routine is her Elvis act, which her parents call "The Old Standby." She pretends to play a guitar and sings, "Ain't Nothin' but a Hound Dog," and he falls over laughing, especially when she makes up a funny second line, like "Yogurt in your shoes." She plans to put a leash on him and take him to the talent show for an act she calls "Elvis and the Laughing Dog," but her parents nix the idea.

Discussion Points / Writing Prompt:
What funny things have you done that made your family or friends laugh?
What makes you laugh?

NO TALENTS

When Clementine's dad won't let her take her little brother to school for the Talent-Palooza, she has to go to the final rehearsal without a talent.

Discussion Points:
Predict: What will Clementine do when she gets to school without a talent?
How does Clementine use her talent at the rehearsal?

CHAPTER 9:

ONE OF A KIND

After Clementine helps the Talent-Palooza go off without too many hitches, thanks to her attention to every detail, her principal, Mrs. Rice tells her "I have the answer for you now, Clementine. About why you can't have a substitute. It's because there is no substitute for you. You are one of a kind" (page 120).

Clementine stops worrying. She says, "Instead, I had the proud feeling: like the sun was rising inside my chest" (page 120).

Discussion Points:
Why does the audience applaud for Clementine, even though she wasn't in the show?
Why was her role important?
Have you ever done something worthwhile and felt the proud feeling? What were the circumstances?

Writing Prompt:
What makes you one of a kind? Instead of writing about yourself (which could be embarrassing or make it seem like you're bragging), interview a partner and write a personal description about what makes him or her unique.

CHAPTER 10:

After the show, Clementine's parents take her out to the Ritz, a fancy restaurant, for a celebration dinner. "I think this is the luckiest day of my life," she says.

Discussion Point:
What was the luckiest day of your life?

NOTE: Judy Freeman's guide for all three of the Clementine books—*Clementine*, *The Talented Clementine*, and *Clementine's Letter*—will be available on Hyperion's website sometime in Spring of 2008. To find it, go to <**www.hyperionbooksforchildren.com**>. Type "Clementine" in the Search Bar, click on the title, and go to its home page, where you'll find the guide listed. You can print out a copy for yourself.

USING READER'S THEATER

Adapted from *Once Upon a Time: Using Storytelling, Creative Drama, and Reader's Theater with Children in Grades PreK-6* by Judy Freeman (Libraries Unlimited, 2007). Reprinted with permission of Libraries Unlimited.

Improvised drama depends on the talents of the actors to make its unscripted production smooth and believable. With Readers Theater, a more structured drama variation, children are given or write their own scripts to act out a scene. Readers Theater stresses reading aloud, and as such, is a boon to the children who are less confidant about extemporaneous speaking.

When my very first edition of *Books Kids Will Sit Still For* was published back in 1984, I recall one reviewer who was disappointed because I didn't include any information on or mention of Reader's Theater. "What on earth is Reader's Theater?" I said as I looked it up. I found it means you hand out copies of a script derived from a book or story, and have readers act it out. "Wait, I do that!" I said.

The inspiration for what we now call Reader's Theater had to be old time radio. Before television, people listened to weekly radio shows like "The Lone Ranger" and "Fibber McGee and Molly." In the radio studio, actors would stand in front of their microphones, scripts in hand, and read their parts.

You can find some of these scripts old online, including Abbott and Costello's famous bit, "Who's On First?" <**www.louandbud.com/WOF.htm**>, and act them out. There are scripts for 117 different vintage radio series from 1930-1960 at <**www.genericradio.com**>.

Here's how I got started with Reader's Theater. It was the week before Christmas vacation and I was gearing up to do a week of storytelling for the students in the elementary school where I was the librarian. Then laryngitis struck.

I got to school that morning, and headed straight for the books of plays on the library shelf—the 812's. Finding several cute holiday-related plays with lots of parts, I ran off scripts for each class, rearranged the chairs into a big semicircle, and crossed my fingers. I wrote instructions on the board. Something like: "Can't talk. It's up to you today. Let's put on a play." It was a huge hit. Necessity was the mother of invention, though I had no idea there was a name for what we were doing and that it was an educationally sound and wise process. We were just having fun with drama. A lot of fun. And I've been doing it ever since.

Reader's Theater is not to be confused with round robin reading where one child after another reads paragraphs aloud from a story. Round robin reading can be deadening.

When I was a child in elementary school, my classmates and I spent a fair amount of time reading aloud from our basal readers, Round Robin–style, up and down the rows. I remember, when it was my turn, trying to read aloud with lots of expression. I never could recall any details from the passage I was assigned, focused, as I was, on the written text in lieu of comprehending its meaning. If I made a mistake, I felt humiliated. Kids would laugh at stumblers, stammerers, and mispronouncers, unless they were too busy nervously surveying the upcoming text for their own turns. That type of Round Robin reading has fallen out of fashion.

So how do we help sharpen children's oral reading skills and encourage their response to literature? How do you get them to think deeper, beyond the usual glib happy-sad-mad-glad-bad responses when you read aloud a picture book like *The Trial of Cardigan Jones* by Tim Egan (Houghton Mifflin, 2004). Cardigan, a moose, is accused of stealing Mrs. Brown's freshly baked apple pie. He says he didn't do it.

Write up a Reader's Theater script of the story for children to act out. After your group has acted out their script two or three times, you can ask them, "How did Cardigan Jones feel when the jury finally declared him not guilty?"

Your actors will not just have seen the book and heard the story and read the story. They will have lived the story. They'll know that story from the inside out. Maybe you'll even bring out an apple pie for the cast party. What a fine way to get children invested in literature.

We all know there are no quick fixes in turning children into readers, don't we? Well, there are a few. And Reader's Theater is one of them. If you're searching for a painless, effective way to get your children reading aloud with comprehension, expression, fluency, volume, and, most important, joy, Reader's Theater is a miracle. It allows children to get invested in the plot of a story, to see it unfold and come together.

What is Reader's Theater (or Readers Theatre, another of its many spellings)? It's nothing fancy. And you can do it yourself. After you read a book aloud to your children, you hand out a photocopied play script of the story with a part for each child, and they simply read the script aloud and act it out. You don't need props, costumes, or scenery, unless you want them. Children don't need to memorize their lines, though they will often do so just because they want to. (They have more brain cells than we do. Memorizing lines is child's play to them.) You don't need to perform your play in front of an audience, though actors may decide they want to do that, too. That's it? Pretty much. It's the process that's important here, not a finished product. And then magic happens.

Students have a script to hold and follow, but they also interact with the other readers as the group acts out its playlet. They bond with their fellow actors and respond to them in character, walking, for a short time, in their characters' shoes. By participating in an activity they love, they become more proficient and self-confident as readers and as performers.

If you are looking for a way to enhance presentation and public speaking skills, to get your children working together in harmony, to enunciate when they speak, to listen to what others have to say, to get to the heart of a story, to boost self esteem, and to hone every reading skill, Reader's Theater is your free ticket to change lives and raise contented, fulfilled, and motivated children. Watch your reading scores soar while children think they're just having a great time.

In my many years as a school librarian, I had each class put on at least one Reader's Theater play each year, starting with first grade (spring is best, when their reading skills are coming along), based on books I read aloud to them. Children thrive, even the quiet ones, on the thrill of being a star for a little while.

SOURCES OF READER'S THEATER PLAYS

How do you get going with Reader's Theater? First off, choose a good book and read it aloud to your group. They need to hear your expressive voice in their heads and have a sense of the characters, plot, setting, and sequence. They will be making an important connection between a book and the play that emerges from the book's text.

When you finish reading aloud or sharing a book, tell children you will then be acting out the story as a Reader's Theater play, they will probably cheer.

Where can you get plays? Look in the 812s on your library shelves for books of plays. Check out *Plays: The Drama Magazine for Young People* (and its website at **www.playsmag.com**), an indispensable magazine which comes out monthly, and is filled with good, royalty-free plays for elementary through high school. These are not always connected with children's books, but they're still good plays to read.

There are wonderful books containing Reader's Theater scripts by Suzanne Barchers, Caroline Feller Bauer, Toni Buzzeo, Anthony Fredericks, Aaron Shepard, and Judy Sierra.

Authors are starting to write Reader's Theater scripts for their own books and put them on their websites. See Margie Palatini's site, <**www.margiepalatini.com**>, and Toni Buzzeo's site, <**www.tonibuzzeo.com**>, for instance.

Another excellent online source is Rick Swallow's Readers Theater/Language Arts Home Page for Teachers at <**www.timelessteacherstuff.com**>, with more than eighty scripts, many from well-known children's picture books.

My favorite source for Reader's Theater scripts is the amazing website of author Aaron Shepard, who has retold and published many wonderful folk tales, most of which he has also adapted into Reader's Theater Scripts. Go to <**http://aaronshep.com/rt**>, where you can easily download his scripts, buy his books, or get in touch with him to have him visit your school to give a workshop.

WRITING YOUR OWN READER'S THEATER SCRIPTS

You can, of course, write up your own scripts, just like Aaron Shepard does, which is far easier than you might think. I write up at least one new Reader's Theater script a year. If you type up just one script each year, pretty soon you'll have a drawerful of interesting plays to use with your kids.

Many books you read aloud or booktalk have scenes or chapters with multiple characters and an emphasis on dialogue. Picture books are a logical starting place, but controlled vocabulary Easy Readers, dialogue-rich scenes or chapters in fiction books, folktales, narrative poems like "Casey at the Bat," picture book biographies, and even science and history books can lend themselves to being turned into plays. Keep an open mind when considering possibilities for drama.

When deciding on a book or excerpt to transform into a script, I consider my own Freeman's Five Essential Ingredients. For the elementary school audience, a story should have:

1. Peppy dialogue
2. A little action
3. Laugh out loud parts
4. Lively narration
5. Enough roles for all

It takes me about an hour to do a good first draft of a picture book, even when typing with my usual two fingers and a thumb. Some of my favorite picture books I've adapted include Matt Novak's *Mouse TV* (Orchard, 1994), Helen Bannerman's *The Story of Little Babaji* (HarperCollins, 1996), Susan Meddaugh's *Martha Walks the Dog* (Houghton Mifflin, 1998), Diane Stanley's *Raising Sweetness* (Putnam, 1999), Doreen Cronin's *Click, Clack, Moo: Cows That Type* (Simon & Schuster, 2000), Shelley Moore Thomas's *Get Well, Good Knight* (Dutton, 2002), Antonio Sacre's *The Barking Mouse* (Albert Whitman, 2003), Tim Egan's *The Trial of Cardigan Jones* (Houghton Mifflin, 2004), Kate DiCamillo's *Mercy Watson to the Rescue* (Candlewick, 2005), and Lane Smith's *John, Paul, George & Ben* (Hyperion, 2006).

SCRIPTWRITING TIPS

If you've ever seen a real script for a play or movie, you'll note that the formatting of a RT script is simpler. It needs to be easy for children to read so they can scan down and find their lines and follow along as the play progresses. Here are some of my script tips:

1. At the top of your script, include a list of all the acting roles, in order of appearance, plus the narrators.
2. Use a good-sized font for your scripts, so students can see and read their lines clearly. I like 14- or 18-point Helvetica or Times, both of which are easy on the eyes.
3. Justify your right margin to give the script a clean look.
4. Add page numbers at the bottom.
5. Always photocopy your scripts single-sided. It's very confusing to try to follow a double-sided script, especially for children. "I can't find the page," they'll wail.
6. Character names, including narrators, are on the left, in caps and in bold. Set up tabs for the dialogue, so actors can scan down the left side of each page to find their names and look to the right for their lines.
7. Single-space each character's lines, but add a double space between lines.
8. Put your stage directions in italics and in parenthesis. (*Explain to children that they don't read these out loud as lines, but that they should follow the stage directions so they know what to do.*)
9. Bold and/or capitalize those lines, phrases, or words you want an actor to say with more **force** or VOLUME or **EXPRESSION**.

10. In writing a script, try to incorporate verbatim as much of the story's actual dialogue and narration as possible, but don't be afraid to change, rearrange, edit, or add, if it will make the play flow better. You don't have to be a word-for-word slave to the book, though you do want to stay true to the author's words.

11. You can condense scenes, or even leave them out, especially if you're doing a long, involved chapter or scene from a fiction book.

12. Try to ensure that everyone will get a good speaking part, both actors and narrators. This means you may need to add lines. You might turn some dialogue into narration, and vice versa

13. Even if you proofread and run your spellcheck, you won't catch all of the typos you made until you run off a script and hand it out. (Then they will jump out at you.)

14. As for problems with the script itself, make notes as you watch your group perform their first reading. Did one character get too many lines? Not enough? Are the stage directions clear? Afterwards, go back to your computer and fix everything that wasn't perfect, and run off a second draft.

15. If you like, you can start with the characters introducing themselves. ("I'm Josh, and I play the Lawyer.") This makes sure the audience knows who's who, and also gives each character an extra line. This isn't necessary, and you don't have to write it in the script if you want your players to do it.

KIDS WRITE SCRIPTS

As a writing exercise, scripting a scene is challenging and fun for children, once you have demonstrated the format and construction. Students in grades two and up can learn to write scripts, adapting published books or their own original stories. Get them started by giving each person a copy of a sample play for reference.

Do your first script together as a class. First hand out copies of a brief story for all to read. With their input, outline the story on the board, chart, or overhead projector. Model how to turn dialogue from a story into play dialogue and how to turn narration into lines for narrators to read. Show them how to write stage directions in italics.

When students are adapting print into a script, photocopy the original story. Have them mark up the copy with highlighters, using a different color for each part. This will make it easier for them to transcribe and keep track of who says what.

The tedious part is copying down or typing the dialogue and narration. Think of it as a good way to practice handwriting or keyboarding.

One excellent source for younger readers is the "I Can Read" genre, those easy-to-read early chapter books like the "Frog and Toad" series by Arnold Lobel or the "Henry and Mudge" and "Poppleton" books by Cynthia Rylant. Short, self-contained chapters which contain snappy dialogue are ideal for small group productions. Break children into small groups to work on their scripts and then act them out.

Students in all grades can also write new dialogue-filled chapters. Just because these stories are easy to read, doesn't mean they're that easy to write. If your students create a couple of new scripts each year, in no time you'll have a lifetime supply of scripts to use.

READER'S THEATER LOGISTICS

How do you give everyone a part? You'll need to do a bit of juggling to make everything come out even. With Reader's Theater scripts, you can expand the number of parts by adding narrators, doubling up on characters, or even splitting a character's part into two or more. When you type up a new script, estimate how many acting parts you have and how many students, and add narrators to make up the difference. If you have 12 narrators and 10 to 12 actors, this usually works fine. If you have more parts than actors, double the lines of the narrators. Have Narrator 11 also read Narrator 10's part as well, for instance.

What about an existing script that has 11 parts when you have 23 kids? You can easily add more parts by doubling or tripling the number of narrators. Tell one child, for example, "You are Narrator 1, pages one to three," and the next one, "And you are Narrator 1, pages four to six." And so on. If necessary, divide the roles of your main characters in the same way.

You can also break the script into three or four smaller scenes, with a separate cast for each. Each group can practice its small scene several times and then put it on for the others.

Or you could have two separate casts, rehearsing on separate sides of the room. Each group can then do the play for each other, giving everyone a chance to be both actors and audience members. You also can have simultaneous rehearsals for two or three separate plays, and then have the casts perform for each other. As long as everyone gets a part, you can make almost any configuration work.

IT'S SHOWTIME!

If you're putting on an all-class production, you'll most likely want to rearrange desks to make space for a makeshift stage or space. In a library, you'll need to move tables, which could be trickier, but certainly not impossible. I like to arrange 24 chairs in a big semicircle or arc so actors can see each other, with open space in the front of the chairs for interaction-a chase scene, for instance-so they can get up and move around. Set up a chair for yourself, facing the actors, so you can be the director, prompter, and appreciative audience all in one.

Once the children are sitting in the chairs, hand out the scripts in order. About half of your group will be narrators. I designate the children who sit on the left side as narrators, and the right side, actors. I hand out the parts sequentially, with Narrator 1 on the left, and then 2, 3, 4, and so on, sitting next to each other. Don't get fancy here. You always want to be able to figure out whose line is next. Someone will always say, "I can't remember which narrator I am." Count over and say, "You're Narrator 5." Easy.

Unless you have a few parts that are particularly difficult to read, don't worry about who gets what role. Some of your shyest kids will shine doing this activity. I do try to make sure the boys get boy parts, as there's usually an outcry if they don't. The girls tend to be a bit more flexible and don't mind as much if they get a boy part.

Give the children a few minutes to go over their lines and practice a bit. When they can't figure out a word or phrase, instruct them to turn to the actors on their left or right for help.

Give a little pep talk as follows:

"This is a first reading, just like real actors do on Broadway or on TV when they start to rehearse a new play or episode. Nobody expects it to be perfect and nobody should care if someone misses a line or stumbles on a word. Never laugh at a fellow actor who makes a mistake. We're all in this together.

"Keep an eye out for your neighbors on either side of you during the play. If you see the person next to you has lost his place, don't say a thing. Just lean over and put your finger on his script to show him where we are.

"I am the prompter for this play. When an actor gets stuck, the prompter helps by giving the correct line or word. Even actors on Broadway look to the prompter if they forget their lines. If you get confused and your neighbors can't help you, then look at me."

Then it's showtime. Each time a child has a line, he or she must stand up to deliver it in a loud, clear, and expressive voice. Prompt them as needed, and laugh with them. That first reading, while exhilarating, can be choppy, but who cares?

Once is not enough with Reader's Theater; try for two or even three readings for it to be truly effective. Even though your group will have heard you read the story aloud, the first time they undertake to plow through the script for themselves, they will stumble and stammer and lose their places. They'll struggle with decoding unfamiliar words, getting a sense of how their parts might sound, and making sense of the plot.

During the second reading, your actors will start to listen to the others' lines, to relax and watch the story unfold, and they'll read with more understanding and expression. If you have time to do it a third time, it will seem like a revelation. Readers will be able to focus on enjoying the performance and their parts in it.

You might want to change parts the third time you run through the script, giving the actors a chance to be narrators, and vice versa. Challenge your actors in a constructive way. Say to them, "How can you make this next reading better? What will you do this time that you didn't do the first time?"

Now when you ask all those lovely interpretive questions to foster higher level thinking and reasoning skills, your children will be brilliantly prepared to discuss a story they have heard, then read, then lived.

Make sure you have extra copies of the script. You want your actors to mark up their parts—they love to use highlighters—and get comfortable with their scripts. If they take them home to read and practice, that's ideal. So don't chew anyone out for leaving her script at home. Just hand out extra copies.

If you expect your students to do well, they probably will. I used my Reader's Theater script of Matt Novak's picture book *Mouse TV* (Orchard 1994) with several classes of first graders in my school library one year. It was the first time these children had ever done RT and I was excited about it. We had read the story the week before.

When the first class entered the library, I had them sit in the chairs I had arranged in a long arc across the room. We talked about the story. I handed out parts and let them find their lines and practice them for a few minutes. Then we started acting. I had written the song "Three Blind Mice" into the script for the whole cast to sing, and when we got to that part in the script, they sang it with great exuberance. They read with expression. They had a ball. Their teacher was amazed. "Wow! I didn't know they could do that!"

The next class came in and I explained what we were going to do. The teacher said, sharply, "They won't be able to read that! This is *much* too hard for first grade!"

Well, guess what. Those children found it much too hard. They whined and said, "I don't know what to do!" and "I can't read this."

Talk about your self-fulfilling prophecy. If I hadn't seen the first class, I would have believed that teacher. Yeah, this is too hard for first grade, I guess. Maybe next year. But I knew they could do it and they did. You will have children and teachers who tell you it's too hard. Don't give up on them. They feel so proud of themselves when they realize they can do it.

In 2002, when Aaron Shepard's book of the West African pourquoi tale, *Master Man: A Tall Tale of Nigeria* (HarperCollins, 2001), was published, I couldn't wait to try out his new script with two classes of third graders at Van Holten School.

In the first production, the boy who played Shadusa, the cocksure man who considers himself the strongest man in the world, was himself a self-assured, brash kid, well-liked for his comic take on the world. He was very funny and brazen in the part.

Then in came the second class eager for their chance to act. I handed out the scripts, giving the lead part of Shadusa to the boy who sat at the end of the semicircle of chairs, on the right. His teacher pulled me aside. "Maybe he's not such a good person to play the main character," she whispered. "He's so shy, he barely talks. We haven't heard him say Boo all year."

"That's OK," I told her. "It doesn't matter if he's not fabulous. The play will still be fun."

And then the miracle happened. The boy playing Shadusa got into his role. And while he wasn't as flamboyant as the first boy had been, he was still plenty expressive and blustery, fitting the part just fine. The other children in the class looked at him in amazement when he started to speak, hearing that quiet boy become a whole new person.

When children finish reading a script, they usually feel pretty good about it. Reinforce that by teaching them how to do their bows, just like on Broadway. I have them face front, join hands, hold their arms up high, and then bow in unison on the count of three. They come up on the count of three, and repeat it three times. They have to watch each other out of the corners of their eyes so they go down and come up together. It looks pretty cool. You keep the count and applaud and cheer like crazy, especially if you are their only audience member.

PERFORMANCE TIPS FOR ACTORS

1. Read over your lines so you know where they are in the script and how to pronounce all the words.
2. Hold your script still. If you rattle the paper, the other actors will be distracted. When you need to turn the page of your script, do it quickly and as quietly as you can. [NOTE: Teachers can circumvent the problem by putting the pages of each script in plastic sleeves and in a notebook binder. Children can either hold their binders or place them on music stands in front of them. For everyday RT, this is more work than necessary, but if you're putting on a performance for parents or an audience, it's a nice professional touch.]
3. If the cast is sitting in chairs, stand up when you have a line. Sit down when you finish.
4. When you stand up to deliver a line, hold your script down by your belly button. (I call this, "Belly It Up.") Make sure it stays there so everyone can see and hear you. Don't let your script creep up to cover your face.
5. If you can't see the audience, they can't see you either. In Reader's Theater, you act with your face. Make sure it's visible at all times.
6. Never turn your back on the audience. People need to be able to see your face, not your fanny.
7. Read your lines slowly and clearly so everyone can understand you.
8. Use your playground voice. Imagine your voice bouncing off the back wall like a rubber ball. You may think you are speaking loudly, but chances are no one can hear you.
9. Always read with expression. Concentrate. Think about how your lines should sound or how you can do them better next time.
10. If your line is funny, don't laugh unless the script calls for it. Let the audience will figure out the funny parts.
11. If you're acting for an audience and they laugh, freeze until they stop laughing. If you say your next line while they are still laughing, they won't hear it.
12. Stay in character. When you act out a play, you become someone else. Try to act like that person would.
13 Follow along in your script so you don't lose your place.
14. If you do lose your place, catch the eye of the actor sitting next to you. Point to his or her script, and shrug your shoulders. That person will know you're lost and will put a finger on the correct line of your script. Return the favor when needed.
15. If you mess up a line, don't worry about it. Just keep going.
16. Be considerate of the other actors. If you fool around while they're delivering their lines, they might do the same to you.
17. Take your script home and practice reading it aloud with someone-a friend, your parents, or a brother or sister. If there's no one around, read it to the mirror.

Dog and Bear: Play with Me! Play with Me!

Adapted from "Play with Me! Play with Me!," a chapter in *Dog and Bear: Two Friends, Three Stories*, written and illustrated by Laura Vaccaro Seeger, Roaring Brook Press, 2007. (For grades K-2.)

Reader's Theater adaptation by Judy Freeman; reprinted with permission of the publisher, Roaring Brook Press.

ROLES: Dog, Bear

NOTE: This is a two-person play. Have your children break into pairs to act this out together. Then have them do it again, switching parts.

DOG: Bear, will you play with me?

BEAR: Not right now, Dog. I am reading my book.

DOG: Please, Bear. Play with me.

BEAR: I am reading a story about a dog and a stuffed bear.

DOG: Oh, Bear. Play with me!

BEAR: In the book, the dog and the bear are best friends.

DOG: Come on, Bear. Play with me!

BEAR:	Although they love to be together, sometimes the bear just needs some time to himself.
DOG:	Play with me! Play with me! Play with me! Play with me!
BEAR:	The bear tried to explain this to the dog, but the dog did not understand.
DOG:	Play with me! Play with me!
BEAR:	After a while, the bear realized that the dog just wanted to be with his friend. All right, Dog. I will play with you now. What shall we do?
DOG:	Read to me! Read to me!

A Reader's Theater Script for
My Friend Is Sad

Adapted from *My Friend Is Sad*, an Elephant & Piggie book written and illustrated by Mo Willems, published by Hyperion Books for Children, 2007. (For grades K-2.) Reader's Theater adaptation by Judy Freeman; reprinted with permission of the publisher, Hyperion Books for Children.

ROLES: Elephant, Piggie

NOTE: This script can be handed out to pairs of students to act out together. After they read it the first time, they can switch roles so each child has the chance to be both Elephant and Piggie. Be sure to explain how stage directions are written in parenthesis and in italics, to be followed by the actors but not to be read aloud. When you photocopy this script, be sure to run it single-sided. Double-sided scripts are confusing for children to follow.

ELEPHANT: Ohhh. . .

PIGGIE: My friend is sad.

ELEPHANT: *(puts hands up to his mouth and looks upset)*

PIGGIE: I will make him happy!

ELEPHANT: *(looks up, puzzled)*

PIGGIE: *(rides in like a cowboy on a horse)* Yee-haw!

ELEPHANT: A cowboy! *(Elephant looks down, sad again)* Ohhh . . .

PIGGIE: Gerald loves cowboys. But he is still sad.

ELEPHANT: *(looks up, puzzled)*

PIGGIE: *(pretends to juggle balls like a clown)*

ELEPHANT: A clown! *(Elephant looks down, sad)* Ohhh . . .

PIGGIE:	Clowns are funny. But he is still sad.
ELEPHANT:	*(looks up, puzzled)*
PIGGIE:	*(walks like a robot)*
ELEPHANT:	A robot! *(Elephant looks down, sad)* Ohhh . . .
PIGGIE:	How can anyone be sad around a robot?
ELEPHANT:	*(looks down, very sad)*
PIGGIE:	*(looks upset)* Gerald.
ELEPHANT:	*(looks up, excited)* Piggie!
PIGGIE:	I am sorry. I tried to make you happy. But you are still sad.
ELEPHANT:	I am not sad now. I am happy!
PIGGIE:	You are happy?
ELEPHANT:	I am happy because you are here! But I was so sad, Piggie. So very SAD! I saw a COWBOY! *(puts arm across his eyes)*
PIGGIE:	But you love cowboys!
ELEPHANT:	I do. I love cowboys. **But you were not there to see him!**
PIGGIE:	Well, in fact, I . . .

ELEPHANT:	**THERE WAS MORE!** Then I saw a clown! *(starts to cry)* A funny, funny clown! But you were not there to see him!
PIGGIE:	But . . .
ELEPHANT:	*(yells)* **THERE WAS MORE!**
PIGGIE:	*(falls over)*
ELEPHANT:	I saw a ROBOT! **A COOL, COOL ROBOT!** *(sadly)* And my best friend was not there to see it with me. *(covers face with his arms)*
PIGGIE:	But . . . Um . . . You see . . . I am here NOW!
ELEPHANT:	You are! You are here now! My friend is here now!
PIGGIE:	*(smiles at Elephant)*
ELEPHANT:	*(smiles at PIGGIE)* I need my friends.
PIGGIE:	*(cups hand over mouth and turns head to the side)* You need new glasses . . .

A Reader's Theater Script for
The Cheese

Adapted from the book *The Cheese*, written by Margie Palatini, illustrated by Steve Johnson and Lou Fancher, published by Katherine Tegen Books, HarperCollins Publishers, 2007.

Reader's Theater adaptation by Judy Freeman; reprinted with permission of the publisher, HarperCollins Publishers, Inc.

For a wonderful free recording of author Margie Palatini reading the entire story, go to <www.harpercollinschildrens.com> and type "cheese" in the search bar.

FOR GRADES K-2

ROLES: Rat, Cat, Dog, Child, Wife, Farmer, Cheese
              Narrator 1, Narrator 2, Narrator 3, Narrator 4, Narrator 5

NOTE: If you need more parts, add more narrators. (When you hand out parts, say, "You are Narrator 1 on pages 1 and 2, and you are Narrator 1 on pages 3 and 4," etc. You can do the same for the Cat and the Rat who have such big parts.) Be sure to explain how stage directions are written in parenthesis and in italics, to be followed by the actors but not to be read aloud. When you photocopy this or any script, run it single-sided. Double-sided scripts are confusing for children to follow.

NARRATOR 1:   The rat looked down in the dell and shook his head.

RAT: *(shakes his head)* What a waste of a chunk of cheddar.

NARRATOR 2:   He turned to go into his hole, and then he stopped.

NARRATOR 3:   He looked back at the cheese standing all alone in the middle of the meadow.

NARRATOR 4:   So yellow.

NARRATOR 5:   So mellow.

NARRATORS 1- 5: So tasty.

RAT: This is ridiculous. What's the point of a hunk of cheese being left out and lonesome when it can be enjoying the company of a perfectly fine rat like me? *(licks his lips greedily)*

NARRATOR 1:	None that he could think of.
NARRATOR 2:	The rat grabbed a napkin, and scurried down the hill for some dinner in the dell.
CAT:	*(jumping down from tree)* And just where do you think you're going?
RAT:	Me? Uh, why . . . just out for a short stroll.
CAT:	You don't look like you're strolling. You look like you're scurrying and sneaking.
RAT:	Scurrying and sneaking! WELL!
NARRATOR 3:	The rat sounded very insulted.
NARRATOR 4:	And, as he was quite a good actor, he almost convinced the cat that he was indeed just out for a walk.
NARRATOR 5:	But the cat, who was very clever herself, caught sight of the napkin.
CAT:	*(grabs napkin and holds it up)* **Aha!** And just what is this?
RAT:	Oh, if you must know, I'm going to get the cheese.
CAT:	The cheese? You can't do that. Everyone knows the cheese stands alone.
RAT:	Give me one good reason why the cheese stands alone.
CAT:	*(thinks)* Well . . . ummm . . . hmmmm . . . It's the song. Yes. It's most definitely the song. The song says, "The cheese stands alone," and that's that.
RAT:	Well, I think it's a silly song. *(grabs back his napkin)* And I'm going to eat that cheese.
NARRATOR 1:	The cat looked at the rat. Then she looked down in the dell at the cheese.

NARRATOR 2:	It did look rather lonely..
NARRATOR 3:	The cat could not argue that the song was silly.
NARRATOR 4:	And as finicky an eater as she was, the cat did have a fondness for a nibble of cheese now and then.
CAT:	You know, I believe you may be correct. That cheese should not stand alone.
NARRATOR 5:	The rat smiled and held out a paw. Care to join me for a bit of cheddar, my dear?
CAT AND RAT:	*(joining paws)*
NARRATORS 1- 5:	So off went the two, down into the dell, headed for the cheese.
NARRATOR 1:	They were about to crawl under the fence when who should come running up but . . .
NARRATORS 2- 5:	**THE DOG!**
DOG:	Where are you going? Where are you going? Where are you going?
NARRATOR 2:	The dog was **such** a bother.
CAT:	Calm down and sit. If you must know, we're going to eat the cheese.
DOG:	The cheese? The cheese in the dell? The cheese in the dell? But the cheese stands alone. Everyone knows that.
RAT:	Yeah, yeah, yeah. Stop your slobbering. We know all about it. But why should good food go to waste because of some silly song?
NARRATOR 3:	The dog thought.
NARRATOR 4:	Which was not an easy thing for him to do.

NARRATOR 5:	He looked across the dell at the cheese. It **did** look very lonely. And even the dog had to admit it **was** a silly song.
DOG:	*(drooling)* You know, I could go for a nosh right about now myself.
NARRATORS 1- 5:	So off went the rat, the cat, and the dog to eat the cheese.
CHILD:	*(calling to dog)* Here, boy! Here, boy!
DOG:	Woof! Woof! Arf! Woof! Arf!
RAT:	That dog can never keep a secret!
NARRATOR 1:	The child looked at the dog. She looked down in the dell.
CHILD:	Why, you aren't thinking of eating that cheese, are you? Naughty, naughty puppy. You know the cheese stands alone.
NARRATOR 2:	The dog rolled over with a whimper and a whine.
DOG:	*(hangs his head)* Woof! Arf! Arf! Arf! Woof!
RAT:	This is pitiful.
CAT:	I'll take care of this.
NARRATOR 3:	The cat walked up to the child.
NARRATOR 4:	Purred.
CAT:	*(purrs)*
NARRATOR 5:	Arched.
CAT:	*(arches its back)*
NARRATORS 1- 3:	Rubbed
CAT:	*(rubs head against child's shoulder)*

NARRATORS 1- 5: And mewed.

CAT: **MEOW!**

CHILD: *(giggles)* You know, that piece of cheese does look awful yummy. And I haven't had my afternoon snack. How about you?

NARRATORS 1- 5: So off went the child, the dog, the cat, and the rat to eat the cheese.

NARRATOR 1: And then . . . Mother called.

WIFE: **YOO HOO.**

RAT: *(to child)* Shush!

CAT: *(to child)* Shush!

DOG: *(to child)* Shush!

CHILD: *(calls to Mother)* I'm going to eat the cheese!

RAT, CAT, DOG: **SHUSH!**

NARRATORS 1-5: That child was completely unshushable.

RAT: What a little blabbermouth.

WIFE: No, no, you can't eat the cheese. The cheese stands alone. Wait until your father comes home.

NARRATOR 1: So they all waited for the cow to come home with the farmer, who was the father.

WIFE: *(to Father)* Your child wants to eat the cheese in the Dell.

FARMER: *(shaking his head no)* Nope. Can't eat the cheese. Cheese stands alone. Everyone knows that.

NARRATOR 2:	The wife looked at the child . . .
WIFE:	*(looks at child)*
NARRATOR 3:	Who looked at the dog . . .
CHILD:	*(looks at dog)*
NARRATOR 4:	Who looked at the cat . . .
DOG:	*(looks at cat)*
NARRATOR 5:	Who looked at the rat . . .
CAT:	*(looks at rat)*
NARRATORS 1-5:	Who looked at the cheese . . .
RAT:	*(looks at cheese, sighs, and rubs belly)*
NARRATOR 1:	It was very quiet until everyone's tummy started to grumble.
NARRATORS 1-5:	Grumble, grumble, grumble, grumble, grumble.
NARRATOR 2:	After a long day's work, the farmer's grumbled the loudest.
NARRATORS 1-5:	**Grumble, grumble, grumble, grumble, grumble.**
FARMER:	I suppose that song is rather silly.
ALL:	*(all turn to cheese and stare, rubbing their bellies and nodding yes)*
WIFE:	It truly is.
FARMER:	*(takes off hat and scratches head)* What should we do?
NARRATOR 3:	The rat elbowed the cat.
RAT:	*(elbows cat)*

NARRATOR 4:	Who poked the dog.
CAT:	*(pokes dog)*
NARRATOR 5:	Who nudged the child.
DOG:	*(nudges child)*
CHILD:	**LET'S HAVE A PARTY!**
DOG:	Woof!
CAT:	Meow!
RAT:	Squeak!
NARRATOR 1:	So the farmer followed his wife.
NARRATOR 2:	And his wife followed the child.
NARRATOR 3:	And the child followed the dog.
NARRATOR 4:	Who followed the cat.
NARRATOR 5:	Who followed the rat, who was already wearing his napkin.
NARRATORS 1-5:	Down into the dell to **EAT THE CHEESE!**
NARRATOR 1:	And then the farmer stopped.
FARMER:	You know, if we're going to have a party, we really should have some apples from the orchard to eat with the cheese.
WIFE:	Delightful idea. And I'll fetch a few pears.
CHILD:	I'll get the crackers.
DOG:	Some sausages would be tasty, too.
CAT:	I insist on milk!

NARRATOR 1:   So off went the farmer.

NARRATOR 2:   And his wife.

NARRATOR 3:   And the child.

NARRATOR 4:   And the dog.

NARRATOR 5:   And the cat.

NARRATOR 1:   To get some apples.

NARRATOR 2:   And pears.

NARRATOR 3:   And crackers.

NARRATOR 4:   And sausages.

NARRATOR 5:   And milk.

NARRATORS 1-5: Everyone left the cheese alone except . . . you know who.

RAT: Take your time. I'll just stay here and hang out with the cheddar. Heh Heh Heh. *(looks at cheese longingly, reaches out to take a piece, and then stops. Sighs. Looks at audience)* Shame on you for what you were thinking. I may be a sneaky rat, but I'm still one big party animal. Hi-ho the dairy-o!

ALL: *(sing)* **Hi-ho the dairy-o, we all ate the cheese.**

A Scene from
Emmy and the Incredible Shrinking Rat

Adapted from the novel *EMMY AND THE INCREDIBLE SHRINKING RAT* (Chapter 1, pages 3-8) by Lynne Jonell. Copyright 2007 by Lynne Jonell. Published by Henry Holt and Company, 2007.

Reader's Theater adaptation by Judy Freeman; reprinted with permission of the publisher, Henry Holt and Company and by the author, Lynne Jonell.

FOR GRADES 3-6
ROLES: Emmy, the Rat

NOTE:
In the first chapter, we meet Emmy, a girl whom no one ever seems to notice. The children in her class, her teachers, and even her parents don't ever seem to know she's even there. She tries being extra good, but it's almost like she's invisible. That's why she likes to sit next to the Rat in school. He isn't good at all. He sneers at the children, snaps at their fingers when they reach into his cage to feed him, and makes cutting remarks when the teacher is out of earshot. Emmy is the only one who seems to be able to hear him, and she wonders if she's just imagining things. In this scene, she and the Rat speak for the first time.

This script can be handed out to pairs of students to act out together. After they read it the first time, they can switch roles so each child has the chance to be both Emmy and the Rat. Be sure to explain how stage directions are written in parenthesis and in italics, to be followed by the actors but not to be read aloud. When you photocopy this script, be sure to run it single-sided. Double-sided scripts are confusing for children to follow.

EMMY: I need to stay indoors for recess today. I have to study my spelling. *(sighs)*

RAT: *(snorts in disgust and scowls)*

EMMY: *(looks down at Rat)* Why are you always so mean?

RAT: *(curls his upper lip)* Why are *you* always so *good*?

EMMY: *(looks at Rat, startled)*

RAT: *(shrugs one shoulder)* It doesn't get you anywhere. Just look at you—missing recess to study words you could spell in your sleep—and the only thing that happens is, you get ignored.

EMMY: *(looks away from Rat, speaks to audience)* It's true. My parents never answer the letters I send, even though I copy them over for neatness and give them to my nanny, Miss Barmy, to mail. My teacher keeps forgetting my name, even though I made a placard for my desk that says EMMY in big red letters edged with silver glitter. And I don't really mind missing recess at all. I feel so alone at recess. *(looks back at Rat)*

RAT: The bad ones get all the attention. Try being bad for once. You might like it.

EMMY: *(looks away from Rat, speaks to audience)* If I were bad, I could stick my tongue out at Miss Barmy. I could call my parents long distance whenever I wanted. I could climb on my desk in school and scream until the other kids *had* to notice me. *(looks back at Rat)* No one will like me if I'm bad.

RAT: No one likes you anyway.

EMMY: Well, they don't *dis*like me.

RAT: That's right. Nobody likes you, nobody dislikes you, nobody cares about you either way. You're a big nothing if you ask me.

EMMY: I didn't!

RAT: That's the first time I've heard you sound like anything but a piece of wet bread. Why don't you stand up for yourself more often?

EMMY: Listen, it's not like I don't *try*.

RAT:	Yesterday, when that girl with the ponytail butted in line, you let her. And when that kid who sits across from you, the soccer star, the freckled one with hair that looks like a haystack—
EMMY:	Joe Benson.
RAT:	Yeah, him. Well, when Haystack Hair was walking backward and stepped on your foot, *you* said "Sorry."
EMMY:	I was just being nice!
RAT:	You're *too* nice. A little meanness is good for the soul. I highly recommend it.
EMMY:	*(lifts her chin)* Being mean doesn't get *you* anywhere. Nobody pets *you*. Nobody plays with *you*.
RAT:	*(shows his long, yellow teeth)* I get what I want. I get respect, which is more than I can say for you.
EMMY:	You get respect? You live in a *cage*.
RAT:	*(looks stunned)*
EMMY:	Well, it's true. Don't tell me you haven't noticed. You know, the bars, the lock on the door . . .
RAT:	*(whiskers trembling)* You're not being very nice.
EMMY:	Nice? I thought a little meannesss was good for the—
RAT:	Most people don't mention it. Most people know better than to taunt a rodent about his . . . unfortunate situation.
EMMY:	Look, you were the one who said—

RAT: *(voice quavering pathetically)* It's not *my* fault I'm locked up! I committed no crime. Have I survived kidnapping from the nest, unjust imprisonment, and absolutely appalling food *(gives his dish of pellets a contemptuous kick)*, only to be mocked by a little child?

EMMY: *(hotly)* I'm bigger than *you*. And you were the one who said I shouldn't be so nice—

RAT: But not to **me**! It's different when you're mean to ***me!***

EMMY: Oh, right. *(looks away from Rat, speaks to audience)* Why are things so different here? At my old school, I had lots of friends. Maybe it's me. Maybe I've turned into some horrible person and I don't even know it.

RAT: *(buries head in forepaws, shoulders heaving, lets out a small sob, and wipes a tear from his eye)*

EMMY: *(speaks to audience)* Poor Rat. For all his tough talk, he's awfully sensitive. I shouldn't have mentioned his cage. *(whispers to Rat, apologetically)* Sorry.

A Reader's Theater Script for
The Boy Who Cried Lunch Monitor

Reader's Theater adaptation by Judy Freeman. (For grades 2-5.)

Adapted from "The Boy Who Cried Lunch Monitor," a chapter in **THE FABLED FOURTH GRADERS OF AESOP ELEMENTARY SCHOOL**, by Candace Fleming, copyright © 2007 by Candace Fleming. Used by permission of Schwartz & Wade Books, an imprint of Random House Children's Books, a division of Random House, Inc.

ROLES: Narrator 1, Narrator 2, Narrator 3, Narrator 4, Narrator 5, Mrs. Bunz, Lenny, Jackie, Victoria, Calvin, Melvin, Students

NOTE: If you want everyone in your class to have a role, expand the number of narrators. One child can be Narrator 1 on pages 1 and 2, and another can be Narrator 1 on pages 3 and 4, and so on. You could have 12 narrators this way. The role of Students can be played by the remaining children. They act as a sort of chorus. When you compare the script to the original chapter, you'll note that the many children have been consolidated into 5 roles, to make sure they everybody gets a decent amount of lines.

NARRATOR 1: The fourth grade class at Aesop Elementary School had a reputation among all the teachers for being—

NARRATOR 2: Precocious.

NARRATOR 3: High energy.

NARRATOR 4: Robust.

NARRATOR 5: Because Mrs. Bertha Bunz, the lunchroom monitor, wasn't a teacher, she felt free to speak the truth.

MRS. BUNZ: Humph! Those kids are just plain naughty!

NARRATOR 1: Mrs. Bunz ruled Aesop Elementary's lunchroom with an iron fist.

LENNY: No kid dared blow bubbles in his milk, or slurp her spaghetti, or stick a straw up his nose. If one of them did . . .

173.

MRS. BUNZ:	*(bellowing into her bullhorn)* **LUNCHROOM INFRACTION! Five minutes . . . on the WALL!**
JACKIE:	On the wall. Those three words struck fear into the heart of every student at Aesop Elementary.
STUDENTS:	*(Students hug arms and shiver and shudder)* **On the wall. Oooooohhhhhh.**
VICTORIA:	On the wall. It was Mrs. Bunz's favorite punishment. A form of torture so horrible that anyone who endured it never again left his bread crusts uneaten, or chewed with her mouth open.
NARRATOR 2:	Still, at the beginning of every school year, there was always one kid foolish enough to tangle with . . .
STUDENTS:	**BIG BAD BUNZ.**
CALVIN:	*(hollering)* **You know what I'm having for lunch?**
NARRATOR 3:	Before anyone could warn him, he would open his mouth wide so all could see the gob of half-chewed baloney with mustard and pickle relish on pumpernickel lurking inside.
CALVIN:	*(opens mouth wide)* **SEAFOOD!!!**
MRS. BUNZ:	*(bellowing into her bullhorn)* **LUNCHROOM INFRACTION! Five minutes . . . on the WALL!**
STUDENTS:	**On the wall. Oooooohhhhhh.** *(Students hug arms and shiver and shudder)*
MRS. BUNZ:	*(bellowing into her bullhorn)* **I think you have something to say to your classmates!**
CALVIN:	*(looks bewildered)* Huh?
MRS. BUNZ:	*(bellowing into her bullhorn)* **An apology. You owe us all an apology!**

NARRATOR 4:	No one could bear to watch.
NARRATOR 5:	One hundred elementary school students would quickly look down at their carrot sticks or stare at their apple slices.
CALVIN:	*(looks embarrassed, stammers)* I . . . I don't understand.
NARRATOR 1:	That was when Mrs. Bunz would pull the note card, yellowed with age and wrinkled from much use, from her pocket.
MRS. BUNZ:	Read it.
CALVIN:	*(in a quivering voice)* I apologize for my rudeness and promise to use my best table manners the next time I sit down to lunch.
MRS. BUNZ:	Thank you.
NARRATOR 2:	Then she'd walk away, leaving the kid to simmer in her own embarrassment for five minutes . . .
NARRATORS:	**ON THE WALL.**
CALVIN:	*(puts arm straight out against wall, palms back, a mortified look on his face)*
STUDENTS:	**On the wall. Oooooohhhhhh.** *(Students hug arms and shiver and shudder)*
NARRATOR 3:	No wonder the children in Aesop Elementary's lunchroom sat up straight, ate in silence, and cleaned up all their trash.
MRS. BUNZ:	Lunchtime isn't about enjoyment. It's about discipline, and maintaining order.
NARRATOR 4:	There was an emergency in the school and Mrs. Bunz was called to help with her bullhorn.
MRS. BUNZ:	I'm on my way! *(stomps out)*

NARRATOR 5:	Left unmonitored, the students sat in silence for a moment. Then . . .
NARRATOR 1:	Lenny glanced furtively around the lunchroom. He took a big swig of his Mr. Fizz and . . .
LENNY:	**B-U-U-U-R-P!**
NARRATORS 1-5:	The doors of restraint were belched wide open.
JACKIE:	**Hey, Calvin. Catch my Cheesy Puffs.** *(tosses one in Calvin's open mouth)*
CALVIN:	*(catches Cheesy Puff and chews it)* Good throw, Jackie!
VICTORIA:	Watch me put a pretzel stick up my nose!
STUDENTS:	*(laugh and yell and gargle their chocolate milk)*
NARRATOR 2:	The only fourth grader not laughing or talking or joining in the fun was Melvin Moody.
NARRATOR 3:	Melvin was used to not joining in. He was used to not being part of the group.
NARRATOR 4:	Somehow, in Mr. Jupiter's class, Melvin always managed to blurt out the wrong thing, or pick his nose when someone was looking, or fumble the ball at recess and lose the championship kickball game.
NARRATOR 5:	Now Melvin was suddenly seized with an uncontrollable urge.
MELVIN:	*(leaps up, cups hands around mouth)* **LUNCH MONITOR! LUNCH MONITOR!**
LENNY:	**Uh, oh!**
JACKIE:	Victoria, get that pretzel stick out of your nose!

VICTORIA:	Whoops!
NARRATORS 1-5:	Fear swept through the room.
STUDENTS:	*(sit up straight, fix their hair, fold hands)*
NARRATOR 1:	A minute passed.
NARRATOR 2-3:	Then another.
NARRATORS 1-5:	And another.
VICTORIA:	She's not coming.
LENNY:	*(to Melvin, angrily)* You did it! You ruined the fun!
JACKIE:	BOOOO!
CALVIN:	*(sticks out tongue at Melvin)*
NARRATOR 1:	Someone threw a banana peel.
NARRATOR 2-3:	It hit Melvin on the back of the head.
NARRATORS 1-5:	And Melvin loved it!
MELVIN:	*(to audience, proudly)* I'm the center of attention!
NARRATOR 1:	Melvin felt like a celebrity.
VICTORIA:	There's that kid from the lunchroom.
MELVIN:	I'm somebody!
LENNY:	What a loser.
JACKIE:	What's his name again?
STUDENTS:	*(shrug and shake their heads)*

NARRATOR 2:   The next day, Mrs. Bunz got a phone call in the office.

MRS. BUNZ: Tell them I'm busy. What? It's from my mother, the marine? She's calling from boot camp? All right. I'm coming. *(stalks out)*

VICTORIA: Hey everyone, watch me squeeze all the cream filling out of my cupcakes.

LENNY: Let's have a cookie race down the table.

JACKIE: *(in sports announcer voice)* And the Oreo takes the lead. Followed by Hydrox and Girl Scout . . .

STUDENTS: *(laugh and yell and blow straw covers in the air)*

MELVIN: *(leaps up, cups hands around mouth)* **LUNCH MONITOR! LUNCH MONITOR!**

LENNY: Quick! Stuff the cookies in your mouth!

STUDENTS: *(sit up straight, fix their hair, fold hands)*

NARRATOR 3:   Flushed and panting, everyone braced themselves for . . . nothing!

CALVIN: Not again! What's your problem, kid?

MELVIN: *(proud, grinning)* They're all talking about and recognizing ME! I am **SOMEBODY!**

NARRATOR 4:   Fame was fleeting.

NARRATOR 5:   By the middle of the following week, Melvin was as forgotten as last month's vocabulary words.

NARRATOR 1:   Then, during lunch . . .

NARRATORS 1-5:   **CRASH!**

NARRATOR 2:	It was the secretary, Mrs. Shorthand, who had been standing on a swivel chair and hanging a sign in the hallway.
NARRATORS 1-5:	**MAYDAY!**
MRS. BUNZ:	I'm on my way! I'm coming, Mrs. Shorthand! *(runs out)*
JACKIE:	Hey, everyone. Let's play Flick Your Peas!
STUDENTS:	*(laugh and yell and flick their peas)*
MELVIN:	*(to audience)* Oh, no. Here comes Mrs. Bunz. *(leaps up, cups hands around mouth)* **LUNCH MONITOR! LUNCH MONITOR!**
LENNY:	Yeah, right!
MRS. BUNZ:	*(starts coming back to lunchroom)*
MELVIN:	*(hops up and down)* **LUNCH MONITOR! LUNCH MONITOR!**
MRS. BUNZ:	*(gets closer)*
CALVIN:	Knock it off, kid. Nobody believes you.
NARRATOR 3:	Mrs. Bunz pushed on the wide swinging cafeteria doors.
NARRATOR 4:	Panicked and desperate, Melvin leaped onto a table.
MELVIN:	*(hops up and down, waving his arms)* **LUNCH MONITOR! LUNCH MONITOR!**
NARRATOR 5:	His behavior finally grabbed their attention.
STUDENTS:	**HUH?** *(All swivel to gape at Melvin.)*
MRS. BUNZ:	*(bursts into lunchroom, bellowing through her bullhorn)* **LUNCHROOM INFRACTION!**

MELVIN: *(hops up and down, waving his arms)* **LUNCH MONITOR! LUNCH MONITOR!**

MRS. BUNZ: Unbelievable! I'm gone just a few minutes and look how you behave! Melvin Moody, that's five minutes . . . **ON THE WALL!**

STUDENTS: **On the wall. Oooooohhhhhh.** *(Students hug arms and shiver and shudder)*

MELVIN: *(puts arm straight out against wall, palms back, a mortified look on his face)*

NARRATORS 1-5: **MORAL.**

EVERYONE: *(shake fingers at Melvin)* **LIARS ARE NOT BELIEVED EVEN WHEN THEY TELL THE TRUTH.**

ACRONYMS OF FAMOUS PHRASES

See how many of these common proverbs you can identify by looking at the first letter in each word?

1.   LBYL =

2.   HWHIL =

3.   ASITSN =

4.   HITBP =

5.   IAFYDSTTA =

6.   BCBC =

7.   DJABBIC =

8.   ARSGNM =

9.   AAADKTDA =

10.   TEBCTW =

For these and many other puzzlers, read
The Puzzling World of Winston Breen
by Eric Berlin (Putnam, 2007).

WORD SCRAMBLE PUZZLE

These six words can all be scrambled to make new words.

Which one does not belong and why?

AMONG   **BEARD**   **CHEAP**

LUMP   **MILE**   **PAGER**

For these and many other puzzlers, read
The Puzzling World of Winston Breen
by Eric Berlin (Putnam, 2007).

Casey Back at Bat: The Book Hunt
Developed by Sharon Boyle, School Librarian
Old York School, Branchburg, NJ
Based on Dan Gutman's *Casey Back at Bat* (HarperCollins, 2007)

Casey at the Bat Lesson Plan for Grade 5

Lesson 1

- Ask students what is going on in the world, related to baseball- playoffs, World Series, etc.
- Sing Take Me Out the Ball Game using lyrics and website with music
- Read "Casey at the Bat"
- Read *Casey Back at the Bat* by Dan Gutman. Have students say rhyming word at the end of every other sentence
- Ask the where else could the ball go? Ask each child to contribute
- Create list on paper

Lesson 2

- Book Hunt in small groups
- Explain book hunt rules and procedures
- Give students time to complete Book Hunt
- Have messenger share items found as teacher reads items to find from card

Team Ground Rules for Students:

Your team must follow all of these rules or you will lose minutes. Teams that do not follow the ground rules will be penalized by having to sit back at their table for 1 minute.

1. Your entire team must work together. You cannot separate for any time during the Book Hunt Game.
2. Everyone on your team must agree to the answers that you find.
3. If another team is in the area your team needs, you must wait until the occupying team leaves.
4. Your team does **not** have to find the answers in the order they are listed on the card.
5. You must keep the shelves in order. If your team drops or pulls out something they don't need, your team is responsible for putting it back correctly.
6. When items have been shared with the class and teacher, all members of the team will put away **at least** one item.

Roles:

Team Leader: Person who motivates and makes sure the ground rules are followed and each player is doing his or her job.

Computer: This is the only team member who is allowed to access the computer in order to locate information.

Shelf Marker: Person who is responsible for placing the shelf marker on the shelf when removing a book and leaving **one** shoe if the book hunt says to do so. You can also designate this person or another student as a Shelver, making sure everyone returns the books to their proper places afterwards and retrieving the shelf markers.

Messenger: Person or people who show all of the items they found in order to complete the book hunt.

Casey Back at Bat
Book Hunt
Team #2

- Go to the encyclopedia and look up the page that tells you how many years ago the Sphinx was built.

- Leave one of the shelf marker's shoes in the section with nonfiction books about planets.

- Find a fiction book about dinosaurs.

- Go to the dictionary and find a definition of the word "masterpiece."

- Find a biography about a baseball player.

- Sit in order based on birthday month (if you were born in the same month, then the day that comes first).

Casey Back at Bat
Book Hunt
Team #1

- Find a fiction book about baseball (more than 100 pages).

- Go to the dictionary and find the page that tells you what sauerkraut is.

- Find an easy fiction book about dinosaurs.

- Leave one of the shelf marker's shoes in the section with nonfiction books about Egypt.

- Go to the encyclopedia and find the page where you would find why the Leaning Tower of Pisa leans.

- Sit in order based on birthday month (if you were born in the same month, then the day that comes first).

Casey Back at Bat
Book Hunt
Team #4

- Find a biography about an astronaut.

- Find a nonfiction book about baseball.

- Go to the dictionary and find a definition of the word "Eureka."

- Go to the encyclopedia and find a picture of a rhinoceros.

- Leave one of the shelf marker's shoes in the section with nonfiction books about space.

- Sit in order based on birthday month (if you were born in the same month, then the day that comes first).

Casey Back at Bat
Book Hunt
Team #3

- Leave one of the shelf marker's shoes in the section with nonfiction books about birds.

- Go to the encyclopedia and find out when the Great Pyramid was built.

- Find a nonfiction book about the Atlantic Ocean

- Go to the dictionary and find the definition of the word "hijinks."

- Find a biography about a baseball player.

- Sit in order based on birthday month (if you were born in the same month, then the day that comes first).

Casey Back at Bat
Book Hunt
Team

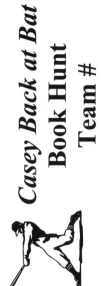

Casey Back at Bat
Book Hunt
Team #5

- Find a poetry book about baseball.

- Go to the dictionary and find a definition of the word "eclipse."

- Go to the encyclopedia and find a map of Egypt.

- Find a nonfiction book about Italy.

- Leave one of the shelf marker's shoes in the section where you would find books about oceans.

- Sit in order based on birthday month (if you were born in the same month, then the day that comes first).

HOW MUCH DO YOU KNOW ABOUT SPIDERS?

Answers to these and other questions can be found in *Nic Bishop Spiders* written and photographed by Nic Bishop (Scholastic, 2007).

DIRECTIONS: You can use this question sheet in several ways. First, have children work in pairs, small groups, or as a class to see how many answer they know of think they know. Ask them listen carefully for the answers as you read the book aloud. Or you can read the book aloud and then see how much they have learned. Or you could have them use the book's index to locate the correct page for each question and skim the text looking for the answer. Have them write each answer as part of a complete sentence.

1.   How many types of spiders are there in the world?

2.   What is the largest spider?

3.   How many legs does a spider have?

4.   What do you call the part of a spider that makes silk?

5.   What color is a spider's blood?

6.   Except for the spiders that live in complete darkness and have no eyes, how many eyes do most spiders have?

7.   What kinds of spiders have the best eyesight?

8.   Where do female spiders keep their eggs after laying them?

9.   How long can a tarantula live?

10.   What are baby spiders called?

HOW WELL DO YOU KNOW ANIMALS?

All of the following animals are described and pictured in the book, *Living Color*, written and illustrated by Steve Jenkins (Houghton Mifflin, 2007).

DIRECTIONS: Read each question on page 189. Using the alphabet of animals below, write the correct letter in the blank to the left of each question

A. HOODED SEAL

B. HYACINTH MACAW

C. LADYBIRD BEETLE

D. LEAFY SEA DRAGON

E. MONARCH BUTTERFLY

F   MONGOOSE

G. MOON MOTH

H. MORAY EEL

I. OLM

J. PERCHER DRAGONFLY

K. PINK SQUAT LOBSTER

L. POISON DART FROG

O. PORTUGUESE MAN-OF-WAR

P. SCARLET IBIS

Q. SHIELD BUG

R. STONEFISH

S. THREE-TOED SLOTH

T. WHITE UAKARI (wah-*car*-ee)

U. WRASSE

V. YELLOW CRAB

W. YELLOW CRAZY ANTS

X. YELLOW MONGOOSE

HOW WELL DO YOU KNOW ANIMALS?

Answers can be found by reading the book, *Living Color,* **written and illustrated by Steve Jenkins (Houghton Mifflin, 2007)**

DIRECTIONS: Using the alphabetical list of animals on page 188, fill in the blanks to the left of each question with the correct letter.

___ *1.* These insects kill or blind other animals by spraying them with acid from an opening in their abdomen. (_____)

___ 2. Found only in flooded caves in southern Europe, this rare, pink, primitive amphibian is completely blind. (_____)

___ 3. Native hunters in the South American jungles rub the tips of their arrows on this creature's skin. (_____)

___ 4. A relative of the seahorse, it looks like a bit of floating seaweed. (_____)

___ 5. This is the largest parrot in the world. (_____)

___ 6. Other animals who try to eat this insect, which feeds on the poisonous milkweed plant, will get very sick. (_____)

___ 7. This male mammal from the North Atlantic ocean tries to impress females by inflating a sac of loose skin that hangs from its left nostril, blowing it up like a big red balloon. (_____)

___ 8. This mammal spends most of its life sleeping upside down in the trees of the rain forest. (_____)

___ 9. Though you can't tell from its name, this South American monkey has a bright red face. (_____)

___ 10. A long-legged wading bird, it takes its colors from the shells of the shrimp, crabs, and insects it eats. (_____)

___ 11. This is the most poisonous fish in the world. (_____)

___ 12. Named after an 18th century sailing ship, this marine animal has long poisonous tentacles. (_____)

DO YOU REMEMBER YOUR FAIRY TALES?

Many children have no concept as to what makes a story a fairy tale, so you may need to start from scratch. After you ask each question below, whether or not your listeners know the answer, hold up a book version of that tale and hand it out to interested readers. Notice how Eurocentric these tales are, for the most part? Introduce your students to stories from every continent except one. (And ask them if they can name the continent that has no stories. Penguins don't tell tales.)

1.   IN WHAT FAIRY TALE does a princess spend her formative years locked in a tower growing her hair?

2.   IN WHAT FAIRY TALE does a princess prick her finger on a spindle on her 16th birthday and take a very long nap?

3.   IN WHAT FAIRY TALE does a boy steal a giant's harp and a hen that lays golden eggs?

4.   IN WHAT FAIRY TALE does a princess accidentally drop her golden ball into a well, and accept the help of an amphibian to retrieve it?

5.   IN WHAT FAIRY TALE does a soldier use his cloak of invisibility to follow a king's daughters at night to find out why their shoes keep wearing out?

6.   IN WHAT FAIRY TALE does a Russian witch with iron teeth live in a house on chicken legs and ride through the sky in a mortar and pestle?

7.   IN WHAT FAIRY TALE does a boy outsmart a powerful magician pretending to be his uncle, and summon a genie who makes him rich.

8.   IN WHAT FAIRY TALE does a girl set off to find her true love, a white bear by day and a man by night, before he can marry a troll princess?

9.   IN WHAT FAIRY TALE does a miller's idle boast lead to his daughter being locked in a room at the local castle to spend the night with a spinning wheel?

10.   IN WHAT FAIRY TALE does a girl's stepmother arrange to have her taken into the forest by a woodsman and killed, just because a talking mirror said the girl was the fairest of them all?

11.   IN WHAT FAIRY TALE do a brother and sister get lost in a forest and find a gingerbread house belonging to a witch?

12.   IN WHAT FAIRY TALE does a poor young lad pass himself off to the king as the Marquis of Carabas, take over an ogre's castle, and win the hand of a princess, thanks to his clever cat?

13.   IN WHAT FAIRY TALE does a man open the door to a robbers' cave with the words, "Open, Sesame"?

14.   IN WHAT FAIRY TALE does an enchanted fish give an ungrateful woman a new house, which only makes her want more?

15.   IN WHAT FAIRY TALE does a merchant's youngest daughter agree to move to the palace of a hideous creature who wants her to say she'll marry him?

LOOKING AT CINDERELLA

Reprinted and updated from *Once Upon a Time: Using Storytelling, Creative Drama, and Reader's Theater with Children in Grades PreK-6* by Judy Freeman (Libraries Unlimited, 2007).

When you ask students to compare and contrast elements of stories, one of the most interesting fairy tales to delve into in some detail is the world's most ubiquitous: "Cinderella." Ask your listeners first to tell you the story as they know it. (This may be the Disney movie version.) Next, read or tell a standard, familiar version, followed with a version from a non-European country. Together, your class can compare and contrast characters, setting, plot, motifs, theme, and style of both stories. Finally, small groups can read other versions and make charts showing the differences and similarities. Below are some elements to consider.

COMPARE AND CONTRAST:

CHARACTERS:
- Cinderella's name
- Cinderella's physical appearance
- Cinderella's personality
- "Prince Charming"
- Fairy godmother
- Other characters (father, stepmother as villain, stepsiblings, fairy godmother type, etc.)
- Relationship of main characters (names and relation to "Cinderella" character)

SETTING:
- Country of origin
- Cinderella's house
- Place the party or ball is held

PLOT:
- How Cinderella's life changes
- Cinderella's work and her place in the family; stepsisters' treatment of Cinderella
- Cinderella's assigned tasks to perform at home before or during the ball
- How the fairy godmother helps Cinderella

CLIMAX:
- Climax: What happens to Cinderella at the ball, party, dance, or celebration
- How Cinderella is found by the prince afterwards
- Endings (What happens to her and to her family)

MOTIFS:
- Lost shoes (what they are made from: glass, gold, straw, etc.)
- Clothing (from rags to finery)
- Magical godmother (human or animal)
- Other magical objects or characters (wands, rats, pumpkins, etc.)
- Magical powers or transformations
- Beginnings and endings (Once upon a time; happily ever after, and variations)
- Use of magical numbers (3, 7, etc.)

THEME:
- How does good win out over evil?
- What lessons or morals are stated or implicit in the story?

STYLE AND FORMAT OF THE RETELLING:
- Language style and how it reflects the country of origin
- Illustrations

ADDITIONAL CINDERELLA LESSON IDEAS

GEOGRAPHY: Keep a globe handy to show the origin of versions of Cinderella from other countries and ask listeners how the story changed in each particular country.

FOOD TIE-INS: For a quick story-related snack, hand out toasted pumpkin seeds.

CREATIVE DRAMA: Conduct interviews with students posing as characters in the story. Holding a real microphone (and taping the proceedings if you like), ask each character a variety of questions, giving students the opportunity to range from yes or no answers to ones that require synthesis and analysis of a character's motives. *If the Shoe Fits: Voices from Cinderella* by Laura Whipple, told in poetry, examines the story from each character's vantage point.

POINT OF VIEW: As a warm up to interviewing, have children get into character by repeating the following statement from a variety of points of view:

"Cinderella went to the ball."

How would each of these characters utter that sentence: the prince, the stepsisters, the fairy godmother, Cinderella, a dancer at the ball, the stepmother, an innocent bystander?

Next have them repeat the same sentence, but using different emotional shadings. Have them say it: disgustedly, jealously, angrily, delightedly, indifferently, quizzically, sarcastically, disappointedly, pityingly, sadly, and eagerly.

WRITING ACTIVITY: Write a Cinderella story which takes place in another time and place, using research to get the supporting details right.

RESEARCH ACTIVITY: When students are researching countries of the world, have them also explore the folklore of their countries.

AND FINALLY, AN URBAN JUMP ROPE RHYME

Cinderella, dressed in yella,
Went downtown to meet her fella;
On her way, her girdle busted,
How many people were disgusted?

CINDERELLA VARIANTS: A BOOKLIST

Here are but a handful of the hundreds of Cinderella variants worldwide. For more information on the story and its variants, go to the SurLaLune Fairy Tales website at <**www.surlalune.com**>.

Adelita: A Mexican Cinderella Story by Tomie dePaola. Putnam, 2002. (Mexico)

Ashpet: An Appalachian Tale by Joanne Compton, illus. by Kenn Compton. Holiday House, 1994. (U.S.)

Cendrillon: A Caribbean Cinderella by Robert D. San Souci, illus. by Brian Pinkney. Simon & Schuster, 1998. (Martinique)

Cinderella by K. Y. Craft. SeaStar, 2000. (France)

Cinderella by Paul Galdone. McGraw-Hill, 1978. (France)

Cinderella by Nonny Hogrogian. Greenwillow, 1981. (Germany)

Cinderella by Barbara Karlin, illus. by James Marshall. Little, Brown, 1989. (France)

Cinderella by Barbara McClintock. Scholastic, 2005. (France)

Cinderella: or, The Little Glass Slipper by Marcia Brown. Scribner, 1954. (France)

The Egyptian Cinderella by Shirley Climo, illus. by Ruth Heller. HarperCollins, 1993. (Egypt)

Favorite Fairy Tales Told in Italy by Virginia Haviland. Little, Brown, 1965. ("Cenerentola"; Italy)

The Gift of the Crocodile: A Cinderella Story by Judy Sierra, illus. by Reynold Ruffins. Simon & Schuster, 2000. (Indonesia)

Glass Slipper, Gold Sandal: A Worldwide Cinderella by Paul Fleischman. Henry Holt, 2007. (Many countries)

The Golden Sandal: A Middle Eastern Cinderella Story by Rebecca Hickox, illus. by Will Hillenbrand. Holiday House, 1998. (Iraq)

In the Land of Small Dragon by Dang Manh Kha, illus. by Tony Chen. Viking, 1979. (Vietnam)

The Irish Cinderlad by Shirley Climo, illus. by Loretta Krupinski. HarperCollins, 1996. (Ireland)

Jouanah: A Hmong Cinderella by Jewell Reinhart Coburn, illus. by Anne Sibley O'Brien. Shen's Books, 1996. (Laos)

Kong and Potgi: A Cinderella Story from Korea by Oki S. Han and Stephanie Haboush Plunkett, illus. by Oki S. Han. Dial, 1996. (Korea)

The Korean Cinderella by Shirley Climo, illus. by Ruth Heller. HarperCollins, 1993. (Korea)

Moss Gown by William H. Hooks, illus. by Donald Carrick. Clarion, 1987. (U.S.)

Mufaro's Beautiful Daughters by John Steptoe. Lothrop, 1987. (Africa)

Oryx Multicultural Folktale Series: Cinderella by Judy Sierra. Oryx, 1992. (Various countries)

The Persian Cinderella by Shirley Climo, illus. by Robert Florczak. HarperCollins, 1999. (Iran)

Princess Furball by Charlotte Huck, illus. by Anita Lobel. Greenwillow, 1989. (U.S.)

The Rough-Face Girl by Rafe Martin, illus. by David Shannon. Putnam, 1992. (Native American)

Smoky Mountain Rose: An Appalachian Cinderella by Alan Schroeder, illus. by Brad Sneed. Dial, 1997. (U.S.)

Sootface: An Ojibwa Cinderella Story by Robert D. San Souci, illus. by Daniel San Souci. Doubleday, 1994. (Native American)

Sukey and the Mermaid by Robert D. San Souci, illus. by Brian Pinkney. Four Winds, 1992. (U.S.)

Tattercoats: An Old English Tale by Flora Annie Steele, illus. by Diane Goode. Bradbury, 1976. (England)

The Turkey Girl: A Zuni Cinderella Story by Penny Pollock, illus. by Ed Young. Little, Brown, 1996. (Native American)

The Way Meat Loves Salt: A Cinderella Tale from the Jewish Tradition by Nina Jaffe, illus. by Louise August. Henry Holt, 1998. (Jewish)

Wishbones: A Folk Tale from China by Barbara Ker Wilson, illus. by Meilo So. Bradbury, 1993. (China)

Yeh-Shen by Ai-Ling Louie, illus. by Ed Young. Philomel, 1982. (China)

SOME CINDERELLA PARODIES AND UPDATES

Bella at Midnight by Diane Stanley. HarperCollins, 2006.

Bigfoot Cinderrrrella by Tony Johnston, illus. by James Warhola. Putnam, 1998.

Bubba the Cowboy Prince: A Fractured Texas Tale by Helen Ketteman, illus. by James Warhola. Scholastic, 1997.

Cinder Edna by Ellen Jackson, illus. by Kevin O'Malley. Lothrop, 1994.

Cinderella by William Wegman. Hyperion, 1993.

Cinderella Skeleton by Robert D. San Souci, illus. by David Catrow. Harcourt, 2000.

Cinder-Elly by Frances Minters, illus. by G. Brian Karas. Viking, 1993.

Cinderlily: A Floral Fairy Tale by Christine Tagg, illus. by David Ellwand. Candlewick, 2003.

Cindy Ellen: A Wild Western Cinderella by Susan Lowell. Orchard, 1997.

Dinorella: A Prehistoric Fairy Tale by Pamela Duncan Edwards, illus. by Henry Cole. Hyperion, 1997.

Ella Enchanted by Gail Carson Levine. HarperCollins, 1997.

Ella's Big Chance: A Jazz-Age Cinderella by Shirley Hughes. Simon & Schuster, 2004.

Fanny's Dream by Caralyn Buehner, illus. by Mark Buehner. Dial, 1996.

I Was a Rat by Philip Pullman, illus. by Kevin Hawkes. Knopf, 2000.

If the Shoe Fits: Voices from Cinderella by Laura Whipple; illus. by Laura Beingessner. McElderry, 2002.

Prince Cinders by Babette Cole. Putnam, 1997.

"Prinderella and the Cince" retold by Judy Freeman in *Hi Ho Librario!: Songs, Chants and Stories to Keep Kids Humming*. Rock Hill Press, 1997. (For the text, see page 195 of this handbook.)

Sidney Rella and the Glass Sneaker by Bernice Myers. Macmillan, 1985.

CINDERELLA WEBSITES:

FOLKLORE AND MYTHOLOGY ELECTRONIC TEXTS
(On D. L. Ashliman's comprehensive folklore site, find the texts to 16 Cinderella variants worldwide.) **http://www.pitt.edu/~dash/type0510a.html**

SURLALUNE FAIRY TALES
(Includes an annotated version of the tale from Andrew Lang's *The Blue Fairy Book* published in 1889; from the book *Cinderella* by Marian Roalfe Cox, published in 1893, detailed abstracts of 345 Cinderella variants; dozens of reproductions of classic illustrations and cover art of scores of children's books of the story.) **www.surlalunefairytales.com/cinderella/index.html**

WIKIPEDIA
(Quite a thorough analysis of origins and history, plot and variations, a discussion of the story, and a list of adaptations.) **http://en.wikipedia.org/wiki/Cinderella#Songs**

PRINDERELLA AND THE CINCE

Reprinted from *Once Upon a Time: Using Storytelling, Creative Drama, and Reader's Theater with Children in Grades PreK-6* by Judy Freeman (Libraries Unlimited, 2007).

This retelling is a composite based on several versions from New Jersey folks, including Carol Phillips, head of Children's Services at East Brunswick Public Library; teacher Betty Butler; author and librarian consultant, Alice Yucht, who originally "cranstribed" all three versions together; and further edited and tampered with by Judy Freeman.

Tonce upon a wime there lived a gritty little pearl named Prinderella. She lived in a hovely louse with her stugly sep-isters and her sticked wep-mother. All lay dong Prinderella had to do all the hork of the wousehold; wean the clindows, flub the scroor, pine the shots and shans, and do all the other wirty dirk, while her sugly isters and sticked wep-mother dept all slay on beather feds. Prinderella was treated bery vadly and had to wear roppy slags that fidn't dit. Isn't that a shirty dame?

Done way, the Quing and Keen prade a mocklimation that there would be a brand drancy-fess gall in honor of the Cince, and all the gelligible irls of the kole wingdom were invited. So the kole whingdom prepared for the brand gall. Prinderella's stugly sep-isters and sticked wep-mother made Prinderella murk all day to wake their drancy fesses.

Then poor Prinderella, in her roppy slags that fidn't dit, had to hay stome as her stugly sep-isters and sticked wep-mother went off to the gall in a covely larriage. Wasn't that a shirty dame!

Prinderella dat in the soorway, crobbing and sying till her gairy fodmother, who lived in a laraway fand, heard her and came to see mat was the whatter.

"Oh! Gairy Fodmother," cried Prinderella, "I feel so serribly tad! Why can't I bo to the gall, and pree the Cince?"

"Near fot, chy mild. You *shall* bo to the gall!" said the gairy fodmother. "Now, so to the geller and bring me some pice, a mumpkin, and three rat fats."

When Prinderella brought the pice, the mumpkin, and the rat fats, the gairy fodmother fapped her sningers, touched them with her wagic mand, and changed the mumpkin into a hoach, the pice into corses, and the rat fats into moachcen.

But Prinderella still had nothing to wear but roppy slags that fidn't dit. Wasn't that a shirty dame? So the gairy fodmother quickly fapped her sningers again, winkled her tye, and there was a garkling spown of gilver and sold, all covered with pubies and rearls. It was the bost dreautiful mess in the kole whingdom! And for her feet, there was a painty dair of slass glippers.

As the gairy fodmother clelped Prinderella himb into the covely larriage, she warned her: "Don't gorfet: you must beave lefore the moke of stridnight, for the brell will be spoken when the twock clikes strelve."

Prinderella was the bost meautiful baiden at the mall. When the Cince saw her fovely lace and her dreautiful bess, all covered with pubies and rearls, he lell in fove with her. They nanced all dight, until the calace plock chegan to bime. Then, just before the last moke of stridnight, Prinderella dan out the roor to her waiting harriage and courses. But as she durried hown the stalace peps, she slopped her dripper! Now wasn't that a shirty dame?

The dext nay, the Ping issued a krocklamation that the Cince was lesperately dooking for the meautiful baiden who had slopped her dripper as she left the brand gall. The Cince hent to the wouses of all the gelligible earls of the kole whingdom in gearch of the sirl he had lallen in fove with, and now manted to warry.

195.

When the Cince came to Prinderella's house, her stugly sep-isters all tried to tit their foes into the slass glipper, but it fidn't dit!

But whuess gat? When Prinderella flipped her soot into the slass glipper, it fid dit! So Prinderella and the Cince mere warried. She wore a gedding wown of wharkling spite, all covered with pubies and rearls. And Prinderella and the Cince hived lappily ever after. That wasn't such a shirty dame, was it?

STORYTELLER'S NOTE:

Finish off your Cinderella unit with Prinderella. (For resources, see the "Looking at Cinderella" section of this handbook, on page 191, for lots of ideas, activities booklists, and websites.) I introduce it to children, grades three and up, by saying, "Do you kids like tairy fails?"

"What?" they always answer. "Do we like what?"

"Tairy fails! Everyone loves tairy fails! You know, like Whow Snite and the Deven Swarves? And Gansel and Hretel? And what about Beeping Sleuty! Everyone loves Beeping Sleuty!"

At which point, someone always says, "Sleeping Beauty! She means Sleeping Beauty!"

"Exactly. Tairy fails. Just like I said. I'm going to tell you a really famous one." And then I launch into Prinderella.

After you read or tell this story, ask listeners just what it was you were doing with the words. They'll observe that you were switching initial consonants.

You can segue into a lesson on Spoonerisms, based on the legendary tips of the slongue, er, slips of the tongue, made by the Reverend William Archibald Spooner (1844-1930), the Oxford Dean and Warden of New College in Oxford, England. He called a well-oiled bicycle "a well-boiled icicle." He once reprimanded a student who, as he said, "hissed my mystery lecture." Officiating at a wedding, he proclaimed, "Son, it is now kisstomary to cuss the bride." And, in church one day, he said, "Mardon me padam, this pie is occupewed. Can I sew you to another sheet?"

The Greeks called this metathesis, or the act of switching things around.

"Prinderella and the Cince" is a prime example of metathesis, and a case of phonics run amok. After you share it aloud, hand out copies of the text and have children pair up and try reading it to each other. They can orally transpose each sentence back into English. And then ask them to bring the story home and read it aloud to their parents.

You can also use the story to fool around with other well-known fairy tales. Have them work in pairs or trios (humor is most satisfying when shared) to read a fairy tale—"Snow White and the Seven Dwarfs," "Hansel and Gretel," and "Sleeping Beauty" do come to mind, among others— and then write a one or two-sentence synopsis of it. Then have them switch some of the consonants. Finally, have each group read aloud its description for the rest of the children to identify. It's an effective way to familiarize children with classic fairy tales we assume they know but often do not.

Shel Silverstein's *Runny Babbit* (HarperCollins, 2005) is an entire book of witty poetry filled with Spoonerisms, ideal to read aloud and share. Children love writing their own rhyming poems about the further exploits of Runny Babbit and his animal friends, and doing Silverstein-like pen and ink line drawings to go along.

For more fun with wordplay, including anagrams, palindromes, Tom Swifties, Malapropisms, mnemonic devices, and more, you and your students will love this site: <**www.fun-with-words.com**>.

SOUND EFFECTS TO USE WITH THE BOOK
The End
By David LaRochelle, illustrated by Richard Egielski
(Arthur A. Levine/Scholastic, 2007)

DIRECTIONS:
Read aloud the story, *The End*. Break your class into the nine groups below. Go over the sound effect or phrase for each part. Now read the story again. As you read, each time you say the name of one of the groups below, pause, and the children in that group will say their phrase aloud, using lots of expression.

When you hear your name, say:

1. **KNIGHT:**   **AHA!**

2. **PRINCESS:**   **OH, YES!**

3. **LEMON:**   **SOUR SOUR SOUR**

4. **DRAGON:**   **ROARRRR!**

5. **BUNNY:**   **HEE HEE HEE**

6. **TOMATO:**   **SQUISH SQUISH**

7. **TEACUP:**   **(sing) I'M A LITTLE TEACUP**

8. **GIANT:**   **FEE FI FOO YUM!**

9. **COOK:**   **SORRY!**

ACRONYMS OF FAMOUS PHRASES

ANSWERS FROM WORKSHEET ON PAGE 181

DIRECTIONS: See how many of these common proverbs you can identify by looking at the first letter in each word?

1. LBYL = Look before you leap.

2. HWHIL = He who hesitates is lost.

3. ASITSN = A stitch in time saves nine.

4. HITBP = Honesty is the best policy.

5. IAFYDSTTA = If at first you don't succeed, try, try again.

6. BCBC = Beggars can't be choosers.

7. DJABBIC = Don't judge a book by its cover.

8. ARSGNM = A rolling stone gathers no moss.

9. AAADKTDA = An apple a day keeps the doctor away.

10. TEBCTW = The early bird catches the worm.

For these and many other puzzlers, read
The Puzzling World of Winston Breen
by Eric Berlin (Putnam, 2007)

HOW MUCH DO YOU KNOW ABOUT SPIDERS?

ANSWERS FROM WORKSHEET on page 187

Further answers to these and other questions can be found in *Nic Bishop Spiders* written and photographed by Nic Bishop (Scholastic, 2007).

(NOTE: Included is the key word from the book's index, and the page where the answer can be found. Photocopy the index and use for a lesson on how an index works. From this exercise, children can put together their own indexes for a book or a report they've written.)

1.   How many types of spiders are there in the world?
     (*Types, page 7:* There are more than 38,000 types of spiders in the world)

2.   What is the largest spider? Where does it live?
     (*Sizes, page 8:* The Goliath birdeater tarantula, the world's largest spider, lives in South America.)

3.   How many legs does a spider have?
     (*Legs, page 8:* A spider has eight legs.)

4.   What do you call the parts of a spider that make silk?
     (*Silk, page 11:* The parts of a spider that make silk are called the spinnerets.)

5.   What color is a spider's blood?
     (*Blood, page 11:* A spider's blood is pale blue.)

6.   Except for the spiders that live in complete darkness and have no eyes, how many eyes do most spiders have?
     (*Eyes, page 15:* Most spiders have eight eyes.)

7.   What kinds of spiders have the best eyesight?
     (*Eyesight, page 27:* Jumping spiders have the best eyesight.)

8.   Where do female spiders keep their eggs after laying them?
     (*Eggs, page 40:* Female spiders keep their eggs in an egg sac, which, depending on the type of spider, she either leaves in a safe spot, guards, or even carries with her, attached to her spinnerets.)

9.   How long can a tarantula live?
     (*Not found in index, so use this question to discuss what term this should have come under—longevity or life span—and how to find this fact, found on page 33:* Some tarantulas can live for 30 years.)

10. What are baby spiders called?
     (*Spiderlings, page 43; also found in glossary. Note that there is no entry under babies or young, so this one's tricky to find in the index, too, unless you already know the answer:* Baby spiders are called spiderlings.)

HOW WELL DO YOU KNOW ANIMALS?

ANSWERS FROM WORKSHEET on page 189

Further answers to these and other questions can be found in *Living Color*, written and illustrated by Steve Jenkins (Houghton Mifflin, 2007)

W 1. These insects kill or blind other animals by spraying them with acid from an opening in their abdomen. *(YELLOW CRAZY ANTS)*

I 2. Found only in flooded caves in southern Europe, this rare, pink, primitive amphibian is completely blind. *(OLM)*

L 3. Native hunters in the South American jungles rub the tips of their arrows on this creature's skin. *(POISON DART FROG)*

D 4. A relative of the seahorse, it looks like a bit of floating seaweed. *(LEAFY SEA DRAGON)*

B 5. This is the largest parrot in the world. *(HYACINTH MACAW)*

E 6. Other animals who try to eat this insect, which feeds on the poisonous milkweed plant, will get very sick. *(MONARCH BUTTERFLY)*

A 7. This male mammal from the North Atlantic ocean tries to impress females by inflating a sac of loose skin that hangs from its left nostril, blowing it up like a big red balloon. *(HOODED SEAL)*

S 8. This mammal spends most of its life sleeping upside down in the trees of the rain forest. *(THREE-TOED SLOTH)*

T 9. Though you can't tell by its name, this South American monkey has a bright red face. *(WHITE UAKARI* [wah-*car*-ee])*

P 10. A long-legged wading bird, it takes its colors from the shells of the shrimp, crabs, and insects it eats. *(SCARLET IBIS)*

R 11. This is the most poisonous fish in the world. *(STONEFISH)*

O 12. Named after an 18th century sailing ship, this marine animal has long poisonous tentacles. *(PORTUGUESE MAN-OF-WAR)*

CONGRATULATIONS!
If you matched all of these animals correctly, what are you?

You're a WILD BEAST PRO!
(Read the letters you filled in from top to bottom, if you don't believe it.)

DO YOU REMEMBER YOUR FAIRY TALES?

ANSWERS FROM WORKSHEET ON PAGE 190

1. "Rapunzel"

2. "Sleeping Beauty"

3. "Jack and the Beanstalk"

4. "The Frog Prince"

5. "The Twelve Dancing Princesses"

6. "Baba Yaga"

7. "Aladdin and the Magic Lamp"

8. "East of the Sun and West of the Moon" (or its American variant, "Whitebear Whittington")

9. "Rumpelstiltskin"

10. "Snow White"

11. "Hansel and Gretel"

12. "Puss in Boots"

13. "Ali Baba and the 40 Thieves"

14. "The Fisherman and His Wife"

15. "Beauty and the Beast"

SURFING THE NET

A GUIDE TO USEFUL AND SCINTILLATING WEBSITES AND LISTSERVS FOR KIDS AND GROWNUPS

**compiled and updated by Judy Freeman,
with much input from posts on LM_NET
and from
Carol Shields, Stevens Institute of Technology
Edited by Jane Scherer**

Spring, 2008

**NOTE: If you have a great site to recommend, or find a dead link
on this list or information that needs updating, please let me know.
E-mail me at: BKWSSF@aol.com.**

In the years since my book *More Books Kids Will Sit Still For* (Libraries Unlimited, 1995) was published, the Internet has bloomed. It has changed the way we access information. In writing *Books Kids Will Sit Still For 3* (Libraries Unlimited, 2006), I was grateful to be be able to sit at my desk and look up definitions, book reviews, details about authors and illustrators, magazine and newspaper articles, publishing info, and almost anything else I had a burning desire to know. And then there's the e-mail that we now check several times a day, for making further contacts with sources or simply to stay in touch with family and friends. It is my lifeline when I am holed up in the attic, writing.

Our computers, as we move from dial-up to speedy cable connections, have revolutionized the way we look at the world and what we know about the world. As new developments spring forth at a dramatic pace, in a few years, we'll look back to today's Internet and it will seem quaint and primitive. Children nowadays have never not known computers, and think of ancient history as being the days before we had a cell phone in every pocket.

I've been accumulating interesting and useful websites related to children's literature and education, and offer them here to provide you with some helpful links, which will in turn lead you to even more links.

LISTSERVS

Stay current in your field, make new friends, and learn something new every single day. That's what you get when you join a free listserv. I couldn't cope without my daily reading of messages on **LM_NET**, the school librarian's listserv. It's better than a second Masters degree, and a whole lot more fun.

LM_NET

LM_NET is a school librarian's listserv with more than 17,000 members worldwide. To subscribe:
1. Send an e-mail message to: **listserv@listserv.syr.edu**
2. In the first line of the message, type: SUBSCRIBE LM_NET Firstname Lastname

Example: SUBSCRIBE LM_NET Judy Freeman

Requests for membership in LM_NET are handled automatically by the Syracuse University listserv computer and software. The LM_NET listserv computer will respond with an informative message, which will ask you for a confirmation. You will then be added if you properly follow the directions (which are easy), and you'll then receive further instructions on how to use LM_NET, one of the most valuable resources you'll ever find.

HELPFUL AND ESSENTIAL TIP: When you subscribe to LM_NET, or any high volume listserv, check the instructions and be sure you ask for your messages in the much-easier-to-handle **DIGEST** form. This means 8 to 10 messages come together in the body of a single message, with a table of contents at the top for easy perusal. Instead of finding 100+ messages in your box every day, you will get, instead, a far more manageable 5 to 10 digests.

If you want to see what's been said on any library-related topic imaginable, search the LM_NET Archives: <**www.eduref.org/lm_net/archive/**>.

LISTSERVS, cont.

PUBYAC

According to its mission statement, "PUBYAC is an Internet discussion list concerned with the practical aspects of Children and Young Adult Services in Public Libraries, focusing on programming ideas, outreach and literacy programs for children and caregivers, censorship and policy issues, collection development, administrative considerations, puppetry, job openings, professional development, and other pertinent services and issues."

The name PUBYAC amalgamates the most important aspects of the discussion: **PUB**lic libraries, **Y**oung **A**dults, and **C**hildren.

PUBYAC's home page, with more instructions and links, is at: **www.PUBYAC.org**

To join the list and receive the mailings from PUBYAC, send an e-mail message (no subject line necessary) to: **listproc@prairienet.org**

In the body of the e-mail, type this message: **subscribe pubyac**

CHILD_LIT

This unmoderated discussion group examines the theory and criticism of literature for children and young adults. Home page with all info: **www.rci.rutgers.edu/~mjoseph/childlit/about.html**

TO SUBSCRIBE: Send an e-mail to: **<listserv@email.rutgers.edu>**

Leave the subject heading blank. In the body of the e-mail, type: **SUB child_lit** [your full name]

Example: **SUB child_lit Judy Freeman**

KIDLIT-L

For teachers, librarians, students, and others interested in the field of children's literature, this discussion list deals with teaching strategies and current research.

TO SUBSCRIBE: Send an e-mail to: **<listserv@bingvmb.cc.binghamton.edu>**

Leave the subject heading blank. In the body of the e-mail, type:
        subscribe KIDLIT-L [your full name]

Example: **subscribe KIDLIT-L Judy Freeman**

PUBLISHER WEBSITES

These days, you don't need to keep a zillion book catalogs filed away. Most of the information about forthcoming and backlist titles is available on the publishers' websites. Here are the major ones.

ABRAMS (Harry N. Abrams): www.abramsbooks.com
ALBERT WHITMAN: www.awhitmanco.com
AMERICAN LIBRARY ASSOCIATION: www.ala.org
ANNICK PRESS: www.annickpress.com
ATHENEUM: www.SimonSaysKids.com
AUGUST HOUSE: www.augusthouse.com
BAREFOOT BOOKS: www.barefoot-books.com/us
BLOOMSBURY: www.bloomsbury.com/usa
BOYDS MILLS PRESS: www.boydsmillspress.com
CANDLEWICK PRESS: www.candlewick.com
CAROLRHODA: www.lernerbooks.com
CHARLESBRIDGE: www. charlesbridge.com
CHILDREN'S BOOK COUNCIL: www.cbcbooks.org
CHILDREN'S BOOK PRESS: www.childrensbookpress.org
CHRONICLE BOOKS: www.chroniclekids.com
CLARION: www.houghtonmifflinbooks.com/clarion
DELACORTE: www.randomhouse.com/kids
DIAL: www.penguin.com/youngreaders
DK: us.dk.com
DOUBLEDAY: www.randomhouse.com/kids
DUTTON: www.penguin.com/youngreaders
FARRAR STRAUS GIROUX: www.fsgkidsbooks.com
FIREFLY BOOKS: www.fireflybooks.com
FITZHENRY & WHITESIDE: www.fitzhenry.ca
    (Includes **Fitzhenry Kids** and **Stoddart Kids**)
FRONT STREET: www.frontstreetbooks.com
GALE: www.gale.com
GODINE: www.godine.com
GREENWILLOW: www.harperchildrens.com
GROUNDWOOD: www.groundwoodbooks.com
HANDPRINT BOOKS: www.handprintbooks.com
HARCOURT: www.harcourtbooks.com/childrensbooks
HARPERCOLLINS: www.harperchildrens.com
HEINEMANN: www.heinemann.com
HENRY HOLT: www.henryholtchildrensbooks.com
HIGHSMITH PRESS: www.accessola.com
HOLIDAY HOUSE: www.holidayhouse.com
HOUGHTON MIFFLIN: www.houghtonmifflinbooks.com/hmcochild
    (Includes **Clarion, Harcourt, Houghton Mifflin, Kingfisher**)
HYPERION: www.hyperionbooksforchildren.com

KANE/MILLER: www.kanemiller.com

KIDS CAN: www.kidscanpress.com

KINGFISHER: www.houghtonmifflinbooks.com/kingfisher

KNOPF: www.randomhouse.com/kids

LEE & LOW: www.leeandlow.com

LERNER: www.lernerbooks.com

LIBRARIES UNLIMITED: www.lu.com
    (Includes **Libraries Unlimited** and **Teacher Ideas Press**)

LINWORTH: www.linworth.com

LITTLE, BROWN: www.lb-kids.com

MARSHALL CAVENDISH: www.marshallcavendish.com

MCELDERRY: www.SimonSaysKids.com

MILKWEED EDITIONS: www.milkweed.org

MONDO: www.mondopub.com

NATIONAL GEOGRAPHIC: www.nationalgeographic.com/books

OXFORD UNIVERSITY PRESS: www.oup.co.uk/oxed/children

PEACHTREE: www.peachtree-online.com

PENGUIN GROUP: www.penguin.com/youngreaders
    (Includes **Dial, Dutton, Firebird, Frederick Warne, Philomel, Putnam, Price Sloan Stern, Puffin, Viking**)

PHILOMEL: www.penguin.com/youngreaders

PLEASANT COMPANY/AMERICAN GIRL: www.americangirl.com

PUTNAM: www.penguin.com/youngreaders

RANDOM HOUSE: www.randomhouse.com/kids
    (Includes **Bantam, David Fickling, Delacorte, Disney, Doubleday, Dragonfly, Golden, Knopf, Laurel Leaf, Random House, Schwartz & Wade, Wendy Lamb, Yearling**)

ROARING BROOK: (NOTE: acquired in 2005 by Holtzbrinck, now Macmillan; did not yet have a website as of Spring, 2008, though they say they're working on it.)

SCARECROW: www.scarecrowpress.com

SCHOLASTIC: www.scholastic.com

SIMON & SCHUSTER: www.SimonSaysKids.com
    (Includes **Atheneum, Little Simon, Margaret K. McElderry, Scribner, Simon & Schuster**)

STENHOUSE: www.stenhouse.com

STERLING: www.sterlingpub.com

TILBURY HOUSE: www.tilburyhouse.com

TRICYCLE: www.tenspeedpress.com

TUNDRA: www.tundrabooks.com

VIKING: www.penguin.com/youngreaders

WALKER & COMPANY: www.walkeryoungreaders.com

WORKMAN: www.workman.com

EDUCATION AND LIBRARY PUBLICATIONS

AMERICAN LIBRARIES: www.ala.org/alonline
AMERICAN SCHOOL BOARD JOURNAL: www.asbj.com
BOOK LINKS: www.ala.org/booklinks
BOOKLIST: www.ala.org/booklist
EDUCATION WEEK ON THE WEB: www.edweek.org
HORN BOOK MAGAZINE: www.hbook.com
INSTRUCTOR: www.scholastic.com/instructor
KNOWLEDGE QUEST: www.ala.org/aasl/kqweb
KAPPAN: www.pdkintl.org/kappan/kappan
LIBRARY MEDIA CONNECTION: www.linworth.com
MEDIA AND METHODS ONLINE: www.media-methods.com
NEA TODAY: www.nea.org/neatoday
NEW YORK TIMES BOOK REVIEW: www.nytimes.com/books
PUBLISHERS WEEKLY ONLINE: www.publishersweekly.com
SCHOOL LIBRARY JOURNAL ONLINE: www.slj.com
SCHOOL LIBRARY MEDIA ACTIVITIES MONTHLY:
    www.schoollibrarymedia.com (Check out the magazine to read Judy Freeman's book
    review column, "Wild About Books")
SCHOOL LIBRARY MEDIA RESEARCH:
    www.ala.org/aasl/pubsandjournals/slmrb/schoollibrary.htm
TEACHER LIBRARIAN: www.teacherlibrarian.com

POETRY WEBSITES

GIGGLEPOETRY.COM
(Poetry site for kids with funny poems, poetry contests, teaching ideas, and more.):
www.gigglepoetry.com/index.cfm

POETRY FOR KIDS BY KENN NESBITT
(Funny poems by Kenn Nesbitt, as well as games, contests, lessons, and a rhyming dictionary.):
www.poetry4kids.com

POETRY ZONE
(For children and teenagers to publish their own poetry and reviews online.):
www.poetryzone.ndirect.co.uk/index2.htm

WRITER'S WORKSHOP WITH JACK PRELUTSKY
(In an online tutorial, beloved children's poet Jack Prelutsky takes children through the steps of writing their own poems. This site will also lead you to Writer's Workshop with Karla Kuskin and Writing *I Spy* Riddles with Jean Marzollo.):
teacher.scholastic.com/writewit/poetry/jack_home.htm

CREATIVE DRAMA AND READER'S THEATER WEBSITES

Look online and find ideas, techniques, lesson plans, scripts, and guidelines for writing, acting, and staging. Try these for starters.

AARON SHEPARD
(Check out author Aaron Shepard's amazing website, download one of his many fine Reader's Theater scripts, or get in touch with him to book him for a workshop at your school.): **http://aaronshep.com/rt**

AUTHORS' WEBSITES
(A few children's book authors are providing Reader's Theater scripts for their books on their websites, which is a wonderful service for all of us.)

Toni Buzzeo:	**www.tonibuzzeo.com**
Katie Davis:	**www.katiedavis.com**
Suzy Kline:	**www.suzykline.com**
Margie Palatini:	**www.margiepalatini.com**

BAD WOLF PRESS
(More than 30 clever, melodious, and entertaining shows for children to perform, all available at very reasonable prices. The Bad Wolf folks advertise their scripts as "Musical plays for musically timid teachers." Each play comes with a spiral bound script and practical guide for the teacher, with permission to make copies of the script for the whole class, and a CD with a recording of each song.): **www.badwolfpress.com**

CREATIVE DRAMA AND THEATRE EDUCATION RESOURCE SITE
(Information and concrete ideas, sectioned into Reader's Theater, classroom ideas, theater games, and an extensive booklist.): **www.creativedrama.com**

CHILDDRAMA
(Matt Buchanan, playwright and drama teacher, has packed his website with resources for drama teachers, including his original plays, lesson plans, detailed curriculum outlines, and a bibliography of professional books.): **www.childdrama.com**

FICTIONTEACHERS.COM
(Bruce Lansky and Meadowbrook Press's wonderful website contains Classroom Theater scripts based on stories from *Girls to the Rescue,* featuring clever, courageous girls and *Newfangled Fairy Tales,* featuring fairy tales with humorous twists; and links to Poetry Theater poems from **www.gigglepoetry.com**.): **www.fictionteachers.com**

LITERACY CONNECTIONS
("Promoting literacy and a love of reading" is the banner for this useful site which has many annotated links to other Reader's Theater sites.): **www.literacyconnections.com/ReadersTheater.php**

CREATIVE DRAMA AND READER'S THEATER WEBSITES, cont.

LOIS WALKER
(Canadian RT maven, Lois Walker, provides a step-by-step teacher's guide to get you started using RT in the classroom. This site links to her site, **www.scriptsforschools.com**, where you'll find more than 250 of her scripts for sale and a few free ones, too**.**):
www.loiswalker.com/catalog/teach.html

PLAYS MAGAZINE
(*Plays: The Drama Magazine for Young People* is an indispensable magazine which comes out monthly, and is filled with good, royalty-free plays for elementary through high school. Find subscription information and a few sample plays you can download for free on their website.):
www.playsmag.com

TIMELESS TEACHER STUFF
(Teacher Rick Swallow's language arts materials and Reader's Theater activities, plus many scripts you can download.): **www.timelessteacherstuff.com**

WEB ENGLISH TEACHER
("Web English Teacher presents the best of K-12 English / Language Arts teaching resources: lesson plans, WebQuests, videos, biography, e-texts, criticism, jokes, puzzles, and classroom activities," including RT.): **www.webenglishteacher.com/rt.html**

FOLKLORE AND STORYTELLING WEBSITES

New Jersey storyteller, Carol Titus, who provided some of the links on this list, says, "These sites shift and change like the sands and this is in no way a definitive list. Put 'storytelling' in as a subject on your favorite search engine and the sea of story will wash over you. Surfing them will turn up lots of shiny pebbles, interesting shells and some buried treasure. Happy hunting and when you find a good story, catch it and cast it adrift again for others to hear and ponder."

AARON SHEPARD.COM
(Check out author Aaron Shepard's amazing website, download one of his many fine Reader's Theater scripts, or get in touch with him to book him for a workshop at your school.): **http://aaronshep.com/rt/**

AESOP'S FABLES
(Contains all 655 of Aesop's fables,—indexed in table format—with morals listed, illustrations, lesson plan links, and Real Audio narrations.): **www.aesopfables.com**

ANDREW LANG'S FAIRY BOOKS
(All the Andrew Lang books with full text of all the stories. Fabulous resource! Find the text of every story in Andrew Lang's 13 Fairy Books, first published in the late 19th century. Access the stories by book, title, or place of origin.): **www.mythfolklore.net/andrewlang/**

DRAWANDTELL.COM
(Richard Thompson, writer and storyteller from Canada, has posted more than a dozen of his own original draw-and-tell stories, wordplay, and general fun and resources for, as he says, "parents, grandparents, teachers, storytellers and other grown-ups to use with children."): **www.drawandtell.com**

FOLKLORE AND MYTHOLOGY ELECTRONIC TEXTS
(Texts and commentary on thousands of stories, arranged by themes, motifs, and, story tiles; compiled by D. L. Ashliman, a retired professor from the University of Pittsburgh.): **www.pitt.edu/~dash/folktexts.html**

INTERNATIONAL STORYTELLING CENTER
(Website of the International Storytelling Center in Jonesboro, TN, "dedicated to building a better world through the power of storytelling," and a sponsor of the National Storytelling Festival in Jonesboro every October.): **www.storytellingfoundation.net**

KIDIDDLES
(Find the lyrics to thousands of children's songs, and playable music for lots of them.): **www.kididdles.com**

LEGENDS
(A comprehensive site providing "guided access to primary source material and up-to-date scholarship; personal essays and extended reviews." Includes texts of King Arthur, Robin Hood, and Andrew Lang's Fairy Books series.): **bestoflegends.org**

FOLKLORE AND STORYTELLING WEBSITES, cont.

MIMI'S MOTIFS
(Fabulous source for storytelling dolls and puppets that tie into children's books and stories.):
www.mimismotifs.com

STORYARTS
(Useful site from Heather Forest, the well-known storyteller and writer, with loads of stories to download, as well as telling techniques, ideas, lesson plans, and activities.): **www.storyarts.org**

STORY-LOVERS.COM
(Comprehensive free archival library for finding thousands of stories, sources, and advice from professional storytellers.): **www.story-lovers.com**

STORYNET
(Website of the National Storytelling Association (NSA)**;** provides a U.S. calendar of events and links to resources for storytelling.): **www.storynet.org**

STORYTELL
(A forum for discussion about storytelling sponsored by the School of Library and Information Studies at Texas Woman's University in Denton, Texas; home page contains all info on how to subscribe to the listserv STORYTELL.): **www.twu.edu/cope/slis/storytell.htm**

STORYTELLING ARTS OF INDIANA
(Teaching guides, games, activities, and resources.): **www.storytellingarts.org**

SURLALUNE FAIRY TALE PAGES
(Annotated texts of 35 well-known fairy tales, with detailed analysis of illustrations, history, variants, and modern interpretations of each.): **www.surlalunefairytales.com**

TALES OF WONDER
(An archive of more than 100 folk tales from Africa, Asia, and Europe, plus a selection of Native American stories.): **www.darsie.net/talesofwonder**

TURNER LEARNING NETWORK
(An "Educator's Guide to Learning Through Storytelling" includes resources, a how-to list for beginners, and practical lesson plans for teaching children how to be storytellers.):
www.turnerlearning.com/turnersouth/storytelling/index.html

CHILDREN'S LITERATURE-BASED WEB PAGES

ADVANCED BOOK EXCHANGE (ABE is the "world's largest online marketplace for books" new, used, rare, or out-of-print, including children's books.)**: www.abebooks.com**

AMAZON BOOKS (Find not only full-text reviews from professional journals, but from regular readers, too.)**: www.amazon.com** and **www.amazon.uk.co**

ALA (American Library Association)**: www.ala.org**
AASL (American Association of School Librarians)**: www.ala.org/aasl**
ALSC (Association for Library Service to Children)**: www.ala.org/alsc**
CALDECOTT MEDAL: www.ala.org/alsc/caldecott.html
NEWBERY MEDAL: www.ala.org/alsc/newbery.html
LINKS TO ALL ALA BOOK AWARDS:
www.ala.org/ala/alsc/awardsscholarships/literaryawds/literaryrelated.htm

THE BOOK HIVE (Short book reviews categorized by age level.)**: www.bookhive.org**

CHILDREN'S BOOK COUNCIL (Features information about new children's books, info on getting published, hundreds of links to authors' websites, and lots of great literacy materials to buy for Children's Book Week and Young People's Poetry Week.)**: www.cbcbooks.org**

CHILDREN'S WRITING RESOURCE CENTER (Useful info for children's writers of all levels, this Best of the Net-nominated site is presented by the editors of the Children's Book Insider newsletter.)**: www.write4kids.com**

CYNTHIA LEITICH SMITH'S CHILDREN'S LITERATURE RESOURCES: (Named one of the Top 10 Writers' Sites by *Writer's Digest* and selected as one of the "Great Web Sites for Kids" by ALA/ALSC, this site contains info on books, stories, articles, teacher/reader guides, links to multicultural booklists, and articles for concerned educators.)**: www.cynthialeitichsmith.com**

FOLLETT LIBRARY RESOURCES (If you're a teacher or librarian, go to Follett's indispensable site and sign up, for free, for **TitleWave**. Search for books and audiovisual materials by author, title, subject, or key word; work on library collection development; build and store lists; and order online. Find full cataloguing info, reading levels and lexiles, the book cover in color, and full text book reviews from *Booklist, Hornbook, Kirkus, Publishers Weekly*, and *School Library Journal*.)**: www.titlewave.com**

A FUSE #8 PRODUCTION (NYC librarian Elizabeth Bird's awesome blog of children's book reviews and news.)**: www.schoollibraryjournal.com/blog/1790000379.html**

GUYSREAD (Jon Scieszka's push for getting boys to read.)**: www.guysread.com**

JIM TRELEASE (America's Reading Guru includes thoughtful commentary on reading, censorship, AR, and getting children to read.)**: www.trelease-on-reading.com**

CHILDREN'S LITERATURE-BASED WEB PAGES, cont.

KAY E. VANDERGRIFT'S SPECIAL INTEREST PAGE (From well-known Rutgers professor, Kay Vandergrift, a rich resource for students of children's literature who are interested in theory and research as they relate to teaching practice.): **www.scils.rutgers.edu/~kvander**

LINDA'S LINKS TO LITERATURE: (Subscribe for $24.95 a year to access 25,000+ links to book units, lesson plans, activities, booktalks, book quizzes, puzzles, games and more. Subscribe **for free** to Linda Bendall's monthly newsletter, *The Bookmark*, for practical classroom ideas related to children's and young adult literature and information on favorite books and authors.): **www.lindaslinkstoliterature.com**

MIMI'S MOTIFS (Fabulous source for storytelling dolls and puppets that can be tied into a variety of children's books.): **www.mimismotifs.com**

NANCY KEANE'S BOOKTALKS (Booktalks, quick and simple. Includes indexes by author, title, subject, and interest level as well as general booktalking tips and student written talks.): **nancykeane.com/booktalks**

NANCY POLETTE (Ideas for using the best of the best picture books, fiction, and nonfiction. Features a monthly sample literature guide.): **www.nancypolette.com**

NOFLYINGNOTIGHTS (Comprehensive graphic novel review site for teens, including a blog and a link to their sister site, Sidekicks for Kids.): **www.noflyingnotights.com**

PLANET ESME (Book reviews and ideas by the extraordinary Esmé Raji Codell, effervescent author of *Educating Esmé*.): **www.planetesme.com**. and **planetesme.blogspot.com**

PURPLE CRAYON (Well-known children's editor Harold Underdown shares his knowledge about writing, illustrating, and publishing children's books.): **www.underdown.org**

SOCIETY OF CHILDREN'S BOOK WRITERS & ILLUSTRATORS (SCBWI) (For professional and aspiring writers and illustrators of children's books.): **www.scbwi.org**

TEACHINGBOOKS.NET (A WOW! of a website, started by Nick Glass, a guy with a mission. "From one easy-to-use website, TeachingBooks makes instantly available original, in-studio movies of authors and illustrators, audio excerpts of professional book readings, guides to thousands of titles and a wealth of multimedia resources on children's and young adult literature. Our hope is that by utilizing TeachingBooks' multimedia resources, educators will better understand the spirit and personality behind books and discover exciting ways to share these insights with children and teens."): **www.teachingbooks.net**

TIMELESS TEACHER STUFF (Scores of Reader's Theater scripts for stories, many of them well-known children's books, scripted by Rick Swallow; Language Arts Activities, Writing Prompts and more.): **www.timelessteacherstuff.com/**

WEBSITES FOR CHILDREN'S BOOK
AUTHORS & ILLUSTRATORS

As the site names for so many the authors' and illustrators' websites use their own names, such as <**www.kevinhenkes.com**>, it's usually easier to type in that web address first. If that doesn't work, look up the person on a search engine such as Google.com. I type in the search bar the author's name, enclosed in quotation marks, plus additional key words as follows: ("Eric Carle" author website children's books). If the author has his or her own site, often you will find it at or near the top of the listings, as in this case, where you'll find it as <**www.Eric-Carle.com**>.

Where else can you find the websites of authors and illustrators? There are many websites with scores of links including the following:

CHILDREN'S BOOK COUNCIL: Author & Illustrator Sites:
    www.cbcbooks.org/contacts

INTERNET PUBLIC LIBRARY (IPL): www.ipl.org/kidspace/browse/rzn0000

INTERNET SCHOOL LIBRARY MEDIA CENTER: Index to Internet Sites: Children's and Young Adults' Authors & Illustrators:
    falcon.jmu.edu/~ramseyil/biochildhome.htm

ONCE UPON A TIME . . .: A CHILDREN'S LITERATURE WEB SITE: Authors' and Illustrators' Pages: www.bsu.edu/classes/vancamp/aaip.html

Of the hundreds of author and illustrator websites I have visited in the past few years, there are some that really stand out. When it comes to innovative design, the illustrators have the edge, of course, as they can beautify their sites with their own gorgeous artwork. Some folks have obviously spent a fortune on their websites, with sound, color, graphics, interactive home pages, games, and video clips. Others are much more print-based. A good author or illustrator website will include a biography, a personal message, photographs, descriptions and pictures of published books, teacher's guides, activities for children, working links to other good sites, and contact information.

When compiling my list of exemplary sites, I was looking for ones that went beyond the everyday and provided surprises and some heart. That doesn't necessarily mean visual hoopla, although that is certainly welcome. Some sites included a series of questions from children and the author's thoughtful, personal responses. Others included revealing essays; a series of well-thought-out teacher's guides for each of an author's books; Reader's Theater scripts; an illustrator's description of how he or she created the art; or useful ways to bring children and adults to reading. When we finish wending our way through one of these sites, we should feel as if we've gotten to know that author or illustrator a bit as a person. I love a website with personality and passion.

Children are using author websites to do research into authors' and illustrators' lives, find out information about their books, and get motivated to read them. Teachers and librarians use them to plan author visits to schools and libraries and to find teaching guides to books they plan to read aloud or use with students.

The possibilities are growing as authors and illustrators grapple with just how much they want to reveal on the now ubiquitous sites. Can they afford to be left behind?

214.

60 EXEMPLARY AUTHOR AND ILLUSTRATOR WEBSITES

Adler, David A.	www.davidaadler.com
Armstrong, Jennifer	www.jennifer-armstrong.com
Arnold, Tedd	www.teddarnold.com
Arnosky, Jim	www.jimarnosky.com
Asch, Frank	www.frankasch.com
Blume, Judy	www.judyblume.com
Brett, Jan	www.janbrett.com
Buzzeo, Toni	www.tonibuzzeo.com
Carle, Eric	www.eric-carle.com
Carlson, Nancy	www.nancycarlson.com
Choldenko, Gennifer	www.choldenko.com
Christelow, Eileen	www.eileenchristelow.com
Cleary, Beverly	www.beverlycleary.com
Cobb, Vickiw	ww.vickicobb.com
Coville, Bruce	www.brucecoville.com
Creech, Sharon	www.sharoncreech.com
Curtis, Christopher Paul	www.ChristopherPaulCurtis.com
Davis, Katie	www.katiedavis.com
DePaola, Tomie	www.tomie.com
DiPucchio, Kelly	www.kellydipucchio.com
DiTerlizzi, Tony	www.diterlizzi.com
Fleming, Denise	www.denisefleming.com
Fox, Mem	www.memfox.net
Frasier, Debra	www.debrafrasier.com
George, Kristine O'Connell	www.kristinegeorge.com
Grimes, Nikki	www.nikkigrimes.com
Gutman, Dan	www.dangutman.com
Henkes, Kevin	www.kevinhenkes.com
Jacques, Brian	www.redwall.org
Kirk, Daniel	www.danielkirk.com
Krosoczka, Jarrett J.	www.studiojjk.com
Krull, Kathleen	www.kathleenkrull.com
Leedy, Loreen	www.loreenleedybooks.com
MacDonald, Suse	www.susemacdonald.com
Martin, Jacqueline Briggs	www.jacquelinebriggsmartin.com
Martin, Rafe	www.rafemartin.com
McDonald, Megan	www.meganmcdonald.net
McMillan, Bruce	www.brucemcmillan.com
Munsch, Robert	www.robertmunsch.com

60 EXEMPLARY AUTHOR AND ILLUSTRATOR WEBSITES, cont.

Numeroff, Laura	www.lauranumeroff.com
Palatini, Margie	www.margiepalatini.com
Park, Barbara	www.randomhouse.com/kids/junieb
Pilkey, Dav	www.pilkey.com
Pulver, Robin	www.robinpulver.com
Reynolds, Peter H.	www.peterhreynolds.com
Riordan, Rick	www.rickriordan.com
Rowling, J. K.	www.jkrowling.com
	www.scholastic.com/harrypotter
Sabuda, Robert	www.robertsabuda.com
Sayre, April Pulley	www.aprilsayre.com
Shepard, Aaron	www.aaronshep.com
Silverstein, Shel	www.shelsilverstein.com
Smith, Cynthia Leitich	www.cynthialeitichsmith.com
Snicket, Lemony	www.lemonysnicket.com
Spinelli, Jerry	www.jerryspinelli.com
Stevens, Janet	www.janetstevens.com
Willems, Mo	www.mowillems.com
Wood, Audrey	www.audreywood.com
Woodson, Jacqueline	www.jacquelinewoodson.com
Yolen, Jane	www.janeyolen.com

JUDY FREEMAN'S TWO FAVORITE
CHILDREN'S LITERATURE BLOGS

I check in to each of these blogs several times a week to see what Esmé and Betsy are reading. I appreciate their good taste in children's books, and admire their stimulating, well-written book reviews. Check out the following:

PLANET ESME: The Planet Esme Book-A-Day Plan: The Best New Children's Books from Esme's Shelf: http://planetesme.blogspot.com/

Esmé Raji Codell, proprietress of this remarkable blog, is the author of several books I consider essential. For adults, there's *How to Get Your Child to Love Reading: For Ravenous and Reluctant Readers Alike* (Algonquin Books, 2003) and *Educating Esmé: Diary of a Teacher's First Year* (Algonquin Books, 2003)

She's also written a batch of terrific children's books, my favorite of which is *Sahara Special* (Hyperion, 2003). And then there's her fabulous blog, about which she says:

"Welcome to the Wonderful World of PlanetEsme! I hope this book-a-day plan will be a boon to anyone who would like to play a supporting character in a child's reading life story. This blog is a supporting page to sister site <**PlanetEsme.com**>, where you will find a silly amount of additional reviews, thematic lists, links, and much more . . . everything you need to become an expert in children's literature.

"I'm a professional readiologist who thinks children's trade literature is our best hope for equalizing education in America. Anyone who says they care about kids and schools and doesn't read aloud is lying, or about to make the discovery of a lifetime. I'm a woman on a mission. Let me rock your pedagogical world."

A FUSE # 8 PRODUCTION:
www.schoollibraryjournal.com/blog/1790000379.html

Elizabeth (Betsy) Bird, children's librarian at Donnell Central Children's Room of the New York Public Library, keeps up a most remarkable blog, writing long, meaty, conversational, honest, and compelling reviews of new children's books—at least one a day. As "Ramseelbird," she has written more than 1,000 children's book reviews on Amazon.com.

If you're looking for other children's literature blogs, Betsy's blog links to dozens of the best. She also has a hilarious feature: Hot Men of Children's Literature, where she features authors, illustrators, and publishing people, and yes, they are hot. About her blog, Betsy writes the following:

"Children's literature is not for the weak. It's a ruthless cutthroat business with lots of gnashes of the teeth. Children's librarianship, in contrast, is a sweet sweet ride. I'm just gonna include links and tips to things I find interesting, while also including a review of a children's book each day."

For links to lots more wonderful blogs on children's literature, go to Betsy's original site, **fusenumber8.blogspot.com,** and scroll down to **"Cream o' the Kidlit Blogger Crop"** on the right hand side.

ACROSS-THE-CURRICULUM WEBSITES
FOR TEACHERS AND LIBRARIANS

A TO Z TEACHER STUFF (Indexes to online lesson plans and teacher resources by subject or grade level from a database of more than 3,500 lesson plans submitted by teachers.): **www.atozteacherstuff.com/lessons** or **www.lessonplanz.com**

ABCTEACH (Easy, online materials for immediate use by kids, student teachers, teachers, and parents and other visitors to the site, including activity sheets and project helpers arranged by thematic unit.): **www.abcteach.com**

BORED.COM (Endless links to quizzes, trivia, games, songs, and humor, with a separate Kids' Section.): **www.bored.com**

CORE KNOWLEDGE (Collection of high-quality units and lesson plans for preschool through 8th grade.): **www.coreknowledge.org**

DISCOVERYSCHOOL.COM (Listings of educational TV programming, lesson plans, teaching tools, brain boosters, clip art, and more. Sponsored by the Discovery Channel.): **www.school.discovery.com**

DISNEY EDUCATIONAL PRODUCTIONS (Cyber lesson plans complete with activity links, plus teacher-tested ideas and sites covering all subject areas.): Disney's Edu-Station: **dep.disney.go.com/educational/index**

EDHELPER.COM (Includes lesson plans, worksheets, webquests, and worksheet generators, plus the latest educational news headlines and articles.): **www.edhelper.com**

EDUCATION WORLD (Websites, lesson plans, activities, and columns on every subject for teachers.): **www.educationworld.com**

THE EDUCATOR'S REFERENCE DESK: (Includes: **Resource Collection**, with links to more than 3,000 resources on a variety of educational issues; **Lesson Plan Collection**, containing more than 2,000 unique lesson plans written and submitted by teachers from all over the U.S.; **Question Archive**, with more than 200 responses to popular questions on the practice, theory, and research of education; and **ERIC Database**, the world's largest source of education information, which contains more than one million abstracts of documents and journal articles on education research and practice.): **www.eduref.org**

EISENHOWER NATIONAL CLEARINGHOUSE (Provides access to ENC's collection of teaching materials for K-12 math and science.): **www.enc.org**

ENCHANTED LEARNING (Delightful site of activities, games, printable activity sheets, and websites.): **www.enchantedlearning.com**

ERIC CLEARINGHOUSE ON READING, ENGLISH, AND COMMUNICATION (ERIC is the Educational Resources Information Center, a federally funded national information system that provides language arts information to teachers, librarians, counselors, administrators, and parents.): **reading.indiana.edu**

FLAT STANLEY (Journaling project in which schools create a paper doll, write a journal, and send their "Flat Stanleys" to other schools. Based on the book, *Flat Stanley*, by Jeff Brown.): **flatstanley.enoreo.on.ca**

FOREFRONT CURRICULUM ONLINE (Internet training and curriculum development for K to 12 educators.): **www.forefrontcurriculum.com**

FUNBRAIN (Site by the Family Education Network that provides free educational games and quizzes in math, grammar, science, spelling, and history, plus resources for teachers and parents.): **funbrain.com**

INTERNATIONAL READING ASSOCIATION (IRA): www.reading.org

INTERNET4CLASSROOMS (Helping Teachers Make Effective Use of the Internet.): **www.internet4classrooms.com**

JOAN HOLUB'S 100TH DAY OF SCHOOL WEBSITES (300 celebration ideas.): **users.aol.com/a100thday/ideas.html**

KATHY SCHROCK'S GUIDE FOR EDUCATORS: (Categorized list of exemplary educational sites for enhancing curriculum and professional growth for teachers.): **www.kathyschrock.net**

KIDiddles (Lyrics to hundreds of children's songs.): **www.kididdles.com**

LEARNING PAGE (Printable lesson plans, worksheets, activities, thematic units, printable stories, and clip art; for PreK-3.): **www.learningpage.com**

MATH WORD PROBLEMS FOR CHILDREN (More than 3500 word problems for elementary grades, aligned with state standards; also available in Spanish; membership required.): **www.mathstories.com**

NATIONAL COUNCIL OF TEACHERS OF ENGLISH: www.ncte.org

THE NEW CURRICULUM (Helping teachers integrate technology into their curriculum.): **www.newcurriculum.com/index.php**

PROTEACHER (Comprehensive site for K to 6 teachers including extensive links to lesson plans, materials, discussion groups, and archives of teaching tips.): **www.proteacher.com**

QUIZ HUB (A free online interactive learning center for elementary school students, featuring educational games, puzzles, and quizzes for language arts, math, science, social studies, and four foreign languages.): **quizhub.com/quiz/quizhub.cfm**

READ ACROSS AMERICA (A project of the National Education Association, Read Across America organizes literacy awareness events to get kids excited about reading.): **www.nea.org/readacross**

READING IS FUNDAMENTAL (Reading links and ideas aplenty for parents, teachers, and children.): **www.rif.org**

READING LADY (Chat, message boards, and lots of info on Four Blocks reading, including guided reading, writing, comprehension, Reader's Theater, and poetry.): **www.readinglady.com**

SCHOLASTIC (Online activities, lesson plans, teaching strategies, as well as monthly online chats and bulletin board discussions with featured authors; separate resources for kids, families, teachers, administrators, and librarians.): **www.scholastic.com**

SITES FOR TEACHERS: (Hundreds of educational websites, rated by popularity.): **www.sitesforteachers.com**

TEACHERS FIRST (A division of Network for Instructional TV, Inc.; web resource for K to12 classroom teachers who want useful resources and lesson plans to use with their students.): **www.teachersfirst.com/matrix.htm**

TEACHING HEART: (Billed as "A Place for K to 3 teachers with sharing hearts." Great links and wonderful collections of printables, lesson plans, and themes.): **www.teachingheart.net**

TEACHNET.COM: Smart Tools for Busy Teachers (Top 100 websites for educators; bulletin board ideas; lesson plans by subject; how to organize, decorate, and manage your classroom; and more.): **www.teachnet.com**

TEACH-NOLOGY: The Art and Science of Teaching with Technology (Free access to lesson plans, printable worksheets, more than 250,000 reviewed web sites, rubrics, educational games, teaching/technology tips, and more.): **www.teach-nology.com**

WEBQUEST (Developed by Bernie Dodge at San Diego State University, a WebQuest is an inquiry-oriented activity in which most or all of the information used by learners is drawn from the Web. WebQuests are designed to support learners' thinking at the levels of analysis, synthesis, and evaluation.): **webquest.sdsu.edu**

WEBSITES FOR CHILDREN

AWESOME CLIP ART FOR KIDS: www.awesomeclipartforkids.com

BETWEEN THE LIONS (From the PBS book-related show.): **pbskids.org/lions**

DISCOVERYSCHOOL.COM (Worksheets and games.): **school.discovery.com**

DISCOVERYSCHOOL'S PUZZLEMAKER: www.puzzlemaker.school.discovery.com

EDUCATION4KIDS: An Internet Resource: www.edu4kids.com

FUNBRAIN: www.funbrain.com/kidscenter.html

FUNSCHOOL: www.funschool.com

JOSEPH WU'S ORIGAMI: www.origami.vancouver.bc.ca

JUST FOR KIDS WHO LOVE BOOKS: A WEBSITE FOR KIDS 8-14: www.alanbrown.com

KABOOSE KIDS DOMAIN: www.kidsdomain.com

KIDLINK: www.kidlink.org

KIDSREADS.COM: www.kidsreads.com/authors/authors.asp

MIKIDS.COM (Elementary kids' site put together by a school librarian.): **www.mikids.com**

NATIONAL GEOGRAPHIC: www.nationalgeographic.com/kids

NINE PLANETS FOR KIDS: AN INTERACTIVE TOUR OF THE SOLAR SYSTEM: kids.nineplanets.org

OH! KIDS (Ohio Public Library Information Network area for kids ages 6 to 11.): **www.oplin.org/ohkids/Webkids/WebKids.htm**

PBS KIDS: (Kid-friendly, easy-to-navigate site includes stories, games, songs, and parent and teacher guides from PBS children's shows including: *Arthur, Berenstain Bears, Between the Lions, George Shrinks, Reading Rainbow, Sesame Street,* and *Zoom.*): **pbskids.org**

SAN DIEGO ZOO (Fun facts about animals, photos, sound clips, and video; accessible by animal groups, habitats/ecosystems, or continents.): **www.sandiegozoo.org/animalbytes**

SESAME WORKSHOP—SESAME STREET: www.sesameworkshop.org/sesamestreet

STORYPLACE: The Children's Digital Library (An interactive bilingual Spanish and English site sponsored by the Public Library of Charlotte-Mecklenburg County including narrated stories children can read along, annotated booklists, and activities.): **www.storyplace.org**

WHITE HOUSE FOR KIDS: www.whitehouse.gov/kids

YAHOOLIGANS FOR KIDS: yahooligans.com

WORLD WIDE WEB
RESEARCH TOOLS AND SEARCH ENGINES

ALA'S GREAT WEBSITES FOR KIDS (Valuable source of links to hundreds of websites organized under broad subjects/interest areas, including reference.): **www.ala.org/greatsites**

ASK JEEVES FOR KIDS! (Just type in a question and click.): **ajkids.com**

AWESOME LIBRARY—K-12 Education Directory (Comprehensive listing of more than 27,000 reviewed resources for teachers, librarians, parents, and children, arranged by subject area.): **www.awesomelibrary.org**

BIOGRAPHICAL DICTIONARY (The lives of more than 28,000 famous people are summarized.): **www.s9.com/biography**

GOOGLE (A user-friendly search engine that works.): **www.google.com**

INTERNET PUBLIC LIBRARY, YOUTH DIVISION: www.ipl.org/div/kidspace

IVY'S SEARCH ENGINE SOURCES FOR KIDS (Clear and easy to use, with scores of links to excellent, high-interest resources and fun activities.): **www.ivyjoy.com**

KIDSCLICK (Links to 600+ subject sites searchable by first letter and by interest area.): **sunsite.berkeley.edu/kidsclick**

LIBRARIANS' INDEX TO THE INTERNET (Reliable, annotated subject directory of and guide to more than 12,000 Internet resources selected and evaluated by librarians for their usefulness to users of public libraries.): **lii.org**

LIBRARY OF CONGRESS (Resources for kids, families, librarians, and teachers.): **www.loc.gov/families**

MULTNOMAH COUNTY LIBRARY HOMEWORK CENTER (Large number of links for every curricular area imaginable.): **www.multcolib.org.homework**

REFDESK.COM (Astonishingly thorough links to every news and reference source imaginable.): **www.refdesk.com**

SCHOOL LIBRARY MEDIA ACTIVITIES MONTHLY
A magazine by and for school library media specialists.
It is a practical resource you will use every day!

"Highly recommended for school libraries"
Magazines for Libraries

"Splendid activities from how to use an author's book to a day-by-day outline for a month of library promotions. This is a professional journal which librarians should share with teachers."
Elementary School Library Collection.

www.schoollibrarymedia.com

School Library Media Activities Monthly is published September – June each year with contributions from regular columnists like **Judy Freeman** (Wild About Books), **Carolyn Brodie** (Connect the Book and Author! Author!), **Greg Byerly** (Web Monthly), **Daniel Callison** (Key Words for Instruction), **Helen Adams** (Privacy Matters), **Barbara Safford** (Reach for Reference), **Gary Zingher** (Thematic Journeys), **Sharron McElmeel** (Between the Pages) and **Pat Franklin and Claire Stephens** (Management Matters). The magazine also hosts regular submissions from library media professionals for feature articles on current professional issues, lesson plans, and other columns such as, Information Skill of the Month, Sharing Skills, The Advocate, and Keeping Current.

Ordering Information

Fill out the form below and mail it in, or subscribe online: www.schoollibrarymedia.com or call: **Voice:** 1-800-225-5800 X 4488 **Fax:** 203-454-8662.

1 year of SLMAM (10 issues) $55.00

_____ *Payment enclosed.*

Please make check payable to **Libraries Unlimited.**

> **Libraries Unlimited Subscription Services**
> **88 Post Road West**
> **P.O. Box 5007**
> **Westport, CT 06881**

_____ *Please bill me:*
*Purchase order number*_____

Send to:

Name:_____

Name: _____

Billing Address:_____

Address: _____

City:_____ **State:** _____ **Zip Code:** _____

City: _____ **State:** _____ **Zip Code:** _____

_____ Credit card (circle one)   VISA   MasterCard   American Express

Number_____ Expiration Date_____

Signature _____

Available in March 2008!

NoveList® K-8 Plus

With over 17,000 juvenile nonfiction titles to support the school curriculum and kids' pleasure reading.

NoveList K-8 Plus is a school media specialist's complete reading resource - with all of the things you love about *NoveList* – PLUS over 17,000 nonfiction titles and value-added editorial content!

1 Colorful, kid-friendly interface.

2 Search bar makes finding information easy.

3 Browse editorial content right from the homepage!

4 Easy access to content for teachers, librarians and parents.

NoveList K-8 Plus
Your Guide to Reading powered by EBSCOhost

Sign In | Folders | Preferences | Help | Feedback

Home | Advanced Search

Search   Search History/Alerts | Search Other Databases | Database Info

Find: [   ]   Go   Clear   ?

Limited to: ☐ Teens   ☐ Older Kids   ☐ Younger Kids   In: Fiction/Nonfiction ▾

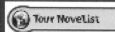

Browse ?

Award Winners

Teens
Author Biographies
BookTalks
Recommended Reads

Older Kids
BookTalks
Recommended Reads

Younger Kids
Recommended Reads

Working with Kids
BookTalks
Curricular Connections
Curricular Standards
Grab and Go Book Lists
Picture Book Extenders

My NoveList

Tour NoveList   My Folders & Alerts

NoveList Newsletters   About NoveList

Spotlight

Latest "Desperate Librarians" Article
Geared toward educators, Judy Freeman's "Desperate Librarians" articles offer countless 'germs'—practical, yet fun ideas for using literature effectively across the curriculum. Previous "Desperate Librarians" articles are always there when you need them—simply enter "desperate librarians" in the *Find* box at the top of your screen.

Just the Facts . . . Just for You
Need an annotated list of quality, readable nonfiction sure to interest students? Bonnie Kunzel's articles, "Just the Facts: Nonfiction Trade Books for the Social Studies Curriculum" and "Just the Facts: Science Trade Books for the Elementary School Curriculum" provide just the thing. Kunzel, a literacy consultant, worked with a team to cull these noteworthy nonfiction titles.

NoveList K-8 Plus

TeachingBooks•net®

All Subject Areas

All Grade Levels

Help students read more ... and enjoy it.

TeachingBooks.net – an online collection of multimedia K-12 book and author resources that help you integrate books throughout the curriculum – for all subject areas and grade levels.

- Author Programs
- Book Guides
- Book Readings
- Author Websites
- Audio Collection of Author Name Pronunciations

The New The Way Things Work

Art
David Macaulay

Less Than Zero

Math
Stuart Murphy

Esperanza Rising

Reading "Esperanza Rising"

Social Studies
Pam Muñoz Ryan

Breaking Through

Spanish
Francisco Jiménez

Walk Two Moons

Middle School
Sharon Creech

Remember: The Journey to School Integration

High School
Toni Morrison

Stills from TeachingBooks original Author Programs.

MIMI'S MOTIFS

www.mimismotifs.com
Email: mimi@mimismotifs.com
Fax: 559-625-1351 or 559-734-6849
Phone: 1-877-367-6464

Explore our line of unique early literacy storytelling "props with a purpose" at www.mimismotifs.com. We are committed to providing our customers with exceptional handcrafted quality, design, and service.

Mimi

CHECK OUT
WWW.MIMISMOTIFS.COM
FOR INFORMATION ON BOTH
VERSIONS OF OUR
EXCLUSIVE MELVIL DEWEY
PUPPET SETS.

Dewey-ing *the* **Decimals?**

Dewey hand Puppet and ten category finget puppets.

www.mimismotifs.com

877.367.6464
mimi@mimismotifs.com

Bear Snores On, etc.

Epossumondus

PURCHASE ORDERS ACCEPTED.

Books Kids Will Sit Still For 3: A Read-Aloud Guide

By Judy Freeman

"This excellent resource will be a favorite with teachers who need assistance finding quality children's literature, and it will also aid librarians and media specialists... She encourages educators to create lifelong learners, library users, and book lovers."—**School Library Journal**

"Every school library must have a copy of this book, and every teacher needs to know about it to freshen his or her own use of literature in the classroom. There has never been a time in education when better children's literature--fiction and nonfiction--existed, and this book will lead you to the best blooms in the garden of print. Essential as a book selection tool and a source to feature, booktalk, read aloud, and tantalize elementary school children."—**Teacher Librarian**

Elementary school teachers, librarians, and parents rejoice! **Books Kids Will Sit Still For 3** by librarian and children's literature troubadour Judy Freeman is here at last. It's an all-new treasure trove of 1,700 all-new, tried-and-true, child-tested favorite read-aloud titles, published since 1995, and a comprehensive source of thousands of inspirational literature-based ideas.

Books Kids Will Sit Still For 3 is the definitive source for the best recent picture books, fiction, poetry, folklore, and nonfiction books to share with children from preschool through sixth grade. Along with the extensively annotated bibliography of 1,705 outstanding recent children's books to read aloud, it incorporates thousands of new and practical ideas for booktalking, creative drama, storytelling, poetry, creative writing, library skills, and other literature-based teaching. There is also a completely new bibliography of professional books.

Extensive all-new chapters offer entertaining, informative, and instantly useful approaches to reading aloud, storytelling, creative drama, Reader's Theater, and nonstop classroom and library activities across the curriculum. Find out "17 Things You Need to Know to Be a Great School Librarian." Learn how to evaluate a new book. See what it's like to be on the Newbery Committee. Each entry in the bibliography now contains five parts: bibliographic information; a lively descriptive annotation; a series of brief follow-up ideas called "Germs"; related titles list and subjects list. You'll find *Books Kids Will Sit Still For 3* to be a goldmine and a godsend!

Children's and Young Adult Literature Reference Series
Libraries Unlimited, 2006
ISBN: 1-59158-163-X; 936 pgs; $70.00 hardcover
ISBN: 1-59158-164-8; 936 pgs; $55.00 paper

JUDY FREEMAN (www.JudyReadsBooks.com) is a well-known speaker, consultant, and writer on all aspects of children's literature, storytelling, booktalking, and school librarianship. A former elementary school librarian, she gives workshops, speeches, and performances throughout the U.S. and the world for teachers, librarians, parents, and children, and is a national seminar presenter for BER (Bureau of Education and Research). Judy writes several children's book review columns, including "Wild About Books" for *School Library Media Activities Monthly*, "Desperate Librarians" for the online fiction database *NoveList*, and "What's New" for *School Library Journal's Curriculum Connections*.

More Books Kids Will Sit Still For
By Judy Freeman

"Liberally sprinkled with titles, chock full of ideas and supplemented with high-quality bibliographies ... librarians will find helpful and few children will be able to resist." —**Booklist**

"Drawing on her years of experience as librarian and storyteller, Freeman offers practical suggestions for numerous literature-based activities to enrich the language arts curriculum." —**School Library Journal**

Based on the author's longtime experience as a school librarian and storyteller, this book offers 1,400 titles—including picture books, folk tales, poetry, and nonfiction—guaranteed to engage children. Annotated entries include brief plot summaries, subject designations, related titles, and curriculum tie-ins. **Libraries Unlimited, 1995**
0-8352-3731-1; 868 pages; 1995; $32.95 (paper)
0-8352-3520-3; 868 pages; 1995; $55.00 (hardcover)

Books Kids Will Sit Still For
By Judy Freeman

"The book talk, creative dramatics, storytelling and book-celebrating activities should be a part of every reading and language arts program."—**The Reading Teacher**

"... detailed annotations of over 2,000 kid-tested titles, curriculum tie-ins and classroom activities, grade-level suggestions, and a comprehensive subject index that alone is worth the cost of the book."—**Library Talk**
Libraries Unlimited, 1990.
0-8352-3010-4; 660 pages; 1990; $55.00 hardcover

Quantity	ISBN	AUTHOR/TITLE	PRICE	TOTAL
	1-59158-163-X	**Books Kids Will Sit Still For 3 hardcover**		
	1-59158-164-X	**Books Kids Will Sit Still For 3 paper**		
	0-8352-3731-1	**More Books Kids Will Sit Still For-paper**		
	0-8352-3520-3	**More Books Kids Will Sit Still for-hardcover**		
	0-8352-3010-4	**Books Kids Will Sit Still For-hardcover**		

Send order to address below **Or call: 1-800-225-5800;** **Or fax: 1-603-431-2214** **Or Online: www.lu.com or** **www.greenwood.com** **For 20% Conference Discount,** **use Code #F238**	Subtotal:		
	Shipping: (add 10% or $8.00 Minimum)		
	Sales Tax: (IL,MA, CO, CT, PA, MD, SD, MO, NJ) Canada residents add GST Tax Or include Tax Exempt #		
	Total:		

If using a purchase order please attach it to this form.
Send order to:
Libraries Unlimited
P.O. Box 6926
Portsmouth, NH 03802

The WINNERS! Handbook
A Closer Look at Judy Freeman's Top-Rated Children's Books of 2007
By Judy Freeman

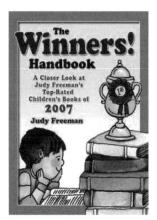

This year's *The WINNERS! Handbook* contains Judy's extensively annotated list of her 100+ best books of 2007 for grades K-6, including this year's Newbery, Caldecott, Sibert, and Geisel Medal winners. For each book she chose, you'll find a thorough description; a "Germ" (if you're looking for a good idea or two or three to try out with your children); a Related Titles list to use for thematic units, follow-ups, read-alouds, and to recommend to readers; and a list of subjects to give you a quick idea of the book's genre and themes. The title, author, and subject indexes will help you locate everything. Next you'll find four fabulous new Reader's Theater scripts; an insider's look at this year's Sibert Medal—Judy was on the 2008 Sibert Committee; lots of lesson plans, worksheets, activities, and book tie-ins; seven new teacher's guides Judy wrote for this year's books, including two major award-winners; a batch of songs and stories; and a chapter chock full of children's literature-based Web sites called "Surfing the Net." What new books do you need to buy and why? Judy's choices are books she thinks no teacher, librarian, or child can live without. She's tested scores of them with children, and says, with gusto, "These books work!" *The WINNERS! Handbook* is based on Judy's popular 24th Annual Winners Workshops she presented in Spring, 2008. **Libraries Unlimited, 2008.**
ISBN13: 978-1-59158-712-5; $35.00; Grades K-6.

The WINNERS! Handbook
A Closer Look at Judy Freeman's Top-Rated Children's Books of 2006
By Judy Freeman

This yearly edition of *The WINNERS! Handbook* starts with an extensive booklist of Judy Freeman's 100 best books of 2006. (If you own Judy's *Books Kids Will Sit Still For 3*, it follows the same format. Indeed, you can consider each year's new *WINNERS! Handbook* an update to that book.) Each entry includes a meaty and thoughtful annotation, a "germ" (a series of practical, do-able, useful, pithy ideas for reading, writing, and illustrating prompts and other activities across the curriculum); a useful list of exemplary related titles; and subject designations for each title to ascertain where the book might fit thematically into your curricular plan or program. There's also a title, author, and subject index for easy access. You find scores of useful and fun ideas, activities, lessons, and ways you can incorporate literature into every aspect of your day and your life. From story hour to school curriculum tie-ins, the many connections include strategies for comprehension, critical thinking skills, research, and problem-solving; songs, games, crafts, songs, plenty of great across-the-curriculum poetry, creative drama and Reader's Theater, storytelling, booktalking, and book discussion. Most of the books are fabulous read-alouds, read-alones, and natural choices for Guided Reading, Literature Circles, or Book Clubs. **Libraries Unlimited, 2007.**
ISBN13: 978-1-59158-510-7; $35.00; Grades K-6.

JUDY FREEMAN (www.JudyReadsBooks.com) is a well-known speaker, consultant, book reviewer, columnist, and writer on all aspects of children's literature, storytelling, booktalking, and school librarianship. A former elementary school librarian, she gives workshops, speeches, and performances throughout the U.S. and the world for teachers, librarians, parents, and children.

For more information or to order, visit the Web site at: www.lu.com; e-mail: orders@lu.com; phone: 800-225-5800 Send purchase orders to:
Libraries Unlimited
P.O. Box 6926
Portsmouth, NH 03802

Once Upon a Time
Using Storytelling, Creative Drama, and Reader's Theater
with Children in Grades PreK-6
By Judy Freeman

Judy Freeman, author of the *Books Kids Will Sit Still For* series, gives personal and practical how-to tips on how to learn and tell a story, how to act out a story using creative drama, and how to write and stage a Reader's Theater script. All are guaranteed to get your children listening, thinking, reading, loving, and living stories with comprehension, fluency, expression, and joy.

Once Upon a Time pulls together a wealth of ideas, activities, and strategies for using folk and fairy tales, songs, chants, and nonsense rhymes. Also included in this handbook are the texts of 10 of Judy's favorite stories you can read today and tell tomorrow; a songbook of songs, chants, and nonsense rhymes; and a Reader's Theater script. You'll also find annotated bibliographies: 400+ children's books every storyteller should know; 100+ great children's books to use for creative drama and Reader's Theater; professional books and Web sites for storytelling, creative drama, and Reader's Theater; and a title and author index.

ISBN13: 978-1-59158-663-0; ISBN10: 1-59158-663-1; $35.00
LIBRARIES UNLIMITED, 2007

Quantity	ISBN	AUTHOR/TITLE	PRICE	TOTAL
	1-59158-663-1	Once Upon a Time		

Send order to address below **Or call: 1-800-225-5800;** **Or fax: 1-603-431-2214** **Or Online: www.lu.com or** **www.greenwood.com** **For 20% Conference Discount, use code #F238**	Subtotal:	
	Shipping: (add 10% or $6.00 Minimum)	
	Sales Tax: (IL,MA, CO, CT, PA, MD, SD, MO, NJ) Canada residents add GST Tax Or include Tax Exempt #	
	Total:	

Name:_____Title:_____

School:_____Address:_____

City:_____State:_____Zip:_____Phone#_____

Email_____

☐ check enclosed made payable to Libraries Unlimited

☐ VISA   ☐ MC   ☐ AMEX   Credit Card #_____Exp date:_____

Signature (required):_____

Print name as it appears on credit card:_____

If using a purchase order please attach it to this form.

Send order to: Libraries Unlimited
P.O. Box 6926
Portsmouth, NH 03802

♬ ♬ *JUDY FREEMAN* ♬ ♬

CHILDREN'S LITERATURE CONSULTANT

JUDY FREEMAN (www.JudyReadsBooks.com) is a well-known consultant, writer, and speaker on children's literature, storytelling, and all aspects of librarianship. She is a visiting lecturer at the School of Information, and Library Science at Pratt Institute in New York City, where she teaches courses on children's literature and storytelling. A former school librarian, she gives conferences, workshops, speeches, and performances throughout the U.S. and the world for teachers, librarians, parents, and children, and is a national seminar presenter for BER (Bureau of Education and Research). Judy served as a member of the Newbery Committee to select the Newbery Award book for the year 2000 and the Sibert Committee for 2008.

Her many courses and workshops include:

WINNERS!: A Closer Look at the Year's "Best" Books for Children
Books Kids Will Sit Still For: Titles Every Classroom Teacher and Librarian Should Know
Literature and Library Skills: An Integrated Approach
Booktalking: Advertising Your Wares
Performance Art: Storytelling, Creative Dramatics, & Reader's Theater
Once Upon a Time: Storytelling for Grades PreK-6
Hi Ho Librario: Songs and Chants to Keep Kids Humming

SCHOOL PROGRAMS FOR CHILDREN: The Musical Booktalk

Judy will give three one-hour assemblies for children, grades PreK-6, per day. She incorporates interactive storytelling, songs, poetry, creative drama, wordplay, and booktalks in a spirited exploration of the power of words, with lots of audience participation. Included are her annotated bibliography of her 100 favorite recent children's books (that you can easily duplicate as a handout for parents, teachers, and children) and a handout for teachers of songs, stories, and reading ideas as a follow-up to her program. If you are interested, Judy will be glad to give, at no extra cost, a one-hour after-school parent/teacher workshop on the latest best books for children, along with an annotated bibliography of all the titles she presents.

JUDY FREEMAN'S latest book, *Once Upon a Time: Using Storytelling, Creative Drama, and Reader's Theater with Children in Grades PreK-6* (Libraries Unlimited, 2007), joins mega-book, *Books Kids Will Sit Still For 3* (2006) and its popular companions *Books Kids Will Sit Still For: The Complete Read-Aloud Guide* (1990), and *More Books Kids Will Sit Still For* (1995) as another indispensable resource for literature-based classrooms and libraries. (To order: 1-800-225-5800; **www.LU.com**) Her *Hi Ho Librario!: Songs, Chants, and Stories to Keep Kids Humming* (Rock Hill Press, 1997) is a book and CD full of her book-related songs. (To order: ssocha@rockhillworks.com; 1-610-667-7431; www.rockhillworks.com) Judy writes several book review columns, including "Wild About Books" for *School Library Media Activities Monthly*, "Desperate Librarians" for the online fiction database *NoveList,* and "What's New" for *School Library Journal's Curriculum Connections.*

For further information about her programs:
JUDY FREEMAN
65 NORTH SIXTH AVENUE
HIGHLAND PARK, NJ 08904
732-572-5634 / e-mail: BKWSSF@aol.com / www.JudyReadsBooks.com

The 25th Annual WINNERS! Conference, 2009:
A Closer Look at the Year's 100 Best Books for Children, Grades K-6

REGISTRATION and ORDER FORM

Libraries Unlimited Prof. Dev. Provider 5568

MAIL or FAX TO: Libraries Unlimited
Professional Workshops Department
7570 Thorn Creek Lane
Tega Cay, SC 29708
PHONE: 803-547-5206 or 1-800-225-5800 ext. 3504
FAX: 803-547-4387   EMAIL: debby.laboon@lu.com
WEBSITE: www.lu.com

Name_____

School_____

Please Check: Teacher:____ Grade:____ Media Specialist:____ Public Librarian:____ Other:_____

Business Address_____

City, State, Zip_____

Home Address (will be kept confidential but needed in event of an emergency)

_____

Phone Number_____ **Email Address** (to get confirmation)_____

Do you want correspondence sent to your: ____Home address ____Work address

Your $179.00 registration includes continental breakfast, lunch, coffee breaks, an extensive conference handbook, and a certificate of participation (5 professional development contact hours).

Hours 8:30am-3:30pm

Registering for (please check):

_____WINNERS in Voorhees, NJ Tuesday, May 5, 2009—LUV1 $179.00

_____WINNERS in Whippany, NJ Wednesday, May 6, 2009—LUW2 $179.00

_____ WINNERS in Edison, NJ Thursday, May 7, 2009—LUE3 $179.00

_____ WINNERS in Edison, NJ Friday, May 8, 2009—LUE4 $179.00

TOTAL Registration Payment to be processed: $_____

Payment Method (Payment must accompany this form)

_____Purchase Order enclosed/attached (fax or mail to the address above)

_____Check enclosed _____Credit Card (mail, fax, or phone orders accepted)

Checks should be made payable to Libraries Unlimited.

To pay by credit card, please complete the following information:

Circle one: Visa   MasterCard   American Express

Name as it appears on the credit card_____

Account # _____**Expiration Date**_____

Cardholder's signature_____

(I agree to pay the above total amount according to my card issuer agreement)

Cardholder's billing address_____

Registration Information:

For directions to the workshop locations please go to www.lu.com/winners. On-Site registrations will be taken and a $10.00 additional fee will be added to the registration cost.

Substitutions & Cancellations: Substitutions are allowed at any time—just let us know. If you are canceling your registration up to one week prior to the date of the workshop, you are entitled to a full refund. If you cancel within one week or less prior to workshop date, we retain a $10.00 cancellation fee. Please note: if you do not cancel and do not attend the workshop, there will be no refund.

PLEASE MAKE COPIES OF THIS FORM AND PASS IT ALONG TO YOUR COLLEAGUES.

CAN'T ATTEND? ORDER *The WINNERS! Handbook* FROM WWW.LU.COM/WINNERS.